COASTAL
DESIGN

COASTAL DESIGN

A GUIDE FOR BUILDERS, PLANNERS, AND HOME OWNERS

Orrin H. Pilkey, Sr. • Walter D. Pilkey

Orrin H. Pilkey, Jr. • William J. Neal.

VNR VAN NOSTRAND REINHOLD COMPANY
New York Cincinnati Toronto London Melbourne

Printed in the United States of America
Designed by Loudan Enterprises

The excerpt on page 126 is taken from *Condominium* by John D. MacDonald
(J. B. Lippincott Company). Copyright © 1977 by John D. MacDonald.
Reprinted by permission of Harper & Row, Publishers, Inc.

Published by Van Nostrand Reinhold Company Inc.
135 West 50th Street
New York, New York 10020

Van Nostrand Reinhold Company Limited
Molly Millars Lane
Wokingham, Berkshire RG11 2PY, England

Van Nostrand Reinhold
480 La Trobe Street
Melbourne, Victoria 3000, Australia

Macmillan of Canada
Division of Gage Publishing Limited
164 Commander Boulevard
Agincourt, Ontario M1S 3C7, Canada

16   15   14   13   12   11   10   9   8   7   6   5   4   3   2

Library of Congress Cataloging in Publication Data
Main entry under title:

Coastal design.

   Bibliography: p. 206
   Includes index.
   1. Building, Stormproof. 2. Coastal engineering.
3. Dwellings—Design and construction. I. Pilkey,
Orrin H., 1905-
TH1096.C63 1983   728.3'7'09146   82-23855
ISBN 0-442-27718-0

Contents

Preface

The beach is America's most precious, most alluring, and most sought after strip of sand. Hundreds of thousands of Americans trek to the ocean beach each year to soak up sun and surf or simply to seek inspiration from the awesome view of a vast ocean. The beach is so attractive, in fact, that we are bringing to the shore the very problems we seek to escape, such as crime, overcrowding, and pollution.

Our population is virtually exploding outward in all directions that lead to the sea. Homes by the thousands are springing up a few feet from the surf zone or a few feet from the edge of bluffs overlooking the ocean. But the shore is a dynamic place. Some small towns have actually disappeared with the ubiquitous and inevitable occurrence of shoreline retreat. In addition, communities such as Green Hill Beach (Rhode Island), Holden Beach (North Carolina), the west Louisiana shore, and Galveston (Texas) that were once totally devastated by hurricanes now sport densely packed houses, some of which are inhabited by people who are actually unaware of these areas' heritage of destruction. The National Hurricane Center predicts that thousands of people will (not may) die when (not if) a major hurricane strikes such places as Miami, St. Petersburg, or Galveston.

Today, people from Indiana and Ohio are flocking to the Carolinas, Georgia, and Florida to build or buy beach houses after only the briefest introductions to the environment. Similarly, people with no "coastal experience" are swarming to the bluffs of the California shore to cantilever houses out over the cliff tops to get the best sea view ever. Helping this rush to the shore is the federal government, ever ready to hand out money for bridges, highways, flood insurance, and sea walls.

What does the citizen from Indiana know about the shoreline, the beach, the storms, the tides and currents, the sea level rise, and the erosion rate? The answer in most cases is very little! Most potential ocean beach property owners are conditioned solely by a few weeks or months of experience during the summer. Few have ever witnessed a winter storm. Fewer have seen the debris from poorly built houses after a hurricane. And fewer yet have any idea how fast the shoreline is eroding in front of their proposed homesite.

More times than we can recount we have talked with shoreline dwellers who have expressed their frustration and even anger over the lack of information given them before they bought or built. We've been asked such questions as: How could we have found out if the shoreline (or bluff) was eroding here? How could we have known that we couldn't trust the building inspector (the health department, the state coastal zone management program) to help us preserve the quality of life we came to the shoreline for? Could we have stopped the shoreline from eroding? Is a seawall a good idea?

These and a thousand other questions inspired us to collaborate on the writing of this book, which we hope will find its way into the homes of the beach property owner and prospective property owner, the offices of the coastal builder and designer, and everyone else who loves the beach. We hope to use the vast amount of already published technical data on our shorelines to open eyes and minds and create a safer and more beautiful American shore.

This book is a principal volume (or an umbrella volume, as we like to call it) of a series of books, entitled *Living with the Shore*, being written for each of the coastal states. The state books have less emphasis on construction and more on the safety of individual sites along specific state shorelines. The state books, which are being prepared in collaboration with recognized local shoreline geologists, will be published by the Duke University Press.

Some studies relating to this volume were funded by the National Oceanic and Atmospheric Administration (NOAA) through their Office of Coastal Zone Management. Their support was administered by the North Carolina Sea Grant Program. The original plan was to emphasize our barrier island coasts, but under the support of the Federal Emergency Management Agency (FEMA), we have expanded our effort to include all American ocean shoreline states in the lower forty-eight. This volume presents our scientific conclusions based on a wide range of published and unpublished information or personal observations of many coastal areas. We do not assume, however, that our conclusions are necessarily the same as those of the federal agencies that supported us.

We owe a debt of gratitude to many individuals for support ideas and encouragement. Peter Chenery and Richard Foster gave us encouragement at critical junctions in the development of the book series. Peter Chenery was responsible for publishing our two earlier books, both concerned with North Carolina: *How To Live with an Island* and *From Currituck to Calabash* (recently reissued by Duke University Press). Doris Schroeder helped us in numerous ways as our agent, confidante, sometime-editor, sometime-typist, and a Jill of all trades. Commander Jim Collins, Jeff Battley, Peter Gibson, Gloria Jiminez, Melita Rodeck, Richard Krimm, and Chris Makris all helped us through the Washington maze. In particular, Mike Robinson of the Federal Emergency Management Agency made a comprehensive critique of the book that added to its accuracy and timeliness. The many individuals and agencies who kindly provided photos and figures are acknowledged in the text. We are grateful to the coastal residents, fellow geologists, coastal engineers, and local, state, and federal government officials, too numerous to name, who willingly provided us with a wealth of ideas, data, and "war stories." Their enthusiastic support made the writing of this book a lot of fun.

Bette Weerstra, Carol Walter, and Ada Maxwell typed some preliminary drafts of some of the manuscript. Cindy Ripley skillfully word processed the complete manuscript. Syu-Cheng Feng, L. Kitis, C. Meyers, and M. Adams drafted several figures.

Last but not least, we wish to thank our wives for lots of help, patience, and support.

COASTAL
DESIGN

Facing the Sea

Hopes, Dreams, and Reality

Learning from History

Some 2,700 years ago, the Phoenicians constructed a harbor at Carthage in North Africa for their merchant vessels that plied the shores of the Mediterranean. The city of Carthage and its harbor might have disappeared into the same historical obscurity of other Phoenician cities if it had not been for the exploits of Hamilcar and his son Hannibal several centuries later. These two warriors sent herds of elephants and mercenary armies from Africa to Europe, sailing from Carthage harbor. They then proceeded to terrorize and nearly conquer the Roman Empire. Unfortunately for Carthage and the Carthaginians, Hannibal eventually returned to North Africa, at which time the Carthaginians surrendered all of their territory except for the city of Carthage. Carthage, being in peace and not allowed to spend money on war and defenses, prospered commercially just as defeated Japan and West Germany did 2,000 years later. The Romans, on the other hand, continued to wage costly war campaigns, and became increasingly jealous and not a little fearful of the rapidly growing harbor city of Carthage. For a while, the Roman orator Cato the Elder ended all of his speeches with the phrase "Carthage must be destroyed." Finally, in 149 B.C. (the way the story is still told in Tunisia), the Romans attacked and overcame the city and then crucified, one by one, the remnants of the army. They tore down the buildings of Carthage and filled the harbor with the debris.

In those days, North Africa was a fertile land, and it became the breadbasket of Europe. The Romans, having destroyed the harbor at Carthage, cast about for a new harbor and eventually settled on Utique (the namesake of Utica, New York) about twenty miles (30 km) north of Carthage. Harbor facilities were built, and the products of much of North Africa soon flowed through this important port. Unfortunately, Utique was situated at the mouth of one of North Africa's largest streams, the Medjerda River, whose delta built out rapidly. Within 200 years the Romans were in need of a new harbor. Hat in hand, back the Romans went to Carthage, excavating and enlarging the harbor they had once glutted, and using it for many years thereafter.

Today both the merchant and the warship harbors of Carthage are still visible and still filled with water. Wind-blown dust and stream-carried sand have greatly shoaled the harbor. About eighty-five years ago a Frenchman filled in part of the harbor to build his villa. In Utique, on the other hand, even when standing atop the highest column at the ruins, one cannot see the shore, which has moved over ten miles (15 km) seaward.

Carthage harbor was guarded by a rocky shore and buffered by a broad, sandy beach. It must have been chosen with much care, observation, and forethought. Many miles of coast must have been studied before the Phoenicians chose that particular site, as it is a uniquely suitable section of the North African shoreline. On the other hand, the Romans made an obviously poor environmental choice for the harbor site at Utique, although it had the advantage of a river to transport foodstuffs from inland.

The moral of this story is that in choosing construction sites, be it beach house or warship harbor, it is wise to work with and not against nature. The Romans were, like Americans, confident of their ability to out-engineer nature, and it led, in the long run, to the loss of their harbor. The Carthaginians, under no such illusions, chose their harbor site with care and with a view to long usage with minimal interruption by nature. Modern man's intervention in the coastal zone could profit from a careful study of how these early cultures dealt with nature.

Sadly, the story of Carthage's harbor does not end with construction of the Frenchman's villa. In recent years, the sandy beach fronting Carthage's rocky shore has been a popular swimming area for the sophisticated tourist wanting to mix fun-in-the-sun with ancient history. But the beach has begun to narrow and disappear. Local citizens who own beach homes are puzzled and disturbed by this turn of events. The cause is simple to understand, and just about any resident of the New Jersey, South Florida, or Southern California shore could explain to the Tunisians what their problem is. A few hundred yards north of the old site of Carthage harbor, Tunisia's first breakwater has been built to provide shelter for small boats. The breakwater has trapped sand and prevented it from travelling its normal path to the Carthage area, thus starving the beach. Unfortunately, in this North African country where one would not lightly criticize a politician, the small boat harbor is right in front of President-for-life Habib Borguiba's palace. Sand trapped by the breakwater is thus successfully building up the presidential beach, while the loss of sand to neighboring beaches is causing rapid erosion. In this way, a shoreline and a beach with which man has lived in harmony for almost 3,000 years is being rapidly altered in a mere decade.

This tiny stretch of North African shore is a microcosm of the thousands of miles of American shoreline. The problems of Carthage are mirrored in the construction here of buildings in safe and dangerous locations, where nature's whim in a storm may save one building and destroy the one next to it.

The rush to the American shore has created many problems. Our beaches are getting narrower and narrower, and many have disappeared altogether. Tens of thousands of people live in low elevation beach communities that will be virtually impossible to evacuate in the next big storm. The sea level is rising, and probably 90 percent of the American shoreline is eroding and threatening thousands of homes even if another storm never occurs. Many if not the majority of shoreline dwellers live in structures that are not built well enough to put up reasonable resistance to the forces they will likely be subjected to.

A lot of our mistakes at the shoreline have come about because we have taken the Roman view concerning our ability to defeat or at least control nature.

But there is good news also. In the early eighties there has been increasing recognition on both the federal and state government levels of the economic and safety pitfalls of our intense coastal development. The economic pitfalls speak loudest, of course. These include the potential tax burden from federal flood insurance and disaster relief when the next hurricane strikes a major coastal city, and the potential multibillion-dollar annual tax bill to stop shoreline erosion.

Optimism and belief in the Roman approach still persist, however. This attitude seems most prevalent among coastal politicians, developers, and anyone who stands to gain economically from present development patterns. Colonel James W. R. Adams, chief of the Jacksonville, Florida, district office of the Corps of Engineers, published a statement in 1981 that epitomizes this philosophy: "Some of the proposed policies for barrier islands are truly plans for negative growth or planned shrinkage. This may be antithetical to the traditional American spirit and to one of the basic instincts of all mankind, namely domination, control and utilization of all the elements of nature, rather than throwing up our hands in despair and slinking away."

Shoreline Types

Francis Shepard, professor emeritus of Scripps Institute of Oceanography, has devised a classification of coastal types that we will use in discussing the American shore. Dr. Shepard classified all coasts as either *primary* or *secondary*. A primary coast is one whose shape or outline on a map results from nonmarine processes such as erosion by rivers, scour by glaciers, or delta buildup. A secondary coast is one that owes its appearance to marine processes such as wave erosion.

Much of the outline of the New England shoreline is related to either erosion or depositional effects of the mighty glaciers that covered all of New England a few thousand years ago. The coast of Maine, which falls in Shepard's primary category, owes its rugged, irregular outline to the thousands of grooves, large and small, carved in solid rocks by the advancing glaciers. Even the direction of movement of the ice sheets can be discerned from the general north–south orientation of Maine's innumerable small harbors.

Cape Cod consists of materials deposited by glaciers. Unlike the Maine coast, which is mostly bounded by hard rock, Cape Cod is made up of unconsolidated or uncemented sands and gravels. Any Cape Cod bluff can be successfully attacked with a pick and shovel. As a consequence, wave erosion has played the dominant role in determining the outline of the Cape as we see it today, and makes Cape Cod a secondary coast type.

The greatest percentage of the open ocean coast of the United States is fronted by barrier islands. Because barrier islands are formed by depositional marine processes, they are a secondary type of coast. The American barrier coast starts from the south shore of Long Island and extends with occasional breaks all the way to the Mexican border. There are also a few barrier islands along the New England shoreline (Plum Island, Massachusetts) and numerous so-called barrier spits blocking river mouths entering the Pacific Ocean (Tillamook Spit, Oregon).

Another type of secondary coast is typified by the Florida Keys, which once were a chain of coral reefs built up thousands of years ago when the sea level was higher.

The southwest corner of the Florida Peninsula adjacent to the Everglades is a coast formed by the outward growth of so-called mangrove swamps.

Delaware and Chesapeake bays are examples of primary shorelines. These huge and commercially important bodies of water are drowned river valleys (as are Pamlico and Albemarle sounds in North Carolina). In other words, the shape of the shoreline here was determined basically by the shape of valleys carved by rivers on land when the sea level was lower. When the ice melted, the sea rose up and occupied former river valleys.

A wave erosion coastline (secondary coastal type) dominates the Oregon–Washington and California coast. Nature tends to strive for a straight shoreline, given enough time. The irregularities of the Pacific shoreline of North America are often caused by the differential resistances of different rock types to erosion by crashing storm waves.

The Beach

Facing the ocean in front of all kinds of coasts is the beach, that most celebrated strip of sand. Although each beach is unique in many ways, there are certain guiding principles and rules that all beaches obey. Some of these rules of nature are positively ingenious. Geologists who have studied beaches find themselves viewing these dynamic bodies of sand as almost living things because of their ability to respond to and survive the changing forces of nature.

The beach is larger than just the strip of sand between high and low tides. The beach is defined as the entire zone of mobile sand that may change its shape over a short period of time. This mobile zone extends seaward to a water depth of about 30 feet (10 m).

One of the principal rules of beaches is that they exist in a dynamic equilibrium controlled by four factors (figure 1-1): the energy of the waves, the shape of the beach, the supply of beach sand, and the level of the sea. When one of these variables changes, the other three shift according to certain rules that marine scientists have spent much time deciphering.

Wave energy (size of the waves) increases during storms. The beach responds by changing its shape, that is, by flattening itself and by building offshore bars. The offshore bars trip the biggest waves before they hit the beach, causing them to expend their energy in deeper water offshore. Flattening of the beach causes the waves that do make it ashore to dissipate their tremendous energy over a much broader area than would have been possible on the previously steeper beach (figure 1-2). During a big storm, in order to flatten the beach profile, the waves may erode sand from the upper beach and even the first or second row of dunes, thus creating a problem to the beach cottage dweller. If a beach cottage is on the dune, it becomes intimately involved in the flattening process. In most cases, a good part of the sand lost to the lower beach during a storm will return to the upper beach and dunes over a period of months and years. The sand is gradually pushed back to the beach by the shoreward push of fair-weather waves.

On most beaches, storms are more frequent during the winter than the summer. The upper portion of the beach between the high- and low-tide lines tends to be narrower and steeper during the winter than in the summer. But when the entire beach is considered, to a depth of 30 feet (10 m) or so, the winter beach tends to be flatter than the summer beach. The narrow upper beach is the reason why shoreline

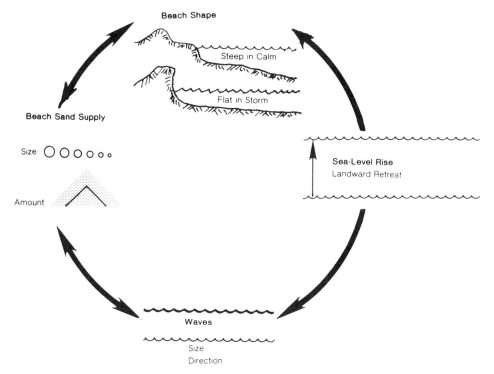

Beach Shape

Steep in Calm

Flat in Storm

Beach Sand Supply

Size ○ ○ ○ ○ ○ ∘

Amount

Sea-Level Rise
Landward Retreat

Waves

Size
Direction

1-1. An illustration of the dynamic equilibrium system that controls beaches. A change in one of these factors produces a response from other factors. For example, during a storm the size of the waves increases and causes the beach to move its sand supply about, which in turn changes the shape of the beach.

community newspapers are filled with stories of beach erosion problems in winter but not in the summer, when the beach is once again broad. This is also why some California developers used to wait for the broad summer beach before they staked a claim by enclosing their land with a concrete bulkhead.

Size of material on beaches is highly variable. Extremes range from the very fine sand of Georgia beaches to the boulder-strewn shores of Washington's Olympic Peninsula. Some Pacific beaches will consist of coarser materials in winter relative to summer because of the bigger winter waves moving the finer sands offshore. In an extreme example of seasonal changes in beach sediment, figures 1-3 and 1-4 both show the same Oceanside, California, beach where waves and tides removed cobbles covering the winter beach by the beginning of summer, thereby exposing the man-made boulder wall or revetment. Other things being equal (such as wave energy), grain size controls the slope of the beach between high and low tide. The coarser the grain size, the steeper the beach; hence, the very broad low-tide beaches of Georgia compared to some much narrower boulder beaches of the Pacific.

Because beaches are moving, dynamic sand bodies, it is not surprising that there is a continuous need to renew the supply of sand. Beaches get their materials from different places, and they lose their materials in different ways. Beach communities must understand where their sand comes from and where it is going if they hope to preserve their beaches. By collectively regulating sand resources to protect beaches, communities will ultimately protect their property. Sand dune ordinances, for example, can protect the rows of dunes the beach needs to respond to a storm. In New England, preventing construction atop unconsolidated and eroding bluffs will allow the bluffs to continue to erode and to function as a supply of sand for the adjacent beaches. Conversely, revetments or retaining walls built up against the first dune row, such as those along East Hampton Beach, New York, will soon cause sand loss and speed up erosion for the neighboring communities to the west (and "downstream" in the sand supply system) such as Westhampton. In California,

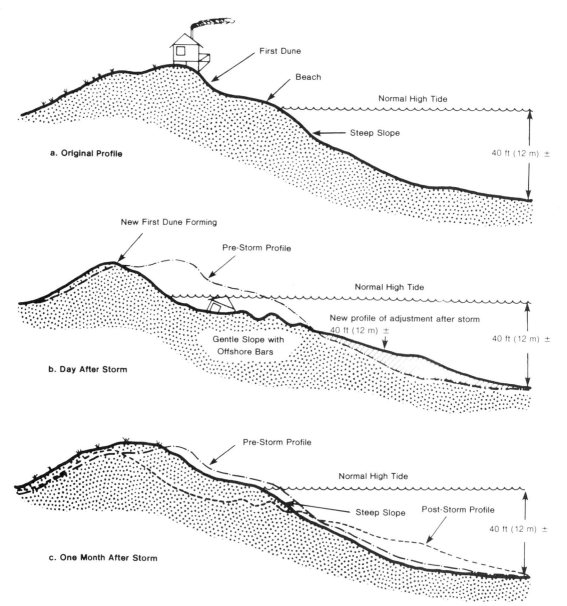

1-2. The natural beach responds to a storm by flattening itself or building offshore bars or both. Whichever the case, these changes, which can be made in a matter of hours, help dissipate the massive storm waves.

1-3. South Oceanside Beach, California, in January, 1978. (Photo: G. G. Kuhn)

1-4. South Oceanside Beach in June, 1978. (Photo: G. G. Kuhn)

stopping dam construction on rivers might halt a significant cause of beach sand loss.

Beach sand is lost from barrier island beaches by transportation through inlets into lagoons behind the island, by overwashing the island during storms, by being blown ashore from beaches into dunes, and by being sucked offshore during storms. Shorelines not fronted with barrier islands, such as our Pacific shore, can lose their beaches in the offshore direction as well as to the dunes in an onshore direction. In California, beach sand is often removed all the way to the deep sea. Submarine canyons whose heads are sometimes within swimming distance of the beach (for example at Redondo Beach and Scripps pier) reach into the nearshore, intercept the sand, and then carry it to deep water via rapidly moving, powerful density flows called turbidity currents. Turbidity currents have been known to cut submarine telephone cables whose misfortune it was to span a submarine canyon.

But the biggest loss of sand from man's beloved beaches is caused by man himself. Engineers and shoreline scientists, in devising all sorts of means of trapping sand to build up certain beaches or to protect harbor entrances, have created other problems elsewhere. They have constructed groins and jetties to trap sand moving laterally along the beach, the trapped sand then widening the beach on the "up-stream" side of these walls, which are perpendicular to the beach. While this improves the recreational and aesthetic value of the "upstream" beach, the problem with trapping this sand is that it was going somewhere, and wherever that some-where was begins to suffer from sand starvation. In other words, the "downstream"

1-5. Offset between Ocean City, Maryland, and Assateague Island, Virginia. Sand trapped by the jetties at the south end of Ocean City has "starved" Assateague, causing very rapid migration (erosion) of this uninhabited island. (Photo: Evelyn Maumeyer)

beach begins to disappear (figure 1-5). Breakwaters such as those off Southern California have the same deleterious sand-trapping effect as the groins of New Jersey.

Robert Morton, a Texas geologist, estimates that 50 percent of the sand supply of the relatively lightly settled Texas beaches has already been tied up by jetties built to protect harbor entrances. No one has made similar calculations for New Jersey, but probably 95 percent of the Jersey beaches' sand supply has been immobilized. Disappearance of buildings near the beach can be directly attributed to jetty-caused erosion in such diverse places as San Diego, California; Tillamook Spit, Oregon; Folly Beach, South Carolina; and Cape May, New Jersey. The question boils down to: Is the protection afforded to shipping worth the shoreline damage caused by the jetties? Sometimes it is. Often it is not.

The natural sources of sand for beaches include rivers, erosion of bluffs, the continental shelf, and wind-blown sand. The beaches of Louisiana and Texas as well as those of the West Coast and some of those in New England depend on rivers for sand sustenance. The problem arises when the rivers are dammed upstream, cutting off sand supply. This causes the beaches to starve and disappear. Southern California beaches suffer mightily because of this problem. On the other hand, the rivers along the East Coast from New York south do not disgorge their loads at the beaches. Instead, the sand is dumped miles inland at the heads of the many bays and estuaries indenting the land. As far as most East Coast barrier-beach sand supplies are concerned, damming the rivers is of little or no consequence.

Erosion of bluffs and cliffs along the shore is a major source of sand for most shorelines not fronted by barrier islands, that is, for the New England and Pacific coasts. In most places the shoreline must erode in order for the beaches to survive. Yet when the shoreline erodes, houses are threatened, and when houses are threatened, people fight back by stopping the erosion, thereby cutting off the supply of sand to their neighbor's beach! Literally hundreds of examples abound along New England's glaciated shores, where individuals have cemented in their future beach in order to save the house that was built because of the original beach's presence.

The continental shelf supplies sand to the beach during times of fair weather. The gentle waves push large volumes of sand ashore, grain by grain. Usually the sand comes from depths of 30 feet (10 m) or less. The same sand may be pushed back by fierce, steeper storm waves that have exactly the opposite effect on sand movement. On most natural beaches a balance is struck between onshore and offshore sand transport. This balance is inevitably changed when man builds seawalls along the shore. Seawalls and similar structures deflect wave energy and cause sand to move offshore in all kinds of weather. Eventually this causes the beach to disappear completely; the lower portion of the beach being steepened to the point where even artificial (replenished) beaches cannot be maintained. The process of beach destruction we call ''New Jerseyization'' has begun (figures 1-6 and 1-7): Shoreline engineering has provided short-term ''erosion-proofing'' that in the long run is calculated to destroy beaches and dunes.

Superimposed on the daily, weekly, annual, and 50-year changes in beach shape, sand supply, and wave energy conditions is the rise in sea level. The sea level has probably been rising for the last 15,000 years or so (figure 1-8). Roughly 4,000 years ago the rise slowed down and probably stayed close to the present level, with the exception of a few minor ups and downs. About 50 years ago the sea level rise began to accelerate to a rate of perhaps one foot (30 cm) per century. We do not

1-6. Long Beach, New Jersey, is an example of how New Jerseyization, generations past, effectively destroyed the beach in order to save the buildings built adjacent to the beach. (Photo: Orrin Pilkey, Jr.)

know whether the post-1930 rise is a brief blip on the curve or the beginning of a long period of change. Mother nature and her beaches and islands are responding as though the sea level rise will continue indefinitely. People should also!

Rising sea level does not just flood land. The vertical rise is not the problem; it is the accompanying horizontal retreat that has the impact (figure 1-9). The amount of horizontal (landward) retreat of a shoreline is largely a function of the slope of the land. A steep slope such as that which exists along our Pacific shores means slow shoreline retreat. A gentle land slope such as that along most of our Atlantic and Gulf coastal areas corresponds to rapid shoreline retreat. For example, a one-foot (30-cm) per century rise in sea level should, in theory, push back the shoreline of much of Florida 500 to 1,500 feet (150 to 450 m) during that century.

We have more to say about the effect of the sea level rise in Chapter 7 and in the barrier island section of this chapter.

Shorelines without Barrier Islands

The basic rule of thumb for living happily ever after on the rocky or bluffed shoreline is to stay far enough back from the cliff edge so that erosion will not catch up with

1-7. Pocket beach swimming: the future of American beaches? Here at Cape May, New Jersey, America's oldest beach resort, the beach has narrowed to the point that at high tide no beach exists at all. This, too, results from New Jerseyization. (Photo: Bill Neal)

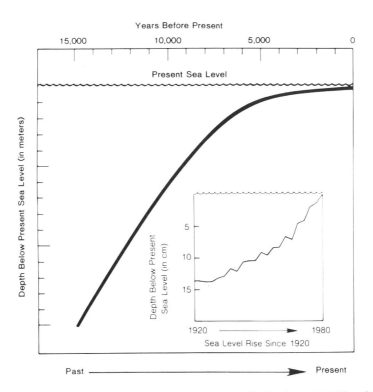

1-8. History of the rise in sea level during the last 15,000 years. During the past 4,000 or 5,000 years, the sea level rise has slowed down considerably. Recently, as shown by the inset, this trend has reversed: the rate of rise is increasing.

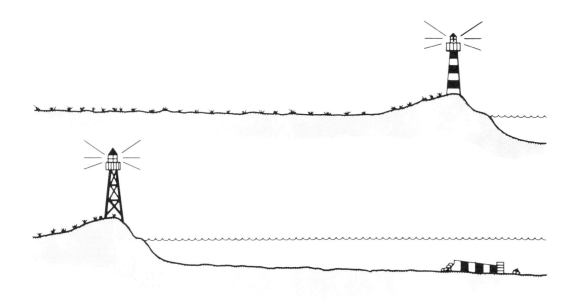

Sea Level Rise

Resulting Horizontal Displacement

1-9. A very small rise in sea level produces a very large horizontal shoreline retreat on America's coastal plain coasts. This figure shows how the shoreline theoretically responds to a sea level rise. The shoreline is pushed back a distance that is in accordance with the slope of the land surface.

you. This sounds simple enough, but it is not always easy to tell just how far back is "safe."

For starters, different types of rock erode at radically different rates—but simple hardness of the rock does not tell the whole story concerning its ability to resist waves. For example, if the rocks are dipping seaward, common sense dictates that they are liable to slip seaward. If a hard and massive rock such as a sandstone rests on top of a finely bedded rock such as shale, the shale will grease the skids for cliff failure. More failures occur in the wet season than in the dry season. Humans even enter the equation. Increased watering of lawns on top of bluffs or cliffs in effect makes the rainy season last all year and in some cases greatly increases the possibility of both the green lawn and the house disappearing into the sea. Loading a bluff face with massive structures, inflicting vibration from construction or increased traffic, diverting storm drains to the bluff, and generally modifying the slope are other human activities that may contribute to bluff failure.

Unlike barrier islands, many of which seem to exhibit a fairly predictable long-range rate of beach retreat on the oceanside, a bluffed shoreline is much more likely to retreat sporadically. Five to thirty years may go by between episodes of bluff failure. The presence of man, however, drastically shortens the time between bluff failure events.

For many Southern California shorelines, only if the storm is a truly big one will the bluff fail in the middle of it. What more often happens is that the bluff falls in long after the storm has gone by. The storm, having removed the pile of sand and gravel at the base of the cliff (the talus), causes the overall slope of the bluff to be steepened, thus putting the bluff into an unstable condition. Rainfall filtering into the ground may cause additional loading and decrease stability. Over the next few days, weeks, and months, chunks of the upper part of the bluff will gradually fall away and accumulate in a new talus pile at the base. So will houses and condominiums if they are there. As the talus pile enlarges, the slope angle of the bluff will be reduced and bluff erosion halted. When the next storm removes the talus pile, the whole process of bluff retreat–talus pileup will begin once more.

Frequently there is a close relationship between the beach sand supply and the bluffs behind the beach. That is, the beaches depend on erosion of the bluffs for part of their sand suppply. "Soft" bluffs like Cape Cod furnish much material for beaches. Tougher rocks such as those fronting Washington state's Olympic Peninsula erode much more slowly and furnish a much smaller proportion of the beach's sand and gravel supply.

Recent studies by Francis Shepard and Gerry Kuhn have revealed a heretofore unsuspected danger for the bluffed Southern California shoreline: the cyclical presence of unusually large and powerful waves. This danger may well affect other Pacific Coast areas also. Having noted a certain periodicity to storm waves striking the San Diego beaches, Shepard was, in the 1940s, personally able to measure a wave larger than 40 feet (12 m) in height striking the La Jolla shore. Such waves have not occurred since, but were they to do so today, they would cause untold damage to the intense development hugging the beach. Shepard and Kuhn find evidence of an earlier period of such big waves in the late 1800s. The question now remains: When will the big one strike again? The 1980 and 1983 winter storm damage to the California coast was a small taste of what to expect in the future.

Barrier Island Shorelines

People have lived on America's barrier islands for a long time, but only recently has this land been considered choice real estate. Indians tended to use the barriers seasonally, usually abandoning them during hurricane season. In 1690, Thomas Budd sold the island that is now Atlantic City, New Jersey, for eleven cents an acre compared to a price of forty cents an acre for adjacent mainland properties. The early Outer Bankers of North Carolina lived in the heavily forested backsides of those barrier islands, where they built their structures at higher elevations. They lived on the islands to pursue a less complex way of life, particularly with respect to such civilized inconveniences as laws and taxes. The black peoples of the South Carolina and Georgia islands (the Gullah and Geeshi, respectively) were able to live a life so independent from the rest of their neighbors that they actually developed their own language, so uninterested were mainlanders in those areas. In all cases, the early American settlers considered building on the beach to be extreme folly.

America's barrier islands probably formed 12,000 to 15,000 years ago when the sea level was 230 feet (70 m) or so lower than at present. The reason the sea level was low and shorelines were out on the continental slope was because massive glaciers covering the polar regions had robbed much water from the oceans. The barrier islands formed at the moment in geologic time when the ice began to melt and the sea level rose up over the lip of the continental shelf (figure 1-10).

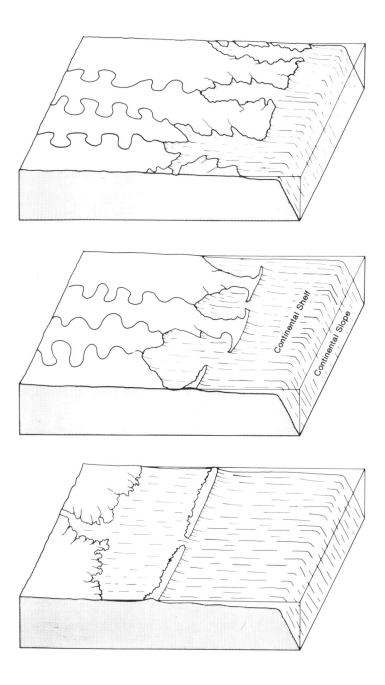

1-10. Barrier islands formed as a result of rising sea level at the end of the last ice age. Geologists believe that the predecessors of present-day barrier islands formed at the edge of the continental shelf. From top to bottom, these diagrams indicate the sequence of how barrier islands form. As the sea level rises and begins to flood the coastal plain, the former river valleys become deeply embayed estuaries. The waves preferentially attack the headlands that protrude seaward. Transportation of sand on the beach builds spits, extending from the headlands, which eventually become islands. Aiding the process of island formation is flooding of the land behind the rows of dunes formed at the beach.

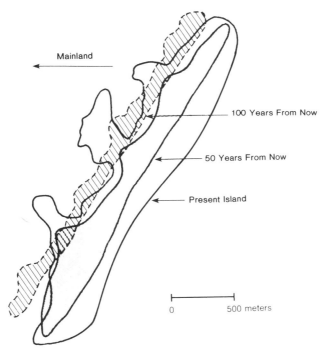

Mainland

100 Years From Now

50 Years From Now

Present Island

0   500 meters

1-11. A diagram showing how a barrier island on the Outer Banks of North Carolina might be expected to migrate during the next 100 years. This hypothetical barrier island migration assumes a sea level rise of 1 foot (30 cm) per century across a very gentle coastal plain surface.

1-12. Trees dying along the Pamlico Sound shoreline, North Carolina. The death of the trees is believed to result from a rising water table that is responding to the rise in sea level. (Photo: Stan Riggs)

After the islands formed, they began to migrate landward in response to the continuing rise in sea level, which in turn was responding to the melting polar ice caps (figure 1-11). Simultaneously, of course, the mainland shores were eroding or flooding (figure 1-12). Over their 12,000- to 15,000-year history of migration the islands probably took many forms and shapes, but they were always there. Possibly some of the sand in modern barriers is from the original islands and has travelled for many miles over thousands of years. The sea level rise probably occurred in fits and starts, sometimes rapid and sometimes slow. When the sea level rose in a particularly rapid spurt, as it did up until 5,000 years ago, the islands were very skinny. Whenever the sea level rise slowed down, the islands "fattened up" (widened) by cannibalizing sand from the inner continental shelf in front of them.

Islands can best migrate rapidly when they are skinny. Almost as though they were thinking objects, barrier islands seem to be planning ahead for the coming sea level rise. Consequently, in response to the post-1930 jump in sea-level rise rate, many American barriers are slimming down by erosion on both frontsides and backsides.

Recently, on Whale Beach, New Jersey, after a winter storm, a patch of dark mud appeared on the beach. The mud contained cow hooves and fragments of colonial pottery and other implements, much to the puzzlement of the stroller who discovered it. But the explanation for cow hooves on the beach is simple: a couple of hundred years ago, a colonist dumped a wagonload of garbage containing hooves and potsherds in the marsh. Subsequently, the island migrated and the backside-buried garbage dump became a frontside garbage dump.

Barrier island migration is a fact of life that must be faced sooner or later by any community of coastal island dwellers. Avoiding this reality will lead to the coastal misuse or "stabilization" of beaches we call New Jerseyization, resulting in a narrow to nonexistent beach covered with the rubble of preexisting seawalls and other structures that have fallen in after being undermined (more about this in Chapter 7). Accepting and working with this fact of island migration, on the other hand, will lead to an attractive island capable of responding to natural forces and of migrating with the rising sea.

All schemes involving the halting of island migration (or beach erosion in general) are lumped under the term *stabilization*. In the short run, that is, twenty to thirty years, stabilization can preserve beaches and buildings successfully. Mounting evidence indicates that in the long run, however, stabilization results in the destruction of the beaches at a great economic cost to local citizens.

A barrier island in its natural state needs no protection. Back in the 1930s, beach erosion on the Outer Banks of North Carolina was not recognized as island migration but rather mistakenly interpreted to mean that the islands were disappearing altogether. A massive and expensive dune-building project was then started along many miles of barrier islands. Not only was the project unnecessary, but recent studies have shown that the dune construction was actually responsible for *increased* rates of erosion on both the backsides and frontsides of the Outer Bank islands.

It is important for barrier island shoreline dwellers to understand how islands work, how they evolve and migrate. Some ways of living with islands will not damage the natural systems, whereas others can destroy the island system entirely. This latter approach, New Jerseyization, is so called not because only New Jersey is guilty of this action, but rather because New Jersey's islands have been developed longer than others, and so most graphically illustrate the problem. Likewise, the impact of shoreline engineering is not restricted to barrier islands and their beaches. Californians too have seen portions of their beaches engineered away. Examples exist from Maine to Washington and across the sea to Hawaii.

Nailing Down America's Shoreline: Taming the Untamable _____

The move to the American shore began shortly after the Revolutionary War. The custom of getting away from the oppressive summer heat by going to the beach spread slowly at first. An interesting beach advertisement was placed by Cape May, New Jersey's, Postmaster Ellis Hughes in a Philadelphia paper in 1801:

> The subscriber has prepared himself for entertaining company who uses sea bathing and he is accommodated with extensive house-room with fish, oysters, crabs, and good liquors. Care will be taken of gentleman's horses. Carriages may be driven along the margins of the oceans for miles and the wheels will scarcely make an impression upon the sand. The slope of the shore is so regular that persons may wade a great distance. It is the most delightful spot that citizens may retire to in the hot season.

The broad beaches of Cape May are now gone (as is evidenced in figure 1-7). What remains is backed by seawalls. Rubble from preexisting structures can be found on the beach. Swimming goes on mainly at low tide. The shoreline at Cape May has been New Jerseyized.

Development of beaches in the late 1800s and early 1900s was restricted to somewhat isolated centers: Galveston, Texas; Miami Beach, Florida; Jekyll Island, Georgia; Wrightsville Beach, North Carolina; and Atlantic City, New Jersey, are all such examples.

The first real indication of the extreme danger of living near the beach came with the furious hurricane that struck Galveston, Texas, head on in 1900. In those days, the first warning of a hurricane came with the first winds of that hurricane. The storm destroyed the city and killed 6,000 people. Today the city is rebuilt and is even undergoing urban renewal. In response to the 1900 storm, the mightiest seawall on any American barrier island was built; running along the island's ocean side, it is 10 miles (16 km) long and 17 feet (5 m) high.

The problem with this is that on most barrier islands the major flooding after a storm comes from the back or mainland side of the island, and not from the open ocean. Storms push water up into the lagoons behind islands, and when these storms move on, or as hurricane winds change direction, the piled-up water moves back suddenly, and often catastrophically. Hence, the Galveston ocean-side seawall, although it offers good protection from storm waves, may be built on the wrong side of the island! As in Singapore during World War II, the defenders may have faced all of their heavy artillery in the wrong direction. Galveston remains as susceptible to storm-surge flooding as it was in 1900. In fact, if the seawall creates a false sense of security on the part of the residents, then susceptibility may have even increased.

With the exception of a few areas such as San Diego, Miami, and Galveston, really intense development of United States beach areas began after World War II with the advent of easily available bulldozers. In earlier times developers and builders had felt no strong compulsion to level building sites before constructing a house; the mule and dragpan approach was just too tedious. The bulldozer, however, allowed removal of huge volumes of sand and soil, unfortunately for man and beach alike. To this day, old developments can be distinguished from newer ones in many beach areas both by their building style and by the presence of unbulldozed higher elevations and unbulldozed rolling hills. Galveston and Miami Beach were exceptions to the general rule of nonsand removal in the early days. Before the 1900 hurricane struck Galveston and the 1926 storm struck Miami Beach, rows of dunes next to the ocean were largely removed to be used in building the cities that were soon to be destroyed.

When humans arrive at the beach and begin developing it, the initial relationship between man and nature can be described as passive. That is, modern man, like the Phoenicians before him, starts out living with nature. Man, providing he remains in a passive role, is an obstacle most beaches can take in stride. Unfortunately, developers treat barrier islands and beach areas as if they were inland suburban cornfields; land is subdivided into small rectangular lots, regardless of the island's topography, vegetation, and water features.

Besides placing houses in dangerous positions, American island dwellers also string power and communication lines in all directions, and sooner or later water and sewer pipelines likewise crisscross the area. Now, what happens in a storm or hurricane? Houses and roads fall in, sewer and water pipes are ruptured, power lines are downed. Man is angered! This affront by nature must be "corrected"; thus, if a new inlet has been formed by the storm, it is filled in by man. The sea is pushed back by bulldozed or pumped sand and held in abeyance by engineering structures. Man, inevitably, has gone from being passive to active. He has "stabilized," he has New Jerseyized, his island or his beach area.

Should We Live Near the Beach?

Our intent in this volume is not to discourage you from living near the beach. We are not totally opposed to all shoreline development, but we hope to promote safe and environmentally sound development that will not obligate future generations to large expenditures of tax money in a contest with nature. Those who live near the beach or who plan to live near the beach must balance a number of hazards and priorities. The beautiful view, the sea breeze, the recreational opportunities must be weighed against the danger, the rapid acceleration of development changing the flavor of the beach, and the specter of high taxes to support shoreline stabilization.

The first step in safe living near the beach is to select a site that will reduce the likelihood of exposure to the more extreme elements of the shore zone environment. The second step is to construct or select a well-built structure.

Development at the beach does not have to be dangerous, aesthetically displeasing, destructive to the environment, or costly to the taxpayer. There *is* a better way. By combining our empirical experience of 150 years of beach living in this country with increased theoretical scientific understanding of beach and island dynamics, it should be possible for us to live at the shore without destroying it or being destroyed by it.

Unfortunately, American beach communities seem to have developed in their own vacuums. Lessons learned about safe siting and construction of buildings on the New Jersey shore have not been applied by Texas. The loss of Bay Ocean, Oregon, had no impact whatever on development of identical beach environments elsewhere in Oregon. So the same mistakes are made over and over. And that is what this book is about: the mistakes, and how to avoid repeating them.

2

Siting a Beach House

Working with Nature

Site Selection: The First Step to Safety _____

The choice of a home site near the beach is far more crucial than it would be in most inland areas. Near the beach, one's life will be enriched by a greater variety of such exciting events as high winds, occasional hurricanes, eroding beaches and bluffs, island migration, sand dune migration, and frequent political battles over what to do about the disappearing beach and how to raise tax revenues to stop beach "erosion." In addition, things that happen far away and out of the control of local citizens may significantly affect them and their environment. For example, dam construction on Texas and California rivers continues to rob beach sand from coastal communities. Jetties and breakwaters or other types of beach construction miles away from a building site may do the same thing. Robbing sand causes beach erosion.

To some extent, the National Flood Insurance Program has actually relieved the potential coastal homeowner of the responsibility and burden of worrying about many of the multiple factors that might affect the quality and safety of living there. For this reason, the attitude of beach planners and home owners has increasingly become: If the insurance will pay for the house if it falls into the surf, why worry about taking care in choosing a homesite? But be advised: federal flood insurance should not be taken for granted. In recent years, the federal government has become painfully aware of the flood insurance program's financial vulnerability, and in 1981 several bills were introduced in Congress proposing to limit the program in one way or another; one devastating hurricane could obligate a payoff that would generate tremendous losses to the program. Furthermore, it has become apparent that the program may be actively encouraging unsafe development practices by reducing the financial risks of developing coastal property—a far cry from the original purposes of the insurance act. In 1982 passage of the barrier island bill eliminated federal insurance coverage and other federal development subsidies for most heretofore undeveloped islands (see Chapter 9). From 1981 to 1983, the cost of federal insurance zoomed upward. Hence, if for no other reason than the possibility of changes in federal insurance coverage, it would be smart to think and look carefully before planning or purchasing a homesite. More important to remember is that both federal and local regulations concerning site safety represent *minimum* standards; thus, the prudent property owner or developer will conduct his or her own site analysis.

When purchasing a lot or a home near the beach, three fundamental decisions must be made. The first is *What type of shoreline should be chosen?* Alternatives include hardrock or unconsolidated cliffs, coastal plain mainland beaches, barrier island open-ocean beaches, lagoon or bay beaches, and rocky shores. Often, the choice is made by economics. Price ranges in different locations may be very great, cutting off an open-ocean view from any but the most well-to-do. One consolation is that from a safety standpoint this may be a distinct plus, as the least expensive lots in beach communities tend to be the least dangerous, and the most expensive, the most dangerous.

Once the general location or type of shoreline has been chosen, the site search must be narrowed down further. The next decision will be: *What lot is best to build on?* Evaluation of individual sites can be very complex, but the single most important factor is clearly and simply elevation. The higher, the better, provided of course it is not high atop the edge of an eroding cliff.

Last, but not least, the final major decision: *What type of structure should be built or bought?* Will it withstand the expected forces of nature? Are the surrounding neighborhood homes of similar construction quality? These particular questions will be discussed in Chapters 3 and 4. Here in this chapter we will probe more deeply into the first two questions, concerning the type of shoreline and the actual lot choice. We will attack these issues by dividing the continental United States shoreline into three regions or shoreline types and covering them separately.

The New England Shoreline

New England has a wide variety of shoreline types, perhaps more so than any other section of the American shoreline. There are rocky cliffs, numerous bluffs of unconsolidated or uncemented glacial material, broad low-lying dune fields behind sandy beaches, and even a few barrier islands.

Because the New England shore was settled well before most of the rest of our coastal areas, one could hope that a vast backlog of experience would be available to help the potential new settler choose a home or a new homesite. But the early New Englanders, wise and prudent people, avoided the dangerous coastal areas altogether! No record exists of the loss of a Pilgrim home from the onslaught of storm waves. One cannot imagine early New Englanders rebuilding in the same spot three times where a home has been destroyed by storms twice before, as have modern residents of Scituate, Massachusetts.

As elsewhere, the great rush to the shore of New England is largely a twentieth-century phenomenon, the product of a mobile and highly affluent society. Nonetheless, a good step in choosing a homesite near New England's turbulent shore is to determine the age of the nearby houses. Needless to say, the presence of a nineteenth-century house would be a reassuring factor. A house near the shore that is 50 or 100 years old has seen many storms. Be careful, though. On some stretches of New England shoreline, a few nineteenth-century houses have survived while neighboring structures disappeared in a storm.

The safest possible open ocean-view homesites in New England are those of rocky headlands, which are particularly numerous on the Maine shore. Care must be taken to choose a high enough elevation to avoid destruction during the spectacular winter storms. At the other end of the spectrum, some of the most dangerous surf-side homesites are atop the cliffs and bluffs of unconsolidated material left behind by the retreating glaciers throughout much of New England. The rapidly eroding bluffs of the Cape Cod National Seashore on the Outer Cape typify this type of home-site.

New England not only has diverse shoreline types but is characterized by a wide variety of wave conditions and by beaches made up of many types of materials. Such diversity of factors makes it difficult to formulate broad generalizations for the home seeker or builder. Nonetheless, some considerations that have wide application are summarized in the following New England checklist, which should be carefully perused before property purchase.

New England Checklist

1. *What is the elevation of the homesite? How does it compare with the 100-year flood level or the reach of waves during the last important storm? The 100-year flood level is the maximum elevation that will be flooded by a storm, which is statistically likely to occur on the average of once in a century.*
2. *Is there a sea view? New England has cold winters. Winter winds whistling past exposed houses may easily increase fuel bills 50 percent or more relative to the same house snuggled in a forest. Is it worth it?*
3. *Is there safe storm egress? Few New England areas have the critical storm evacuation problems facing the barrier island shores. Nonetheless, it is well to remember that the worst winter storms smashing into the shoreline frequently bring with them heavy traffic-snarling snows.*
4. *What is the cultural history of the shoreline area? How old are the houses? (A row of old houses is always a good sign.) Has the community suffered storm destruction in the past?*
5. *What is the site like after a storm? If possible, visit the proposed homesite then—the bigger the storm, the better. If you cannot, take a gander at the beach in the wintertime to get a general idea of what natural protection stands between winter storm waves and the potential property.*
6. *What kind of bluff is between the site and the beach? If it is not solid rock, stay far, far back. If it is solid rock, unstratified rocks such as the granite bordering the Maine shoreline are always better than stratified or layered rocks. If the bluff consists of layered rock that dips seaward, there may be potential for landsliding.*
7. *What is the history of local shoreline erosion? Usually this can be determined only from various state publications. For the more technically oriented person, much information can be gleaned by comparing aerial photos from the late 1930s with ones from the 1980s. On the whole, developers and realtors are poor sources of shoreline erosion history.*
8. *How have humans altered the local shoreline? Have jetties and groins cut off the sand supply? Have bluffs that once supplied sand to the beach been blocked off by seawalls or the inplace cementing of boulders? If the answer is yes,*

expect the beach to narrow and gradually disappear. Open-ocean beaches are much more susceptible to the adverse effects of man's structures than shorelines sheltered behind islands or in bays.

9. *Has the beach been replenished? Ask someone in the community; if it has, beware! Replenishing beach sand is only a temporary solution to a retreating shoreline and is a sure indication a community's erosion and tax problems have just begun.*

10. *What is the community attitude toward beach erosion? Are they trying to work with or against nature? Do they respond to beach erosion by structural or nonstructural means? Nonstructural is preferred; no response is best of all if long-range preservation of the beach is to be achieved. Any response other than doing nothing will result in an increased tax load on the local citizens.*

11. *Does the local government have teeth? How do they respond to violations of regulations promoting safe development?*

12. *What building code is in effect? Is it really enforced? Was it enforced when most of the buildings were built?*

13. *What type of insurance coverage is available? Is the community eligible for the National Flood Insurance Program?*

14. *Last but not least, the final piece of research: What happened to the site in the 1962 Ash Wednesday storm and the 1938 hurricane? For much of the area these are the landmark storms.*

Because of the wide variety of shoreline types, the New Englander would be well advised to also read the Barrier Island and the Pacific Shores checklists that follow. The Barrier Island checklist is pertinent to understanding sand and gravel spits as well as New England barrier islands such as Plum Island, Massachusetts, and Green Hill Beach, Rhode Island. The Pacific Shores checklist will add to one's understanding of cliffs and bluffs along New England's shores.

The Barrier Island Shoreline

Over much of the length of the Gulf of Mexico shoreline, as well as along the entire Atlantic Coast from Long Island to the south, the mainland shores of the United States are protected by barrier islands. On barrier islands we can distinguish open-ocean shorelines and lagoon or "backside" shorelines, each having unique attributes and problems as homesites. Across the lagoon from the island lies the mainland shore with its own different character. On the islands proper, a wide variety of environments exist, each with differing physical conditions, materials, and vegetation.

Regardless of the type of shoreline or barrier island environment, the single most important fact of life for eastern and southern coastal dwellers in this country is that most barrier and mainland shores are eroding today. The way your community decides to respond to the sea level rise and the erosion it is causing will determine whether or not your grandchildren will have a beach on which to play.

Barrier islands are migrating landward. The National Academy of Sciences warns that the sea level rise, which is partly responsible for island migration and beach erosion, is likely to continue and even increase. The probable villain is the greenhouse effect: increased CO_2 in the atmosphere trapping heat and causing a warming of the atmosphere with a corresponding acceleration of melting of the ice caps.

The barrier island migration problem is not going to lessen. Very likely it will worsen, and if you want to live on such an island you must take this into account.

Actually, as discussed in Chapter 1, it is an oversimplification to say that American barrier islands are all migrating. At this time it appears that many islands are narrowing by erosion on both the ocean side and the lagoon side. Geologists suggest that this narrowing phase of island evolution is an essential preliminary step to more rapid and efficient landward migration.

The Outer Banks of North Carolina are an example of this more rapid migration phase, and Capes Island, South Carolina, is the ultimate in a rapidly landward-moving (migrating) barrier island. Capes Island is nothing more than a broad beach moving across older salt marsh deposits.

If you live on a barrier island and have a good view of the sea, the chances are you are in a particularly dangerous place. All American barrier islands are subject to hurricanes and storms, and to one degree or another the whole island is affected by such events. One can, however, maximize the likelihood of one's grandchildren inheriting the house by understanding some commonsense rules.

- No barrier island is a safe place on which to build.

- No two islands are alike. Each island must be understood in its own context.

- In order to build as safely as possible on an island, developers must understand how the particular island evolves, how it responds to a storm, and how fast it is migrating.

- A barrier island must not be developed like a Kansas cornfield.

The Kansas cornfield mentality of development in which a block of farmland is subdivided into identical lots has been the main problem in barrier island development. While the inland field represents a single environment, the barrier island represents several environments quite unlike those we find inland. The problem arises when island lots are apportioned in rectangles with no regard for the relative safety of each different environment.

For example, a maritime forest site is safer than an overwash pass, but rectangular lots are often laid out in both. Most dangerous of all are waterfront lots that are often just deep enough to build a house on without actually infringing on the surf zone. Ironically, these lots, which will be the first to erode away, are also the most highly priced and sought. Most American barrier islands in private hands are too far along in their stage of development to retreat from the aforementioned Kansas cornfield mentality.

In the old days at Nags Head, North Carolina, ocean-front lots were sufficiently long or deep (600 feet, or 180 m) to allow the owner to move his house from time to time as the yearly 6-foot (2-m) erosion rate gradually ate away the shoreline. The island dwellers could "roll with the flow." Today's Nags Head lots are no longer so long and deep, and so a severe erosion problem exists.

The Nags Head situation illustrates another principle. Some of the realtors of today deny that the shoreline is eroding, although in the 1950s some of the same realty companies sold the old 600-foot-deep lots clearly recognizing the fact that an erosion problem existed. This change in outlook comes simply and purely from the much inflated prices of sea-view property.

A large number of considerations should be taken into account in choosing a homesite. The relative importance attached to each of the items in the checklist below of course will vary from individual to individual, depending on such things as practical economics, availability of insurance, and personal preferences.

Barrier Island Checklist

1. *What is the elevation of the homesite? Is it above the 100-year flood elevation plus an allowance for wave impact (which can vary from 2 to 6 feet—0.6 to 2 m—depending on location).*

2. *How did the island and its man-related accoutrements respond to the last winter storm? To the last hurricane? To the largest hurricanes of record, e.g., Camille (1969) or Frederick (1979) in the Gulf Coast? To the 1962 Atlantic storm?*

3. *What is the erosion rate of the frontside and backside of the barrier island? A natural salt marsh on the backside often offers good erosion protection.*

4. *Take a walk on the beach. Do you see scarps (cliffs) or small bluffs of sand dunes with roots protruding? Do you see layers of mud, peat, or stumps on the beach? If so, the beach is eroding rapidly. Usually such evidence is best seen on the winter beach or after a storm.*

5. *How wide is the barrier island? A wide island is less likely to overwash during a storm or have an inlet cut through it than a narrow island. Wide expanses of open water on the sound side of the island may favor inlet formation. Extensive salt marsh on the lagoon side generally suggests new inlet formation is less likely.*

6. *Are there trees that will afford some shelter in the next big blow? Does the community protect such trees? One of the authors of this book lived near a beach, in an area with many trees. During Hurricane Camille some big trees blew down and made holes in his roof, whereas many of the neighboring houses that were not sheltered by trees were much more severely damaged. Better a few holes in the roof than no house at all.*

7. *Are there protective dunes along the front of the island? Dunes protect property and at the same time are necessary for evolution and survival of the beach during a storm. On some barrier islands in New Jersey, the 1962 Ash Wednesday storm damage was a direct function of the width of dunes next to the beach: wide dunes, less damage.*

8. *Is there vegetation on the dunes? Unvegetated sand dunes are usually moving sand dunes (figure 2-1). You may soon be using a bulldozer for a lawn mower. In general, the more vegetation and the greater the diversity of plant species, the safer the homesite. Do not forget to protect the vegetation during and after construction. If a builder insists on having a bulldozed, flat lot, get another builder.*

9. *Look at the shells in the sand of the homesite. Shells similar in color and type to those found on the beach probably indicate that the site is where storm overwash occurs. Keep away. If the shells are black and white, unlike those on the beach, the site may be where an old inlet was filled in or where the island was artifically elevated. Keep away.*

10. *Dig a ditch. Is there a soil profile in the sand? Is there a foot or two (30 to 60 cm) of white sand, containing some organic matter, above yellow sand? If so, the site is probably a relatively safe one. You can also look for soil profiles by looking at nearby road cuts. Soil profiles develop only on long-stabilized areas*

2-1. Wind has removed more than 4 feet (1.2 m) of sand around this property marker near Nags Head, North Carolina. What if a house had been built here? (Photo: Orrin Pilkey, Jr.)

where no storm overwash occurs. But this criterion is not always valid: eroding coastal plain mainland shores may reveal an old soil profile right on the beach, as do some barrier islands. If you see such a profile in a beach scarp, the latter is more significant than the former.

11. Look at the lot during the wet season. Does it drain slowly or turn marshy? Do not build where it is marshy. Among other problems, septic tank drainage will be poor.

12. Look at the road construction, particularly on those roads leading to the shoreline. Such roads should wind and go over, not through, dunes. Roads that cut straight to the beach and through, not over, dunes act as overwash passes during storms. Avoid them. Notches cut or worn through the dune to allow public access to the beach may also allow storm flooding.

13. How close is the nearest inlet? A general rule of thumb is keep at least half a mile (1 km) away from the nearest inlet. Inlets tend to widen during storms and they tend to migrate. Migration patterns are documented in some areas and published in Corps of Engineers or sea grant publications.

14. Is there safe egress from the island in case of a storm? Many heavily populated barrier islands are considered impossible to evacuate completely even with twenty-four hours' storm notice. Part of the problem is human nature; many people will not try to evacuate until the wind begins to blow. Ask, too, what the lowest elevation on the escape route is (often the approaches to a bridge), and how quickly during a storm this low is likely to flood. Purchase a storm evacua-

tion map from the National Oceanics and Atmospheric Administration, National Ocean Survey, U.S. Dept. of Commerce, Rockville, MD 20852. Then consider if the escape bridge is a fixed span or a drawbridge. Always assume that a drawbridge will be stuck in its open position at the moment of greatest need.

15. Is the site on an artificially excavated canal (finger canal)? These frequently become polluted because of poor circulation and poor drainage of septic tank effluent, a problem that usually does not rear its ugly head until after the lots have been built on. There are also cases in which finger canals become over-wash passes or inlets during hurricanes.

16. Is the site on fill, such as a filled-in marsh? In times past, covering salt marshes on the backside of islands was a common way to gain more land for development. Such land has poor drainage and septic tank characteristics and usually is well below storm-surge flood level.

17. Has the beach been stabilized? The presence of seawalls, groins, or revetments is a sure sign of the beginning of the end of the beach. Stabilized beaches end up costing local citizens a lot of tax money. Sometimes a replenished beach is difficult to distinguish from a natural beach. Make sure your beach is natural if you are going to build or buy near it.

18. Do nearby beaches or islands have seawalls or groins? Island beaches often obtain their sand supply from many miles of adjacent shoreline. If nearby islands have been stabilized with seawalls or groins, your island may begin to erode more rapidly as a result of the loss of its sand supply. Likewise, new inlet modification such as dredging for navigation or emplacement of jetties may interrupt the beach's sand supply.

19. What is the community and state attitude toward beach erosion? Will the community flex with nature? Will they choose to spend tax money to stop island migration and hence ultimately destroy the beach?

20. What is the attitude of the voting public toward issues of importance to you (e.g., future development trends)? Remember, on most barrier islands, the vote is held by a very tiny minority of year-round residents, and those residents generally make a living from island development.

21. What are the local regulations? Be aware of laws concerned with the following aspects of barrier island living:
    - Dune and beach buggies. Dune buggies destroy dunes or cause them to begin moving.
    - Sand removal, particularly frontal dunes. The less sand removed, the better.
    - Setback regulations. Setting buildings back from the beach lengthens their life, although it is a temporary solution.
    - Building codes. Even if your house is built well, its neighbor may not be and may fly apart during a storm and batter yours down.
    - Community planning. Multistory buildings generally should not be allowed near the beach. Such buildings obstruct sea views but most important reduce a community's option to respond to the eroding beach.
    - Public access, sanitation, vegetation removal.

22. How well are building laws enforced? How well qualified are the enforcers? On many American barrier islands, building code regulations are only lightly enforced and often by unqualified building inspectors. On one southeastern U.S. barrier island the inspector is a retired pharmacist with no engineering experi-

ence! The National Flood Insurance Program requires a building inspection program but its quality is seldom checked on. The rate of reconstruction in Gulf Shores, Alabama, after Hurricane Frederick (1980) was such that it is doubtful that inspection kept pace with construction.

23. What insurance coverage is available? Is the community eligible for the National Flood Insurance Program?
24. Where are the pipelines supplying water, the lines supplying electricity, the phone lines? Do they cross low, narrow portions of islands that are liable to break through in the next storm?
25. What is water quality and quantity like and, if the water is pumped, is it from wells? What will it be like when all lots are sold and built on and all septic tanks in use?
26. What is septic tank drainage like? Frequently, a layer of impermeable mud is found a few feet below the surface of barrier islands, which may block effluent percolation.

The Pacific Shoreline

The Pacific shoreline, like New England's, is highly variable in nature. It differs from the New England shore in that glaciers have not left their mark, and since the Pacific shore is ringed by mountains, the cliffs and bluffs are often much grander than anything to be seen in the Northeast.

Relatively few studies of our Pacific shores have examined the dangers to shoreline dwellers. Some of the developing low-lying areas adjacent to sandy beaches are similar to barrier islands in terms of what home dwellers and builders should watch for. In particular, the problems faced on the sandspits across the mouths of estuaries (e.g., Tillamook Spit, Oregon, and Crescent City, California) are essentially identical to those on barrier islands.

A quick look at our Pacific shores reveals that the shoreline system is often more difficult to evaluate and understand than that on barrier islands. Gerry Kuhn and his associates at Scripps Institution in La Jolla, California, have most thoroughly studied shoreline retreat mechanisms for any stretch of the Pacific Coast. A quick summary of their conclusions has application to the entire Pacific shore.

The frequency of storms along the Southern California coast appears to be cyclical. Between 1884 and 1893, historical records and shoreline maps indicate a simultaneous occurrence of high rainfall and unusually large storm waves. The same is true for the early 1940s, when waves up to 40 feet (12 m) in height were measured by Francis Shepard of Scripps. Partly because of the cyclical nature of storm waves, the shoreline of California will erode or retreat in an erratic fashion. You cannot put a meaningful rate on most retreating bluffs because they may go from as little as one year to as many as forty or more years between sudden and catastrophic retreats as the bluff caves in. This is quite a different system from barrier islands, which tend to beat a steady and predictable retreat.

In January, 1983, the giant Pacific storms that struck California beaches produced banner headlines across the country, as did smaller storms in 1979 and 1981. The 1983 storms were particularly newsworthy because the waves were crashing into the living rooms of television and movie stars in Malibu. Numerous interviews of stars flashed across the country on the evening news, and the endangered homes of celebrities dominated conversation on late-night talk shows. A recurrent theme in the interviews was the notion that the damage was high simply because the storms were so big. What few coastal residents of California seem to realize is that the damage was high because more and more homes crowd closer and closer to ever-narrowing, retreating beaches. Americans can be assured that during the eighties more and more headline space will be devoted to disasters on California beaches.

Many beaches of Southern California and other Pacific areas as well are short of sand and much narrower than they were fifty years ago. This is probably because of the construction of a large number of agricultural storage dams on coastal rivers, trapping sand that would have gone to the sea. Man is replacing part of that sand by causing increased erosion of farmlands and also increased erosion of the shoreline itself. Some of the most common causes of increased erosion of Southern California bluffs include grading bluff tops to enhance the sea view, emplacing storm drains on cliff faces, which causes runoff down the face of the bluff; and removing vegetation or placing lifeguard towers and other structures at the bluff edge. Seepage of ground water through sea cliffs has a lubricant effect, aiding in cliff failure.

The early railroad connecting Los Angeles to San Diego generally spanned stream valleys with trestles. Subsequent highway construction has utilized culvert construction instead of trestles. Culverts concentrate runoff to the extent that erosion in coastal gullies and canyons leading to beaches has increased tremendously.

On and on it goes. Just like on a barrier island, it seems as though just about anything humans do to the shoreline has some impact on the system's behavior, and almost always this impact is a negative one. Successful Pacific shore living should minimize our negative impact on nature's shoreline processes and thereby maximize our own safety and our own enjoyment of shoreline living. Of course there is the added hazard of earthquakes along portions of this coast, which makes Pacific site selection even more challenging.

Pacific Checklist

1. *Before choosing a California site, first look over the* Assessment and Atlas of Shoreline Erosion Along the California Coast *(1977) published by the California Department of Navigation and Ocean Development. If a proposed homesite is described in this volume as having an erosion problem or being artificially protected, beware! If a sea view is imperative, build on what this publication describes as "stable rock."*
2. *If a sandy, nonbluffed shoreline at one of the many sandy spits in front of river mouths is being considered, read our barrier island checklist.*
3. *What is the elevation of your proposed site? The higher the elevation, the better. Remember that in La Jolla, California, 40-foot (12-m) waves were measured near the beaches in 1940, and that although since that time few waves over 12 feet (4 m) have been spotted, the big ones will return some day!*
4. *If investigating a bluff or cliff homesite, how solid is the cliff? Solid rock with few joints and no layering is the ideal, but such rock types are not the rule along our Pacific shores. Walk to the bluff and hit it with a hammer. Does it ring? If so, that is a good sign. If the bluff is made up of lightly cemented material (can be scraped away with a shovel or hand-pick), avoid it altogether.*
5. *Is the bluff made up of layered rock and do the layers dip seaward? If so, the*

bluff may someday slide seaward. Only the force of gravity aided by a bit of lubrication from lawn watering is required to get things moving. Glide planes commonly occur along clay layers (shale or old volcanic ash beds). Avoid such bluffs.

6. Does the bluff have cavities in it? Features such as small caves may be widened by storms or by ground water seepage and will contribute to bluff failure. Abrasion by beach cobbles thrown up during a storm is a common villain, as is cavity enlargement by the dissolving of rock, particularly limestone.

7. Is there historical or physical evidence of previous bluff failure? Do you see a jumble of landslide material at the base of the cliff on the beach? Do local residents and public records indicate a history of bluff collapse? Take a long walk on the beach. Consult with local or state offices for maps showing land-slip hazard areas. Do not consult with realtors or developers on this matter.

8. If possible, walk on the beach below both developed and undeveloped sections of the bluff. Signs of excess water seepage (springs, clumps of green vegetation) in front of developed sections probably are from septic tanks or watered lawns. Watch out! Such seepage can lubricate cliff failure.

9. If the bluff top of your prospective development has been bulldozed to better the view, if drainpipes have been installed on the bluff face, or if other things have been done that might increase the rate of bluff erosion, stay away. Again, walk on the beach and look for evidence of fresh erosion or bluff failure.

10. What is the community's, county's, city's, or developer's understanding of bluff erosion problems? What is the "party line" on how to solve the erosion problem? If you hear there is no erosion problem, be skeptical. If you hear that erosion can be stopped, be very skeptical. Even if this is true, the means to do so will come out of your pocket.

11. What is the winter beach or bluff like? Try to see for yourself before you buy or build. The broad summer beach sometimes disappears altogether during the winter, exposing the bluff to direct erosion from winter storms. Best of all, try to observe the beach after a storm.

12. Are nearby rivers dammed upstream? If so, the sand supply from river to beach may be greatly reduced, which may lead to drastic reduction in the size of your beach and ultimately a perceived need for costly engineering measures.

13. Have the beaches been stabilized? In general, avoid living adjacent to seawalls, groins, and even replenished (replaced) beaches. The long-range prognosis for beaches that have been stabilized or held in position against the forces of nature is increasing destruction of the beach environment at ever-increasing economic cost. If you do locate in such an area, what is the long-term (fifty-year) commitment to maintaining such structures? Who will pay for it?

14. Are there groins, jetties, and seawalls on adjacent beaches to the north or south? These may result in a cutoff of sand supply to your beach, causing it to erode.

15. What type of insurance coverage is available? Is the community eligible for the National Flood Insurance Program? If so, local officials will have flood maps that can tell you if you are at a dangerous elevation from the standpoint of storm flooding.

16. Is your site in an earthquake hazard area? If so, the danger of associated landsliding may be increased. We recommend Peace of Mind in Earthquake

Country *by Peter Yanev* as a guide for evaluating your site and structure relative to earthquake hazards.*

17. *Is the homesite in a potential tsunami (tidal wave) zone? Depending on the part of the coast, this hazard may determine the minimum safe elevation.*

18. *Are landslides likely to occur? They are frequent along the West Coast, more so than on the Atlantic Coast, because of the hilly terrain and the existence of earthquakes. The cause of landslides may be either a natural geologic deficiency or a man-made problem. Evidence of a previous landslide should raise a warning flag to a prospective buyer or builder. Spotting old landslides by a walk on the beach is usually easy, even for the nongeologist. Common conditions inviting landsliding include:*
    - *A bluff in which natural soil rests upon a thin clay seam or layer, which acts as a lubricant to enhance the sliding of this upper soil.*
    - *A hillside graded by man to provide a flat lot to build upon. Part of the lot is cut into the hill and part is made up of a landfill. The landfill part especially is subject to both settlement and sliding.*
    - *A hillside that has been cut into to provide a flat lot without a landfill. The danger here is that on the uphill side the cut is too steep and the soil above it slides down on the house. This was a major cause of destruction in the 1981 mudslides of Northern California.*

Protecting the Site

Once a homesite has been chosen near the beach, the work has just begun. A lot of political and environmental alertness will be required in order to maintain neighborhood standards.

To begin with, in many beach areas—Pacific, Atlantic, and Gulf—the actual voting public is a very small minority of the community's summer population. Thousands of beach community homeowners have watched helplessly as their community changed its flavor with increasing density of development. The most common development problems are caused by condominiums and high-rises. Ocean City, Maryland, is the type example of "overnight" change of a community through encouragement of high-rise construction immediately adjacent to the (eroding) beach.

A very common problem along the southeastern Gulf and Atlantic shores is the disappearing developer. Figure Eight Island, North Carolina, is on its fourth developer, for example. The problem is that Developer #1 may have made all sorts of promises regarding high-rises and commercial development that Developer #4 is not obligated in the slightest to honor.

Strong homeowner associations are essential to the maintenance of a desirable community life. They must be alert not only to their own neighborhood, but also to what is happening to the beach for miles on either side of them. Twenty miles (30 km) in either direction is a good rule of thumb for a community "zone of alertness." Events concerning beaches miles away can adversely affect one's own beach within a matter of a few years. Following is a list of some of the events within the "zone of alertness" that must be watched for:

---

*For details of publication for this and other books, articles, or pamphlets cited, consult Bibliography in the back of this book.

1. Deepening of a channel or inlet.
2. Construction of seawalls, groins, jetties, revetments or any other type of fixed structure at the beach.
3. Replenishment of a beach or bulldozing of sand from the lower to the upper beach. Borrowing of offshore sand for such replenishment.
4. Development of a beach community in a heretofore undeveloped area.
5. Construction of finger canals or filling of marshes.

We advise communities to hire a consulting geologist to advise them of the possible ramification of any of these events. The need for alertness and quick action cannot be overemphasized.

At any homesite it is best to maintain the vegetative cover as is or encourage the growth of native plants (figure 2-2). Admittedly, this is partly for aesthetic reasons; no more displeasing sight exists to coastal purists than the neatly cut, perfectly flat, and beautifully manicured green lawns of barrier island communities such as Brigantine, New Jersey. Rolling sand dunes and grass flats are part of the beauty of the coast. Beautiful manicured lawns belong in inland suburbia. Maintenance of natural vegetation also has some practical value in terms of sand trapping and maintaining a volume of sand for storm protection. In southern Florida natural dune vegetation has often been replaced by Australian pines. Although the pines are beautiful, they are poor dune builders. Beachfront property owners who desire to build up dunes (always a good idea) should revert to natural vegetation.

2-2. Beach access walkways over the dune minimize damage to dune vegetation on Figure Eight Island, North Carolina. (Photo: Paul Foster)

Again, communities are advised to hire consulting geologists or botanists to recommend the best path of site maintenance. This is especially true for the Pacific Coast bluff dwellers. The minor expenditure of hiring a consultant may pay off many times in future community well being. Some state coastal management agencies have experts available just for this purpose. Every state has publications available (from, for example, the Sea Grant Office) concerning coastal zone development. Many such publications are very generalized, and some tend toward the any-development-is-good mentality. Get expert advice before you buy or build.

Egress: Escape from Disaster

An important aspect of general site choice is availability of emergency egress. Although mentioned in each of the checklists, it is nonetheless worth discussing in greater detail.

Anyone who has been through an evacuation of a community will be aware of the chaos that can occur and the need for preplanning and order. Depending on location, the evacuation can be "vertical" into high-rise buildings or "horizontal" to safe inland locations. Certain congested coastal cities such as New Orleans, Galveston, and Miami have designated specific high-rise buildings as hurricane-safe structures. This vertical evacuation may be necessary if a rapid, total evacuation to safe inland sites is impractical in the case of a large urban population. A combination of vertical and horizontal evacuation may be employed in some instances.

Vertical evacuation is not truly an evacuation, but a move to a position of possible greater safety *within the danger zone*. Most coastal experts have grave reservations about this alternative to evacuating the hazard zone. Some of the serious concerns raised include:

- Will high-rise buildings with large expanses of glass and screen partitions hold up in hurricane winds, or be gutted? High-rise buildings are essentially untested with respect to hurricanes.

- Who will certify these structures as safe for storm refuges?

- Who is responsible for liability when private structures are used?

- Knowing that vertical refuge is a possible alternative, will people delay evacuation from an area until it is too late, thereby increasing the risk and potential injury and loss of life?

- On islands and cut-off spits, how will secondary evacuation problems that will exist after the storm, for example, continued flooding, loss of bridges and roads, blockage by debris, downed power lines, and similar secondary hazards, be handled?

Truly, storm egress is a critical problem for many locations. The escape route you select that seems satisfactory for the population in the area in which you are living should be reviewed over time. If this area grows to any great extent, it would be worthwhile to reevaluate that route to see whether, with more people using it, it is still as satisfactory as you once thought it was.

Escape to inland sites is complicated by bottlenecks. For some locations the bottlenecks are routes leading to the bridges. Depend on it—excited and hysterical drivers will cause wrecks, run out of gas, have a flat tire; the cars behind will be lined up for miles with scared occupants. Be sure you can get out when the warning comes, and have your plans made as to where you will go, with alternatives in mind when you find your refuge is fully occupied or in danger itself from something unforeseen.

Hurricane Carmen, which hit the Gulf Coast in September, 1974, illustrated the desirability of leaving early to miss the traffic jam. Over 75,000 people are said to have evacuated what was thought to be danger areas in Louisiana and Mississippi. On the few roads leading north, the traffic was bumper to bumper. In one case an accident stopped traffic, which then backed up for 19 miles (31 km). Imagine the feelings of a family in a stopped car 17 miles (27 km) back in a pouring rain, wondering what was the matter, not knowing when they could move again, worrying about the approaching storm, and coping with the demands of nature on the children and dogs in the rain. The lobby of the motel where one of the authors stayed was filled with people trying to book a place, but every room in town was taken. These people were forced to continue their journey north. Fortunately for New Orleans and Mississippi, the hurricane came ashore farther west.

3

Beach House Construction

Better Safe Than Sorry

Heeding Biblical Advice

Many words have been written on how to build structures that can best resist storms, hurricanes, and floods. But no better advice can be given than that contained in Matthew 7:24–27 (or Luke 6:47–49), which we quote in part:

> A wise man . . . built his house upon a rock and the rain descended and the floods came, and the winds blew, and beat upon that house, and it fell not for it was founded upon a rock . . . . A foolish man . . . built his house upon the sand and the rain descended and the floods came, and the wind blew, and beat upon that house; and it fell and great was the fall of it.

From earliest history humans have learned to protect themselves from weather by building a shelter. We now know how to design a house so that the roof will not blow away and the walls will not crush under pressure. It is therefore extraordinary that tens of thousands of people in countries subject to hurricane winds and waters live contentedly in houses that will provide no protection from extreme weather.

A house or building designed for inland areas is built primarily to resist vertical loads. It is assumed that the foundation and framing must support the load of the walls, floor, and roof, and relatively insignificant wind forces.

A well-built house in a hurricane-prone area, however, must be constructed to withstand a variety of strong wind forces that may come from any direction. While many people think that wind damage is caused by uniform horizontal pressures, it is in fact mostly caused by uplift (vertical), suctional, and torsional (twisting) forces. High horizontal pressure on the windward side will be accompanied by suction on the leeward side. The roof is subject to downward pressure, and more important, to uplift. Often a roof is sucked up by the uplift drag of the wind; some towers and signboards adequately designed for straightforward winds have fallen from torsional or twisting winds. Usually the failure is in the devices (or lack thereof) that tie the parts of such structures together. Another wind-related force is caused by the drop in barometric pressure as the eye of the storm passes. Other forces that should be taken into account during shoreline construction include those from waves, rising water, flying debris, movement of the land under the house, erosion, and landslides. Figure 3-1 illustrates some of the effects of storm forces on buildings.

Destruction from these forces can be minimized by sagacious location of the house. Having done as much as possible by proper location selection, the next step is to select the type of house and then to design it to withstand the damaging forces.

The big difference between a house designed for inland areas and a well-built

a. Wind Forces

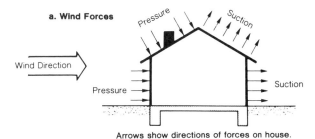

Arrows show directions of forces on house.

b. Drop in Barometric Pressure

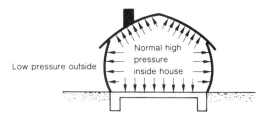

This can occur as the eye of the storm passes; it creates different pressures inside and out, so that the high pressure inside attempts to burst the house open.

c. Wave Forces and Debris

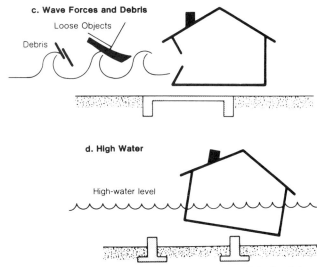

d. High Water

Unanchored house can float off the foundation.

3-1. The forces to be reckoned with at the shoreline: winds, barometric pressure, waves, and high water. (This figure and several others in this chapter are from Defense Civil Preparedness Agency, Publication TR-83.)

beach cottage is that the one on the beach must be held together much more soundly. The ideal to approach is to be able to pick the house up, turn it upside down, shake it, and have it still remain intact. Of course we know this is asking a bit too much. On the other hand, we should have no such expectation for the typical inland house. If the same exaggerated procedure were to be followed for that kind of structure, it would surely fall quickly apart, even though the design and construction were proper and appropriate for its location.

If the rules for safe living in a coastal region were condensed to one sentence, it might well be: Put the building or dwelling at an elevation high enough so the highest high water will not reach it, and build it sturdy enough so the strongest wind will not destroy it. If building on an eroding shoreline (for example, on a bluff), place it far enough back so shoreline (that is, cliff retreat) will not catch up with it. It is fundamental that any structure, be it beach cottage, building, signboard, or tower, be built to withstand the forces to which it may be subjected.

This chapter should be read together with Chapter 4, "The Older House: To Buy or Not To Buy," as the two are related, and it would be redundant to repeat the same principles of construction. Two other chapters which cover relevant material are Chapter 8, with its treatment of wind forces, and Chapter 9 on building codes.

General Rules for Building on the Coast

Safe Storm Egress

First of all, there must exist a means of egress or exit to a safe location inland within a reasonable length of time. As mentioned in the previous chapter, even if you have selected an escape route that seems satisfactory for the population in your area, it should be reviewed from time to time. If the area has grown to any great extent, reevaluation might be helpful in ascertaining whether, with more people using it, the route is still as satisfactory as you once thought it was.

A Good Building Site

On an island, the least desirable areas are where the island is narrow or low or lacks much dune protection. Keep away from the vicinity of flat, straight roads that extend to the beach. Keep at least 100 feet (30 m) back from the first dune, preferably 200 feet (60 m). Beware of unstable bluffs. See Chapter 2 for an in-depth treatment of how to choose a suitable building site.

Adequate Fastenings

A conventional structure is normally built to resist vertical, downward loads (its own weight), plus live loads (contents, people, snow) on the floor and roof. It is a gravity structure. Only token regard is given to transverse or sideward loads or forces, such as wind and waves. But when a storm hits, the forces can be upward (uplift), sidewards, or from any direction. There is not only pressure but also suction. Ordinarily, rafters, concrete blocks, bricks, and other structural elements are laid on top of each other with minimal fastening. On the coast, however, all the components need to be well connected. Rafters to columns, columns to trusses, truss rafters to walls must be securely fastened together with adequate anchors or clips. All structural members (beams, rafters, columns) should be held fast to each other on the assumption that about 25 percent of the vertical load on that member may be a force coming from either the transverse (sideways) or upward direction. Building it right (connecting all elements soundly) adds very little to the cost of the frame of a dwelling, certainly under 10 percent of the frame and a very much smaller percentage of the total cost of the house. Thousands of houses that have been destroyed by storms, hurricanes, or the fringes of a tornado would be standing today if their components had only been fastened together more securely. It is an unforgivable waste to build a structure wherein the lumber cannot develop its capacity for strength because of poor connections.

Secure Foundations

The foundations, whether wood posts, piling, concrete piers, or footing walls under slabs, must be securely anchored (fastened) to the ground, and the superstructure must be anchored to the foundations. In other words, the whole structure must be anchored to the ground so it will not float or blow off its foundation.

Among the lessons learned from inspecting the damages to the Florida Panhandle from Hurricane Eloise in September 1975 was that slabs poured directly on the ground perform poorly. Often wave action washed out the sand underneath the slab, removing the structure's support and resulting in failure. The storm revealed some shoddy construction. Wire mesh for the slab was often placed directly on the sand and the concrete poured on top of it, leaving the mesh out of the concrete but below it and in the sand, where it served no structural purpose. To be effective the mesh should have been set on blocks or chairs before pouring, or pulled up into the slab during the pouring of the concrete. This was typical of most of the failed slabs on grade in the area and is a practice to be avoided.

Proper Material Selection

A structure must be built of materials that are tough and ductile, so as to resist shock and impact. Wood, steel, and reinforced concrete are good. Hollow masonry, brick, and precast concrete panels are poor, unless adequately reinforced and anchored.

Avoidance of Irregularities

The design of a house or building in a coastal area should minimize structural discontinuities and irregularities. That is, a house should have a minimum of nooks and crannies and offsets on the exterior. Experience shows that damage is concentrated at points of structural discontinuity. When irregularities are absent, the house reacts to storm winds as a complete unit.

Appropriate Aerodynamic Shape

The shape of a house, and particularly the roof, affects its ability to resist high winds. In Hurricane Camille damage was less for hip roofs, which slope in four directions, than for gable roofs, which slope in only two directions. The shape of the horizontal cross section (the house as viewed from above) is important. The effect of the same wind on a round or elliptical shape will be about 60 percent of what it would be on a square or rectangular shape; on a hexagonal or octagonal cross section, about 80 percent of what it would be on a square or rectangular shape.

Failure Modes

Some of the rules to be followed in selecting or designing a house are illustrated in figure 3-2. Several possible failure modes along with suggested corrective measures can be found in figure 3-3.

Wood Structures

Wood is one of the best materials for absorbing short-duration loads such as those caused by wind. Whether or not the building will survive a storm, however, depends on how well the components are connected and how solid the anchoring is to the ground. A wood-frame house properly braced with well-fastened connections is hard to beat for safety against dynamic lateral forces such as wind or earthquakes. As illustrated in figure 3-4, proper construction can also reduce the effect of weathering and lengthen the life of wood.

The framing and sheathing of a wood-frame house should be nailed together according to good nailing practice, as detailed in figure 3-5. To help understand this, figure 3-6 relates the length of the nails to the pennyweight designation. Figures 3-7 and 3-8 will also help clarify the terms in figure 3-5. In hurricane areas proper nailing should be supplemented by additional anchoring and reinforcing with metal strips, plates, and bolts, which strengthen the connections between the different components of the frame. They will significantly improve the continuity and strength of the house, at very little added cost. The basic premise is to make sure that the footing is tied to the foundation is tied to the floor is tied to the wall is tied to the roof. More details can be found in the U.S. Forest Service report *Houses Can Resist Hurricanes.*

Bracing

A wood-frame building is most likely to suffer damage when it has insufficient lateral bracing or inadequate connections between lateral bracing and other structural elements. Lateral bracing may consist of shear walls of plywood or a series of lumber strips or metal straps at about a 45-degree angle across the studs (figure 3-9). A shear wall is one which in its own plane provides resistance to racking forces from the action of wind on the adjoining walls at right angles to it. Racking (lateral or sideways collapse) occurs when the strain or deformation levels are beyond what is normal. To prevent this, lumber diagonals should be made of 1 by 6s long enough to reach from the top plate (horizontal beam supporting the roof) to the sill (horizontal beam immediately above the foundation) at a 45-degree angle. The 1 by 6s should be nailed to each of the studs, the top plate, and the sill. Two cross-diagonals (X-bracing) are stronger than single diagonals.

An alternative to 1 by 6 lumber for diagonal bracing is to use a special steel strap 1 to 1¼ inches (2.5 to 3 cm) wide with holes for nailing to the top plate, sill, and each of the studs where they intersect, the same as with the wood. For either type bracing

a. Pick a good site.

b. Plan your escape route.

c. Forces may come from any direction.

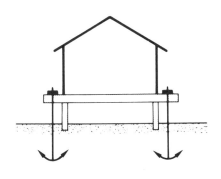

d. House should be well anchored to ground.

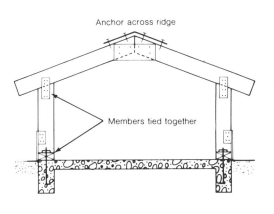

Anchor across ridge

Members tied together

e. Structure should have continuity.

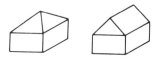

f. Hip roof is better than gable.

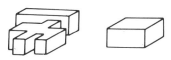

h. Avoid irregular shapes; keep it simple so it can act as a unit.

g. Wind has less effect on curved surfaces than on flat.

3-2. Some rules in selecting or designing a house.

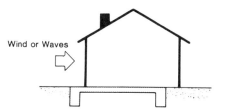

a. Horizontal displacement (lateral movement).

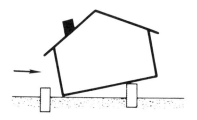

Cure: Shear connection (anchorage) to foundation.

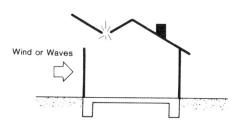

b. Loss of parts of house by material failure or connection separation.

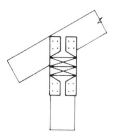

Cure: Adequate connections and anchorage; properly sized and spaced material.

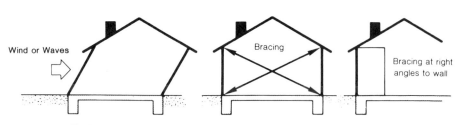

c. Racking (lateral collapse).

Cure: Bracing, such as diagonals; plywood sheets well nailed to studs and floor plates; reinforcing in masonry houses.

d. Collapse caused by connection separation or material failure.

Cure: Adequate connections (see b above and figure 3-2e); properly spaced and sized material.

3-3. Modes of failure and suggested cures.

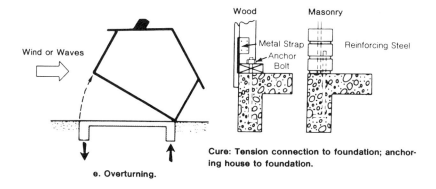

Cure: Tension connection to foundation; anchoring house to foundation.

e. Overturning.

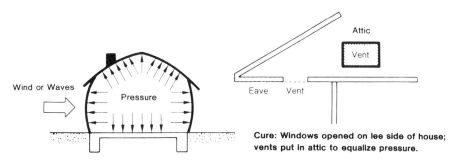

f. Atmospheric differential (higher pressure inside than outside).

Cure: Windows opened on lee side of house; vents put in attic to equalize pressure.

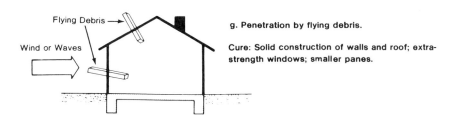

g. Penetration by flying debris.

Cure: Solid construction of walls and roof; extra-strength windows; smaller panes.

3-3 (cont'd). Modes of failure and suggested cures.

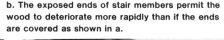

b. The exposed ends of stair members permit the wood to deteriorate more rapidly than if the ends are covered as shown in a.

a. Shown in these figures are two examples of stair construction with much different degrees of exposure of board ends. The less exposure the better.

3-4. Wood weathers and deteriorates very rapidly in structures next to the beach. (Photos: Paul Foster)

the minimum-size nail should be 8d; a 10d is preferable. The metal strap may often be easier to use for reinforcing an existing house.

Better than diagonal bracing is shear-wall bracing—a continuous cover of plywood paneling over the studs. Where possible, extend the panels from the top plate to the sill. If the ceiling is too high for the usual 4- by 8-foot (1.2- by 2.4-m) plywood panel, use two panels of equal length instead of one 8-foot panel with a fill-in of a few inches. The edges of the paneling should be nailed securely with nails at least 8d in size at 6-inch (15-cm) centers. The intermediate nailing of panel to stud can be at 12-inch (30-cm) centers. The plywood should be a half-inch (1.3 cm) thick, or it can be thinner if backed by Sheetrock.

Figure 3-10 shows details of tying the wall paneling to studs at the corners, connections between interior and exterior wood-frame walls, tying the wall system to the floor system, and a method of fastening wood floor joists to a masonry wall.

Trussed Rafters

Wooden trussed rafters (see figure 3-7) are widely used in the construction of houses and small buildings, as they save in labor and material. The trussed rafter uses 2 by 4s, whereas conventional rafters and ceiling joists employ 2 by 6s and 2 by 8s. Further, the trussed rafter is supported completely by the outside walls, allow-

3-5. Recommended Schedule for Nailing the Framing and Sheathing of a Well-Constructed Wood-Frame House.

Joining	Nailing method	no.	size	placement
Joist header to joist	endnail	3	16d	
Joist to sill or girder	toenail	3	8d	
Header and edge joist to sill	toenail		8d	16 in. (40 cm) on center
Bridging to joist	toenail each end	2	8d	
Ledger strip to beam, 2 in. thick		3	16d	at each joist
Subfloor, boards:				
1 X 6 in. and smaller		2	8d	to each joist
1 X 8 in.		3	8d	to each joist
Subfloor, plywood:				
at edges			8d	6 in. (15 cm) on center
at intermediate joists			8d	8 in. (20 cm) on center
Subfloor (2 X 6, tongue and groove) to joist or girder	blind nail (casing) and facenail	2	16d	
Sole plate to stud, horizontal assembly	endnail	2	16d	at each stud
Top plate to stud	endnail	2	16d	
Stud to sole plate	toenail	4	8d	
Sole plate to joist or blocking	facenail		16d	16 in. (40 cm) on center
Doubled studs	facenail, stagger		10d	16 in. (40 cm) on center
End stud of intersecting wall to exterior wall stud	facenail		16d	16 in. (40 cm) on center
Upper top plate to lower top plate	facenail		16d	16 in. (40 cm) on center
Upper top plate, laps and intersections	facenail	2	16d	
Continuous header, two pieces, each edge			12d	12 in. (30 cm) on center
Ceiling joist to top wall plates	toenail	3	8d	
Ceiling joist laps at partition	facenail	4	16d	
Rafter to top plate	toenail	2	8d	
Rafter to ceiling joist	facenail	3	10d	
Rafter to valley or hip rafter	toenail	3	10d	
Ridge board to rafter	endnail	3	10d	
Rafter to rafter through ridge board	toenail	4	8d	
	endnail	1	10d	
Collar beam to rafter:				
2 in. member	facenail	2	12d	
1 in. member	facenail	3	8d	

continued . . .

Joining	Nailing method	no.	size	placement
1-in. diagonal let-in brace to each stud and plate (4 nails at top)		2	8d	
Built-up corner studs:				
studs to blocking	facenail	2	10d	each side
intersecting stud to corner studs	facenail		16d	12 in. (30 cm) on center
Built-up girders and beams, 3 or more members	facenail		20d	32 in. (80 cm) on center
Wall sheathing:				
1 X 8 in. or less, horizontal	facenail	2	8d	at each stud
1 X 6 in. or more, diagonal	facenail	3	8d	at each stud
Wall sheathing, vertically applied plywood:				
$\frac{3}{8}$ in. and less thick	facenail		6d	6 in. (15 cm) edge
$\frac{1}{2}$ in. and more thick	facenail		8d	12 in. (30 cm) intermediate
Wall sheathing, vertically applied fiberboard:				
$\frac{1}{2}$ in. thick	facenail			$1\frac{1}{2}$ in. roofing 3 in. (7.5 cm)
$\frac{25}{32}$ in. thick	facenail			$1\frac{3}{4}$ in. roofing 6 in. (15 cm)
Roof sheathing boards, 4, 6, 8 in. width	facenail	2	8d	at each rafter
Roof sheathing, plywood:				
$\frac{3}{8}$ in. and less thick	facenail		6d	6 in. (15 cm) edge and
$\frac{1}{2}$ in. and more thick	facenail		8d	12 in. (30 cm) intermediate

SOURCE: U.S. Forest Service, Research Paper FPL 33

3-6. Size of Nails

Pennyweight	6d	8d	10d	12d	16d	20d	30d	40d	50d	60
Length	2''	2½''	3''	3¼''	3½''	4''	4½''	5''	5½''	6''

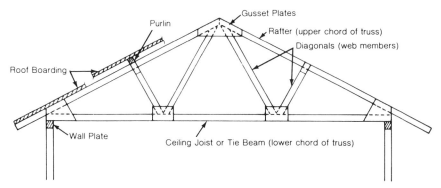

a. Roof truss or trussed rafter. Note that there is a clear span end to end (between walls) with no interior columns.

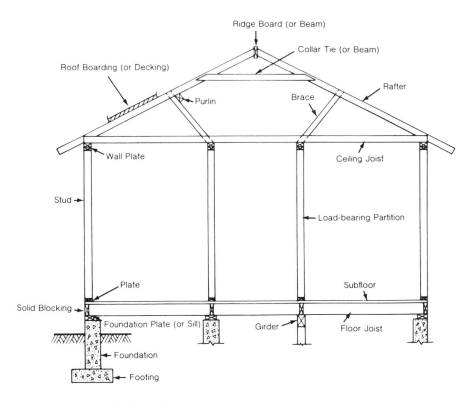

b. Braced Rafter Framing.

3-7. Nomenclature of wood house framing. (This figure and several others in this chapter are from U.S. Forest Service, Research Paper FPL 33.)

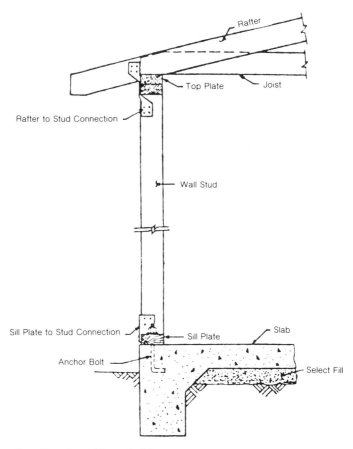

3-8. Typical wall section of wood-frame building.

ing the partitions to be put anywhere, giving complete freedom of floor plan design.

The Forest Products Laboratory conducted a study (U.S. Forest Service, Research Paper FPL No. 204) of different connection systems to join the wood members of a trussed rafter (figure 3-11). These included nailed plywood gusset plates, nail-glued plywood gusset plates, and sheet metal gusset plates. The trusses were loaded and deflections measured at intervals of up to ten years. The relative performance was determined by comparing deflections. The nail-glued trussed rafters (see figure 3-11) experienced the least deflection—twice the initial deflection at the end of 10 years; the metal-plate gusset-trussed rafters deflected a bit more—two and a half times the original; and the nailed plywood experienced the most—three times the original—deflection.

A generally recognized arbitrary criterion for acceptable deflection is the span divided by 360. (It is probable that this was established back in the days of plastered walls and ceiling to inhibit cracking of the plaster.) In the 28-foot-long (8.5-m) trusses used in the experiments by the Forest Products Laboratory, the permissible deflection would therefore be

$$\frac{28' \times 12''}{360} = 0.93 \text{ inches (2.36 cm)}.$$

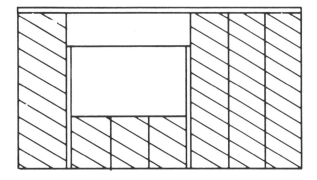

a. Diagonal sheathing—will rack and twist.

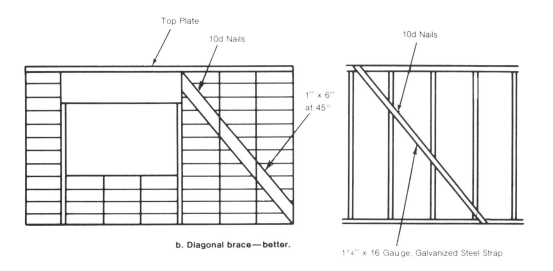

Top Plate

10d Nails

1″ x 6″
at 45°

b. Diagonal brace—better.

10d Nails

1¹⁄4″ x 16 Gauge, Galvanized Steel Strap

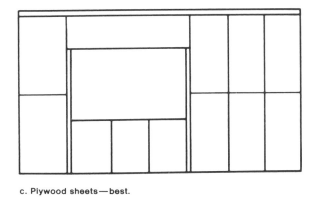

c. Plywood sheets—best.

3-9. Comparison of lateral bracing of walls (see also figure 4-4).

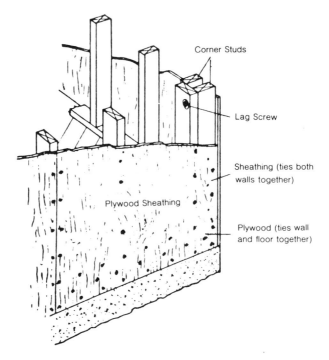

Corner Studs

Lag Screw

Sheathing (ties both walls together)

Plywood Sheathing

Plywood (ties wall and floor together)

a. Improved corner construction

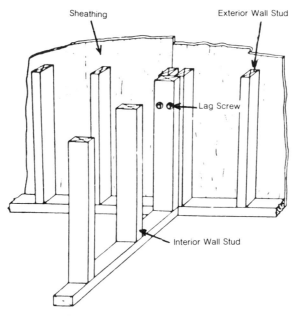

Sheathing

Exterior Wall Stud

Lag Screw

Interior Wall Stud

b. Connection between interior and exterior wood-frame walls

3-10. Methods of tying structural elements together to assure continuity.

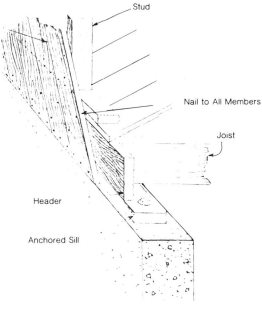

Diagonal Sheathing (or Plywood)

Stud

Nail to All Members

Joist

Header

Anchored Sill

c. Floor-to-wall tie

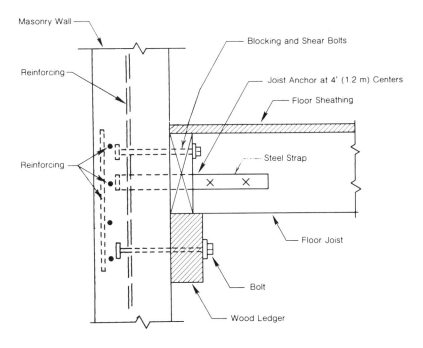

Masonry Wall

Blocking and Shear Bolts

Reinforcing

Joist Anchor at 4' (1.2 m) Centers

Floor Sheathing

Reinforcing

Steel Strap

Floor Joist

Bolt

Wood Ledger

d. Connection of wood joists to masonry wall

3-10 (cont'd). Methods of tying structural elements together to assure continuity.

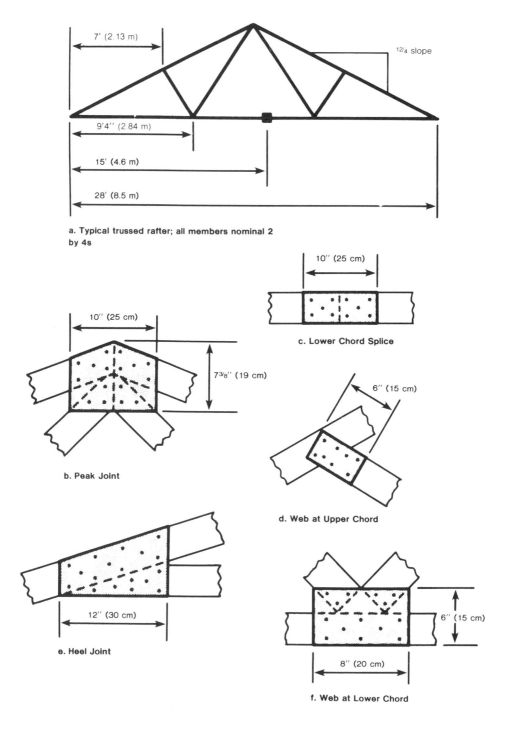

7′ (2.13 m)

¹²/₄ slope

9′4″ (2.84 m)

15′ (4.6 m)

28′ (8.5 m)

a. Typical trussed rafter; all members nominal 2 by 4s

10″ (25 cm)

c. Lower Chord Splice

10″ (25 cm)

7³⁄₈″ (19 cm)

b. Peak Joint

6″ (15 cm)

d. Web at Upper Chord

12″ (30 cm)

e. Heel Joint

6″ (15 cm)

8″ (20 cm)

f. Web at Lower Chord

3-11. Joint details for nail-glued trussed rafters, the type with least long-term deflection. Gussets were ¹⁄₂″ plywood; 4d nails were used to apply pressure on glue. (From U.S. Forest Service, Research Paper FPL 204).

3-12. Steel plates shown here help strengthen the rafters. (Photo: Paul Foster)

All of the trussed rafters proved acceptable in their performance after ten years except the nailed plywood trussed rafters. The moral to the above is that any builder would be well advised to employ a connection system that performs satisfactorily: either the nail glued or the metal plate.

Rafter Construction

Some rafter construction details are shown in figures 3-12 and 3-13. The use of steel plates to strengthen the connections between members is shown in figure 3-12. A tie should be provided between opposite rafters on the two sides of the roof underneath the ridge. This can be a 1- by 6-inch or 2- by 4-inch collar beam (the horizontal base of a triangle) or a plywood gusset (figure 3-13).

Roof Construction

When the roof is too flat for the usual framing and consists essentially of wood decks, use metal plates at the ridge and at the eaves to anchor the decking as indicated in figure 3-14. On flat or low-sloped roofs, the surfacing aggregate on built-up roofing should be fully embedded in the surface coating. Loose gravel will be blown by strong winds and will damage adjacent windows. This was well illustrated during Hurricane Camille, when over 1,000 people took refuge in the solidly built administration building at NASA's Mississippi test facility, opened to the public in this emergency. To get to the building, however, people had to drive cars; hence, the parking lots were jammed. The storm blew gravel off the solid building's roof, and the high winds made missiles of this gravel, which peppered the parked cars. The next morning when the people emerged, they were aghast at the condition of their vehicles—broken windows, mottled finish, and dents. This does not have to happen with your property. For a discussion of such roofing materials as asphalt, wood shingles, and shakes, see Chapter 4.

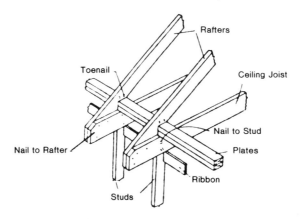

a. Cornice connection—rafter and ceiling joist tie

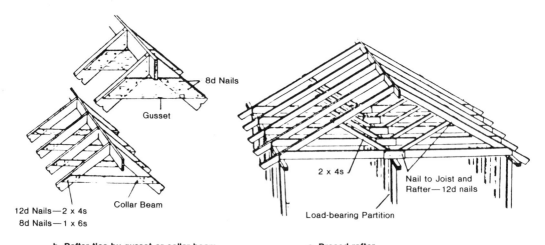

b. Rafter ties by gusset or collar beam

c. Braced rafter

3-13. Rafter construction.

The use of proper roof sheathing will increase the racking resistance of the roof. For flat or low-pitched roofs, diagonal sheathing is more than four times as rigid and eight times as strong as horizontal sheathing (as the U.S. Forest Service attests in its paper *Houses Can Resist Hurricanes*). Plywood sheets applied with the length across the rafters and with end joints staggered give good resistance to racking of steeper roofs. The plywood should be 4- by 8-foot sheets (1.2 by 2.4 m) ½ inch (1.3 cm) or thicker; nails should be 8d in length spaced about 4 to 6 inches (10 to 15 cm) apart at the end of the sheet and 8 to 12 inches (20 to 30 cm) at the intermediate rafter crossings.

Tie Down the House

If the house is supported by a poured concrete foundation wall, a concrete block foundation wall, or on piers, tie the floor system to these foundations with anchor

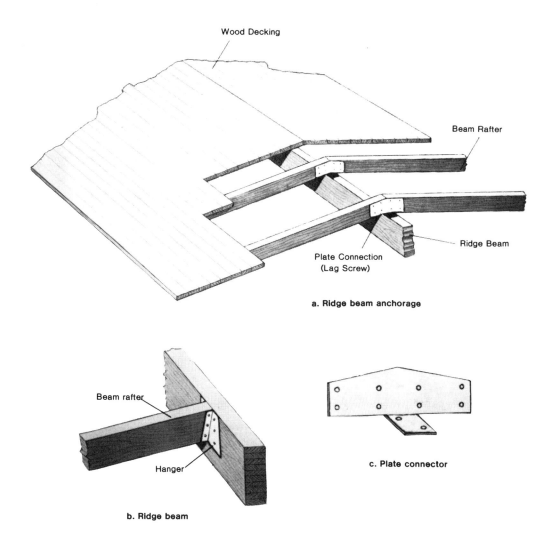

a. Ridge beam anchorage

b. Ridge beam

c. Plate connector

3-14. Reinforcement for a flat roof.

bolts or straps that are placed when the concrete is poured. In turn, anchor or tie the foundation wall or pier to the footing on which it rests (figure 3-15). Hooked reinforcing rods ½ inch (No. 4) or larger in diameter can be used to tie the wall and footing together. They should extend at least 7 inches (18 cm) into the concrete, be located near the corners, and spaced 4 to 6 feet (1.2 to 1.8 m) apart in concrete block walls or 6 to 8 feet (1.8 to 2.4 m) apart in poured concrete walls (see figure 3-15). If concrete block walls or piers are used, the hooked rods should extend to a poured concrete cap. This type of anchoring is an essential part of a continuous tie system between roof and footings. This tie system is needed to resist overturning and uplift forces.

Use metal plates or straps to tie the vertical wall studs to the floor system (figure 3-16). Metal strapping or metal connectors that tie the roof framing to the wall are needed to improve uplift resistance over that provided by a nailed connection (figure 3-17).

In a major storm, the ultimate building securely constructed to withstand all these modes of failure is probably a concrete pillbox. But do not be discouraged; by paying close attention to the "cures," the risk from these modes of failure can be greatly reduced.

Masonry, Brick, and Concrete Block Walls

One of the oldest construction systems is to use stone or brick set dry or with mortar to enclose the space of the building. Many structures so built have stood for thousands of years. This long experience with masonry, however, has not eliminated failures. Sometimes an old wall will collapse from the accumulated effect of traffic vibration on a rough surface street, or from the vibration caused by nearby railroad tracks, or from winds or earthquakes. Sometimes this vibration will cause the wall to

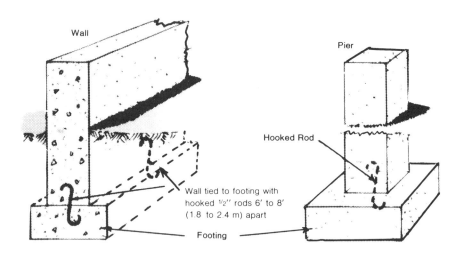

a. Tying a concrete wall or pier to the concrete footing

3-15. Proper foundation anchorage.

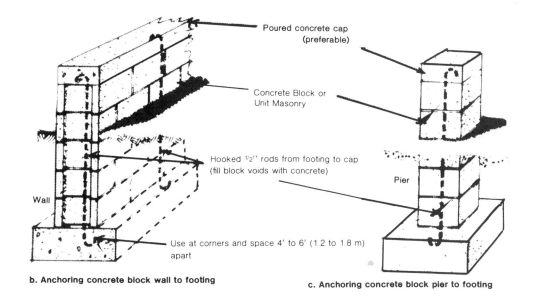

Poured concrete cap
(preferable)

Concrete Block or
Unit Masonry

Hooked ½'' rods from footing to cap
(fill block voids with concrete)

Wall

Pier

Use at corners and space 4' to 6' (1.2 to 1.8 m)
apart

b. Anchoring concrete block wall to footing

c. Anchoring concrete block pier to footing

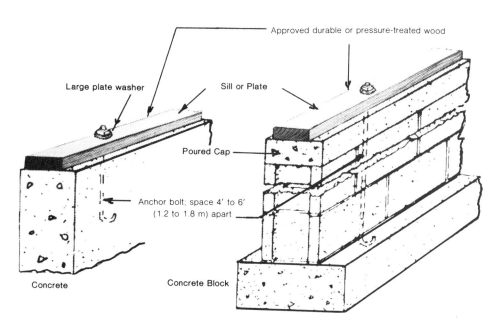

Approved durable or pressure-treated wood

Large plate washer

Sill or Plate

Poured Cap

Anchor bolt; space 4' to 6'
(1.2 to 1.8 m) apart

Concrete

Concrete Block

d. Anchoring wood sill or plate to foundation

3-15 (cont'd). Proper foundation anchorage.

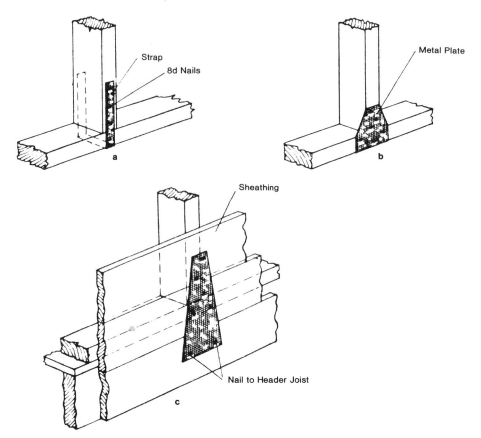

3-16. Stud-to-floor, plate-to-floor framing methods.

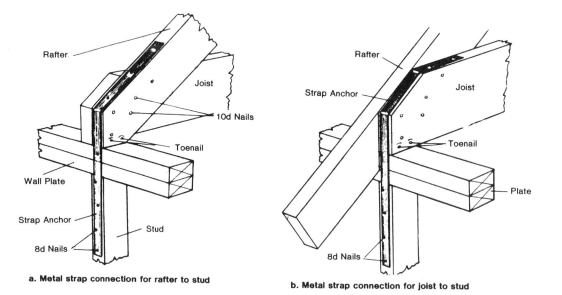

a. Metal strap connection for rafter to stud

b. Metal strap connection for joist to stud

3-17. Roof-to-wall connections.

shift outward and allow the floor beams to drop. Masonry block walls should be stabilized by being tied together by the roof and held by the floor (figure 3-18). Water or weather tightness has always been a problem; it has not yet been solved in all cases, even in modern structures.

Velocity, or V, zones are areas affected by wave surges during flooding. Masonry, brick, and concrete block structures are unsafe constructions within V zones. The discussion that follows applies to construction on sites above the V zone, or for that matter, above the A zone, where water, but no wave action, is expected.

Unreinforced concrete block and brick masonry buildings are often completely destroyed by the wind during a hurricane, even in areas where there was no direct

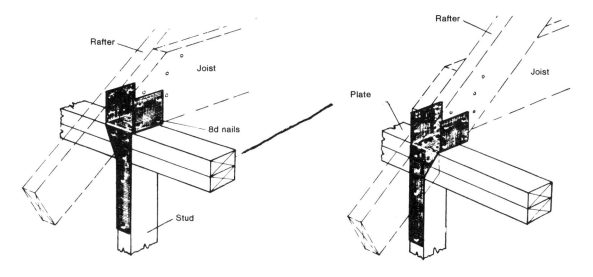

c. Double metal plate connector with joist to the right of the rafter and to the left of the rafter

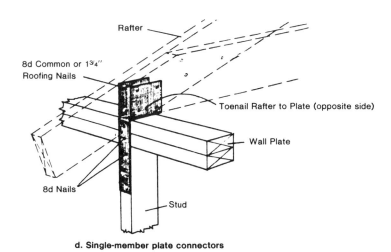

d. Single-member plate connectors

3-17 (cont'd). Roof-to-wall connections.

wave action. The typical form of destruction is failure of masonry walls, apparently from vibration and wind pressures, followed by roof structures either collapsing or blowing away. The need for adequate reinforcing in a masonry wall was clearly demonstrated after Hurricane Camille. Often a properly built building that sustained only minor damage stood right next to a poorly built building that was completely destroyed, even though both were subjected to the same forces. There is no excuse for building an unreinforced concrete block or brick masonry house near the coast.

Unreinforced masonry construction is the most vulnerable to forces other than gravity (the weight of the building). Houses constructed of brick unreinforced by

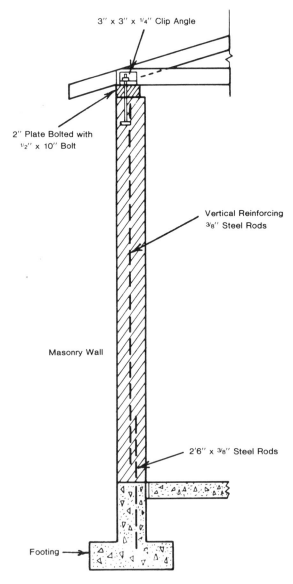

3-18. Anchoring the roof to the footing.

steel or poured concrete framing have a high record of damage from hurricanes because the unreinforced brick walls simply cannot withstand the lateral forces. Building codes applicable to high-wind areas specify the type of mortar to be used, the reinforcing in the walls, and the anchoring of the roof structure to the footing. The codes may vary in some of the details, but all have the purpose of tying the building together to make it act as a unit. It should again be emphasized that building codes specify *minimum* requirements. The prudent owner or builder will make a few additional, low-cost design changes that will greatly enhance the ability of the structure to withstand the onslaught of a hurricane wind. Some examples of code recommendations follow.

The South Florida Building Code specifies methods of tying the building together with both tie columns and tie beams. Reinforced tie beams are to be placed around the perimeter walls at each floor level and the roof level, and shall be a minimum of 8 inches (20 cm) wide and 12 inches (30 cm) deep, with four $5/8$-inch (No. 5) reinforcing bars, two at the top and two at the bottom (figure 3-19). Under certain limitations a U-type beam block may be used, reinforced with two bars.

Another code, the North Carolina State Building Code, specifies:

> For masonry buildings, the roof structure, including rafters and joists, shall be securely anchored to the footing by $3/8$ inch (vertical) steel rods not more than 8 feet apart, one of which should be no more than 2 feet from each corner [this is illustrated in figure 3-18]. All mortar used for masonry walls must be type M, which is one part Portland Cement, $1/4$ part hydrated lime or lime putty, and not over 3 parts aggregate. This is frequently called Portland Cement Mortar.
>
> All girders and large beams into which small joists are framed which bear on masonry foundation walls or piers shall be anchored to the footing with $5/8$ inch steel rods embedded at least 6 inches therein. . . . .

An experienced Florida consulting engineer, Herbert S. Saffir, recommends in *Civil Engineering Magazine* (February, 1971) that the ends of steel joists be bolted, welded, or embedded at each bearing to provide a resistance in any direction of not less than 50 percent of its expected vertical or downward gravity load. Steel joists should also be checked for their ability to withstand uplift.

Some architects today design a concrete block house or building with one block directly above the other block rather than overlapping. Normally, in a brick or concrete block wall or hollow clay tile wall, a block overlaps the block below. In other words, the joints are staggered (figure 3-20). This gives a much stronger wall that will resist a lateral load such as wind much better than the wall in which one block is directly above the other. If stack bond is used, the wall should be more heavily reinforced, very much more so in coastal regions. The Masonry Institute of America has put out several excellent publications on constructing concrete block and brick houses. One of these, *Standard Details for One-Story Concrete Block Residences*, contains nine foldout drawings illustrating details. Principles of reinforcement and good connections are given for design in seismic zones, but these apply equally well for hurricane zones, where a house must also resist lateral force. One example of a seismic zone code difference is that vertical reinforcement must be $5/8$-inch (No. 5) bars at 4-foot (1.2-m) maximum centers, rather than $3/8$-inch (No. 3) bars at 8-foot (2.4-m) centers.

Similarly, the Standard Building Code states that "in hollow masonry unit construction each unit cell shall be reinforced with at least one No. 5 bar ($5/8''$) at all corners;

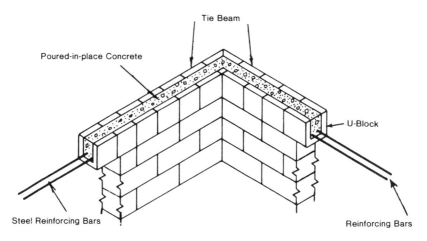

a. Concrete Block Wall

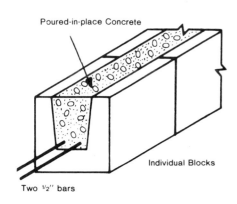

b. U-Block Tie Beam

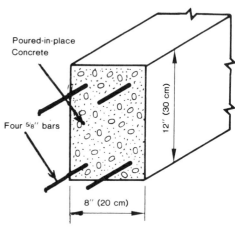

c. Poured Concrete Tie Beam (alternative suggestion)

3-19. Reinforced tie (bond) beam for concrete block walls. This should be used at each floor level and at roof level around the perimeter of the exterior walls.

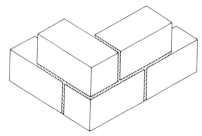

a. Typical broken-joint masonry wall construction.

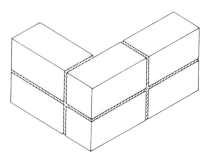

b. Stacked bond with the vertical joints in line.
Weaker than the one above with the staggered configuration, it should be used only for ornamental surfaces in panels or contained areas.

3-20. Concrete block patterns.

poured solid and tamped with concrete, such reinforcing shall be properly tied into the footing and spandrel beam." (A spandrel beam is the concrete beam in the wall at each floor level and at the roof.)

Continuity is stressed, especially at corners, as well as adequate overlapping. Whenever a reinforcing rod passes through the hollow of a concrete block, that hollow must be filled with concrete grout carefully compacted. Additional horizontal and vertical reinforcement should be used at corners and at the intersections of all walls. The walls must be tied together so they will act as one continuous unit.

In the case of windows, reinforcing should be both horizontal and vertical, above and below, and on either side of window openings (figure 3-21).

Masonry Veneer on Wood-Frame Buildings

Masonry veneers are highly susceptible to flood damage. The anchorages between the wood frame and the brick or stone facing are often weak or insufficient, allowing the veneer to crack or be torn away from the frame. Poor-quality mortar is another cause for damage to masonry veneers, especially lime mortar. In building a new house, insist on mortar containing less than 10 percent lime. Masonry veneer should be anchored by noncorrodable metal ties capable of withstanding a horizontal force twice the weight of the veneer. There should be at least one tie anchor for each 200 square inches of wall area.

If the walls of a wood-frame building are to be stuccoed, applying the stucco directly to conventional wire lath and Sheetrock or plasterboard backing will not be sufficient. Rather, apply the stucco to strong wire mesh that has been securely nailed to plywood sheathing; this will properly stiffen the walls. In coastal areas

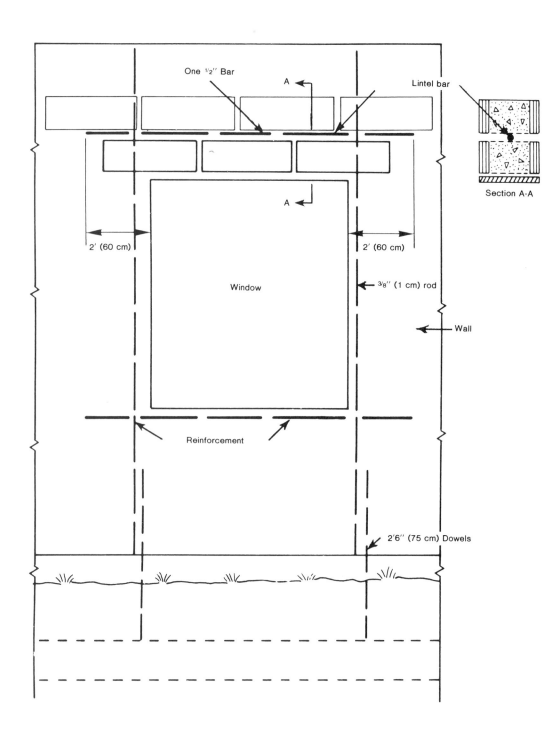

One ½'' Bar

A

Lintel bar

2' (60 cm)

2' (60 cm)

Section A-A

A

Window

³⁄₈'' (1 cm) rod

Wall

Reinforcement

2'6'' (75 cm) Dowels

3-21. Hollow concrete unit construction with window reinforcement.

subject to high wind, the stucco will be too weak if applied to Sheetrock or plaster-board backing, and may crack, break, and even fall off the walls (figure 3-22).

Precast Concrete Panels

The use of precast concrete panels in building construction is fairly common throughout the world because of its low cost. In some countries, particularly in the U.S.S.R. and those Eastern European countries where earthquakes are common, considerable reinforcement is used, both in panels and through the joints, to provide a high degree of structural continuity.

In some other countries and localities, buildings of precast panels have been designed essentially as gravity structures (that is, for vertical loads), with no signif-icant continuity provided through the joints. This practice has led to some serious failures. One of the most spectacular of these was the collapse from top to bottom of part of a twenty-four-story apartment building at Ronan Point in England on May 16, 1968. The failure put the acceptability of the gravity design into question, since the damage caused by an unusual load or an accident at one point may spread progressively to other parts of the building. The cause was attributed to lack of continuity between panels and the absence of alternative load paths. As a result, Great Britain and Canada tightened their building regulations to prevent a recur-rence.

The Ronan Point collapse also illustrates that simply complying with a code may not ensure a safe building. Any design, particularly of a new form of construction, must be examined critically and carefully by a competent structural engineer to make sure that no chain reaction or failure such as at Ronan Point can occur. Certainly, on a building that may feel the force of waves or extremely high winds, the design should be such that damage to one portion of a building will not cause progressive collapse of other parts of it.

The need for good details (fastenings or connections) between prefabricated

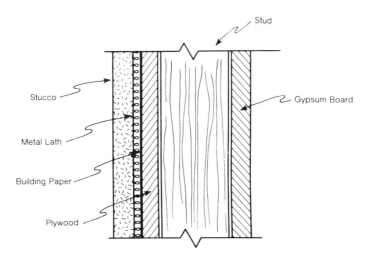

3-22. One method of applying stucco.

components is to be emphasized, details that will incorporate continuity and ductility in the structure. (Ductility in a member is its toughness or ability to withstand large deformations or stretching before fracturing; in other words, a ductile piece will bend or stretch before it will break.) A prefabricated assembly is a structural unit whose integral parts have been built up or assembled prior to construction at a site.

Monolithic concrete frames and continuous steel-frame construction with infill panels are examples of building methods that offer resistance against progressive collapse, as they provide the necessary strength, ductility, and alternative load paths. Great care must be exercised with precast construction, especially connections. Joints, usually the weak link of precast panel construction, must be adequately reinforced. The key is that all elements be anchored or tied together so as to provide continuity in the structure to enable it to resist lateral and upward loads as well as the usual gravity loads, and to prevent a chain reaction of progressive failure in the event of a local failure.

Glass

Hurricanes can inflict severe damage to glass, especially the non-load-carrying glass walls used on the exteriors of some steel-and-concrete-framework buildings (such as motels). Glass can be obtained in various strengths, and in a high-wind area a stronger glass will provide better resistance. Greater strength can also be obtained by reducing the horizontal or vertical distances between the adjacent members that support the glass—in other words, by using smaller panes.

In some cases the frame holding the glass gets yanked out of the wall by the wind forces. This can be overcome by stronger fastenings. In new skyscrapers in New York and Boston, where large glass areas with metal skin walls are the latest vogue, glass panes and a complete wall panel assembly have been sucked out on the lee side of the building. Thicker and stronger glass panes and frames will prevent that.

The answer to glass damage boils down to better and more competent design. Many well-designed structures withstood Hurricane Camille with little or no damage to their glass from the extremely high winds. Remember that a broken glass panel means additional damage from the heavy rains. Heavy interior drapes can lessen the chances of personal injury in the event of broken glass. Even when glass is not broken, however, a window may be ruined by the sandblasting effect resulting from wind-blown sand on exposed glass during high winds. Shutters or movable covers can help prevent sandblasting, as well as glass breakage from flying debris. Figure 6-4 in Chapter 6 gives limits on the size of glass for various heights above grade and for various thicknesses of glass, assuming a wind velocity of 140 mph (224 kph) at 30 feet (9 m) above grade. The table provides width-to-length ratios from 2:10 to 10:10 and applies to regular plate and sheet glass used in exterior walls. A table of multiplying factors is given for other types of glass.

Steel and Reinforced Concrete Frames

A steel or reinforced concrete frame is one in which the main structural members (the columns or posts, and beams) are made of steel shapes or concrete reinforced with steel bars. A well-designed steel or reinforced concrete frame will quite often remain intact even when the side walls and roof have blown away. One reason, perhaps, is that the frame is stronger than the walls and roof, and when the wind destroys the weaker covering, the remaining frame is subjected to a lessened total force.

One should not be lulled into a false feeling of security simply because the material of construction is steel or reinforced concrete. Actually, from the standpoint of material alone, wood is tougher, more ductile, and better able to withstand shock than either. It is how the material is used and connected that counts. It is easier to obtain continuity with steel and reinforced concrete than with wood, but this is achieved only through proper design and fabrication. Steel and reinforced concrete are more commonly used in larger buildings than in single residences.

The premier material for light residential framing for floors, load-bearing walls, and non-load-bearing partitions is wood. Galvanized steel shapes may, however, become competitive for small residential buildings, as they are now for large-volume builders, if current marketing practices change. This will especially be the case if lumber prices increase more rapidly than steel prices, which seems quite possible. The various steel members, whether joists, columns, or cross-bracing, must be properly connected, as the framing system must resist forces from all directions as well as downward. The main thing that must be kept in mind is continuity when constructing houses subject to high winds near the coast.

High-rise buildings made of reinforced concrete seem to have suffered more damage from lateral forces than have steel-frame buildings, although they ought to perform equally well when properly designed and built. One problem is that a concrete *shear wall* (used for lateral stability) is often pierced on the job to provide more openings for plumbing, air conditioning ducts, electrical conduits, and windows. These openings weaken the wall. Concrete building construction requires close supervision, as more of the actual work is done at the site itself than with steel, hence allowing more opportunity for error.

The relative performance of two types of concrete columns is of interest. In the failure of one building, a column was reinforced with vertical steel bars tied together at intervals with individual steel loops. These ties pulled apart, permitting the concrete core to burst. Other columns on the same building were also reinforced with vertical steel bars, but these were tied together with a continuous steel spiral. This spiral did not pull apart and the concrete core remained intact.

Rigid frame construction performed extremely well in Hurricane Camille. A rigid frame (figure 3-23) is a steel skeleton frame made up of two vertical columns and a roof beam, quite often peaked, in which the end connections of all members are securely fastened together so that the angles they make with each other do not change. The roof beam is usually more shallow at the center of the span (the peak of the roof) and deeper at the ends where it is solidly connected to the columns. This solid connection is the secret of its continuity, and hence its ability to resist lateral force.

Apparently, no elevated water tanks failed in Hurricane Camille. These are steel structures designed by qualified engineers backed by special experience in this field. The allowable stress used in their design provides a substantial safety factor. Equally important is the attention to detail. It is of no avail to have a strong structural member if it is not adequately fastened. Suppose the elevated water tank itself had been superbly designed but not securely anchored to the foundations with strong anchor bolts. In a high wind the structure would topple over as an entire solid unit.

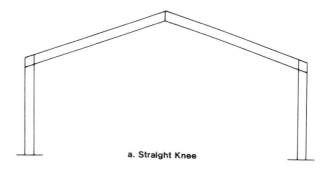

a. Straight Knee

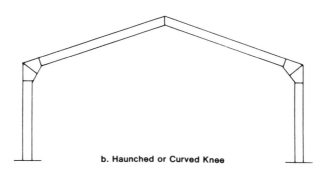

b. Haunched or Curved Knee

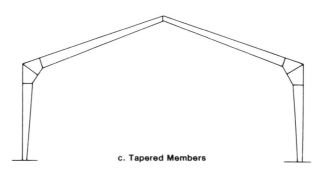

c. Tapered Members

3-23. Types of rigid frame construction.

"A chain is no stronger than its weakest link." This old adage also applies to buildings and dwellings. Steel and concrete frames must be securely anchored to the ground, and the elements fastened to each other to resist lateral and upward loads as well as the usual vertical downward weight of the structure.

Sacrificial First Floor

One solution that many people arrived at for older homes in an area subject to flooding was to assume the first floor would flood. They use it for a playroom, a garage, or storage. The furniture is light and easily moved; the more expensive and heavier items are located on the second floor, out of reach of the rising waters. When a storm of major proportions is imminent, the family simply gets in the car, drives to a high location to stay with friends or in a motel or refugee center, and after the storm recedes, returns to the house to clean out the mud and wash the walls and floor of the first floor. The structure was built in the expectation of a flood and in such a way as to minimize the damage and the clean-up process.

A sacrificial floor on new structures built in flood plains is no longer acceptable under the National Flood Insurance Program. Some additional comments applicable to a sacrificial first floor are provided in the following section. Because of poor attachment of the second floor to foundations or posts and the tendency to close in the ground floor, many people after hurricanes found they had sacrificed the whole house. As we have said already: MAKE SURE FASTENINGS ARE ADEQUATE.

Elevated Residential Structures: Pole Houses

At the start of this chapter, we stated that if the rules for safe living in a hurricane region were condensed to one sentence it might well be: Put the building or dwelling at a high enough elevation where the highest high water will not reach it, and make it sturdy enough so the fastest winds will not destroy it. One of the requirements to comply with local regulations of communities in the National Flood Insurance Program (Chapter 9) is that the lowest habitable floor be above the "100-year flood" level. Not only must the foundation elevate the building above the level of the 100-year flood, it must also be able to withstand the forces from flowing and surging water including scouring from high water (the "washing out" of soil), and from the impact of waterborne debris. To aid in this it should be constructed to offer as little resistance as possible to flow.

Because of the above stipulations, all future coastal-zone residences in V zones will be elevated on pilings or columns with the area below the structure free of obstruction. Two general methods are available to raise the lowest floor of a residence to a higher elevation. One of these is to build up a mound with compacted soil and then to construct the house in the conventional manner. This method is *not* suitable for a coastal zone, since the mounded fill soil erodes easily during flooding and overwash. The other method is to construct an elevated foundation to such a height that the lowest floor resting on these foundations will be at the desired elevation. The most common types of foundations for this purpose are poles (piles or posts) and piers. Poles are sometimes called stilts. Anyone intending to build an elevated residence would do well to consult the useful guide issued by the Federal Insurance Administration on elevated residential structures, details about which can be found in this chapter's reference section at the back of this book.

Hillside lots can often be utilized by building the house with *poles* in place of other types of construction that might either be impossible, impractical, or certainly more expensive. The problems of steepness of the site, severe erosion, loss of topsoil, and blocked drainage can frequently be solved by hand digging the post holes and removing as little as possible of the natural vegetation.

3-24. The ideal way to use pilings (or posts) is shown here. The posts are single timbers extending from deep in the soil to the roof of the house. This house will likely withstand much stronger wind forces than a similar one sitting on pilings. (Photo: Paul Foster)

Piles are long, slender shafts of treated wood, steel, or reinforced concrete driven into the earth to a sufficient depth to support both the vertical load of the house and the horizontal forces of flowing water, wind, and waterborne debris. The capacity of the pile to carry loads is determined by the frictional resistance between the surface of the pile and the soil and by the end bearing of the pile. The depth to which the pile should be driven depends on such considerations as soil type and anticipated scour, or erosion. Pile construction is especially suitable where scouring is a problem.

The majority of piles used to elevate houses are of treated wood. They are usually cut off at the first-floor deck, but they may be extended to the roof line (figure 3-24). When this is done, however, alignment problems are invited, as it is difficult to drive a pile in a precise enough position to match the framing of the house, and jacking and pulling are required.

For reasons of economy and suitability, *posts* are frequently used in elevated construction. They may be of treated wood or of steel. When made of steel they are called columns. Unlike piles they are not driven into the ground, but rather are placed in holes predug either by hand or by machine. Deeply embedded posts or piles are desirable where the soil is subject to erosion by waves and wind. Posts may rest on a concrete pad at the bottom of the hole or be secured with a concrete footing. They may be held in place by backfilling and tamping earth or by pouring concrete into the hole after the post is in place (figure 3-25). The depth of embedment necessary depends on the type of soil, its condition, and the anticipated scour (figure 3-26).

Posts can extend up to the first-floor deck, which is slightly above the base flood level, or they may extend through the deck to the roof, in which case they serve to tie the structure together to improve its wind or lateral resistance. A combination of full- and floor-height poles is used in some cases, with the shorter pieces supporting the floor inside the house and the longer pieces on the perimeter.

If the poles (either piles or posts) are to extend to the roof, it is better to use posts rather than driven piles, as the posts are more readily aligned. In general, treated wood is the cheapest and most commonly used material for both posts and piles.

Piers are vertical supports, usually thicker than posts or piles, made of reinforced concrete or reinforced masonry (concrete blocks or bricks). They are set on footings of a size appropriate for the soil conditions, and in some cases they rest on concrete pile caps where conditions are such that this type of piling is appropriate. The spacing of the piers is determined by the floor framing and the loads they must carry. They extend from the footing to the underside of the floor frame.

The height of reinforced concrete masonry piers should not exceed ten times the least dimension. Square piers are preferred, but if rectangular, the longer dimension should not exceed the shorter by more than 50 percent. As a guide, spacing between piers should not exceed 8 feet (2.4 m) in the direction perpendicular to the joists, nor 12 feet (3.7 m) in the direction parallel to the joists. The residence should be so oriented that the direction of maximum spacing is perpendicular to the flow of floodwaters.

Foundation walls can be used to raise the first habitable floor of the residence to the desired elevation above the level for the base flood. Walls should be built of materials resistant to water damage, such as reinforced concrete, brick, or concrete block, and in flood situations be located parallel to the flow of the floodwaters. In any possible flood situation, the foundation walls should be arranged to provide open

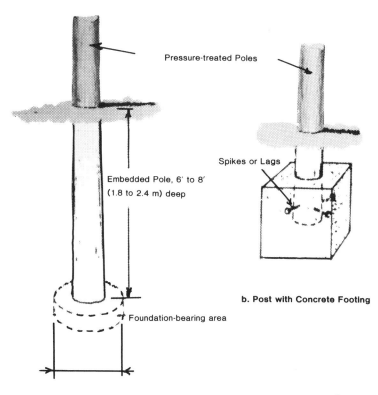

Pressure-treated Poles

Embedded Pole, 6' to 8'
(1.8 to 2.4 m) deep

Foundation-bearing area

a. Embedded Pole on Treated Timber or Concrete Pad

Spikes or Lags

b. Post with Concrete Footing

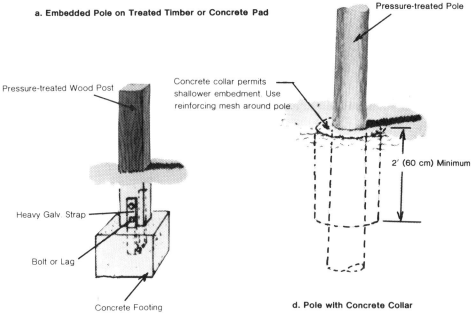

Pressure-treated Wood Post

Heavy Galv. Strap

Bolt or Lag

Concrete Footing

c. Timber Post Anchored to a Concrete Footing

Pressure-treated Pole

Concrete collar permits
shallower embedment. Use
reinforcing mesh around pole.

2' (60 cm) Minimum

d. Pole with Concrete Collar

3-25. Shallow and deep supports for posts.

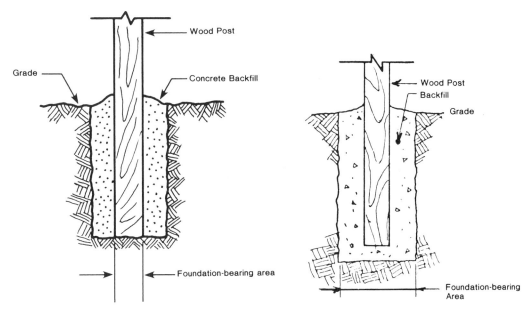

e. Post Resting on Undisturbed Good Earth, then Backfilled

f. Post Resting on Concrete to Increase Bearing Area with Concrete Backfill

3-25 (cont'd). Shallow and deep supports for posts.

3-26. A house that almost went out to sea during a November, 1981, storm at Topsail Island, North Carolina. Here one can see the concrete collars once used to hold posts in place. (Photo: Orrin Pilkey, Jr.)

spaces through which water can flow, to permit equalization of pressure on both sides of the wall to prevent its overturning. Masonry walls should be reinforced with steel.

The Space under the House

As mentioned in the previous section, it is often advisable to have a sacrificial first floor. From a structural standpoint, the space under an elevated house must be kept free of obstructions in order to minimize the impact of waves and floating debris. In some instances it may be desirable to enclose part or all of the space under the elevated structure. If this is done, the enclosing walls should be designed so as not to allow the pressure from the velocity of the water and waterborne debris to overload the structure. This can be done in several ways: The wall can be made to break away or fall under flood loads but either remain attached to the house or be heavy enough to sink (in either case so it will not float away and add to the waterborne debris problem); the wall can be constructed so it can be detached and stored before a storm; it can be designed to be hinged so it can be swung up out of the path of floodwaters and debris; or where no debris is expected, the wall can be built with louvers that will allow the water to pass through.

Piles

A good figure to shoot for is a load of about 8,000 pounds (36 kN—kiloNewtons) per pile. Much lower loading tends to be inefficient, requiring more piles than necessary, and much higher loading requires careful engineering. Driven piles should extend to a depth of 8 feet (2.4 m) or more. Approximate spacing of piles is a minimum of 8 feet (2.4 m) and a maximum of 12 feet (3.7 m). Some guidelines for soil bearing capacities may be useful in determining how deep the pole or pile should go into the ground. The load on the pole must be estimated and correlated to the bearing capacity of the soil. A rough classification follows.

1. *Below-average soil:* soft clay, poorly compacted sand, clays containing large amounts of silt (water will stand in it during the wet season).
   Bearing (vertical load supporting) *capacity:* 1,500 pounds per square foot (psf) (72 kiloNewtons per square meter—kN/m^2).
   Lateral bearing (sideward resistance) *capacity:* 100 psf (4.8 kN/m^2) per linear foot of embedment.
2. *Average soil:* loose gravel, medium clay, or any more compact composition.
   Bearing capacity: 3,000 psf (144 kN/m^2).
   Lateral bearing capacity: 200 psf (9.6 kN/m^2) per linear foot of embedment.
3. *Good soil:* compact, well-graded sand and gravel, hard clay, graded fine and coarse sand.
   Bearing capacity: 6,000 psf (287 kN/m^2).
   Lateral bearing capacity: 400 psf (19.2 kN/m^2) per linear foot of embedment.

Wood posts are generally embedded 6 to 8 feet (1.8 to 2.4 m) to provide anchorage. Holes deeper than 8 feet are usually uneconomical. If the load per post is small and the allowable soil bearing capacity is adequate, the post may be set on undisturbed earth at the bottom of the hole and then backfilled with concrete or earth (see figure 3-25e). For larger loads on the post or for poorer soil conditions, the lower end of the post should rest on a concrete pad, spreading the load to the soil over a greater area to prevent settlement (see figure 3-25). The pad should be about half as thick as its diameter, with a minimum thickness of 8 inches (20 cm).

The holes in which posts are embedded can be backfilled with concrete, soil/cement, pea gravel, sand, or crushed rock (see figure 3-25e). Soil/cement can be made by mixing the earth removed from the holes with cement in a 5:1 ratio. When wetted and tamped into place, it provides an effective and economical backfill. The earth should be free of organic matter. Concrete backfill, of course, is the best material, but it costs more.

Where the soil permits the embedment to be less than 6 feet (1.8 m), it is best to tie the post down to the footing with straps or other anchoring devices. It is wise to drill the holes 8 inches (20 cm) larger than the posts to allow for alignment when the major framing members of the floor and the roof are installed. It is only after these members are installed and squared that the hole should be backfilled and tamped or a concrete collar poured. A concrete collar has to be a minimum of 2 feet (60 cm) deep and should be reinforced with wire mesh to be effective (see figure 3-25d).

Bracing

Bracing the foundation poles or piles can help minimize storm damage. Bracing should be considered to be just as critical as the poles and the floor beams. Both knee braces (figure 3-27a) and diagonal braces (figures 3-27b and c) are used. A knee brace is a corner brace with a diagonal member placed across the angle between two members that are joined, for the purpose of stiffening and strengthening a framework so constructed. The diagonals may be of wood or of steel rods. The bracing for a high elevation (distance between ground and floor) should be more substantial than for a lesser elevation, and the bracing in the direction of the flow of water should be more substantial than that parallel to the beach.

Shear walls, that is, a wall that, in its own plane, carries shear resulting from a lateral force such as wind or flowing water, can be used to brace piles and posts and prevent distortion. They should be placed parallel to the direction of flow and be firmly attached to the piles or posts to make a rigid structure.

Connecting the House to the Foundation

The importance of securely connecting the house to the foundation could have been demonstrated by a tour along the waterfront of the Gulf Coast after Hurricane Camille, where any number of good, solid platforms atop piles or posts were completely denuded of the houses that once rested there. Some of these bare platforms still exist.

The two commonly used methods of framing into pile or post foundations are platform construction and pole-frame construction (figure 3-28). In *platform construction* the posts or piles are cut off at the desired elevation and framed with beams to support floor joists and deck to form a platform that serves as the first habitable floor. Platform construction is also used for pier and wall foundations (figure 3-28c).

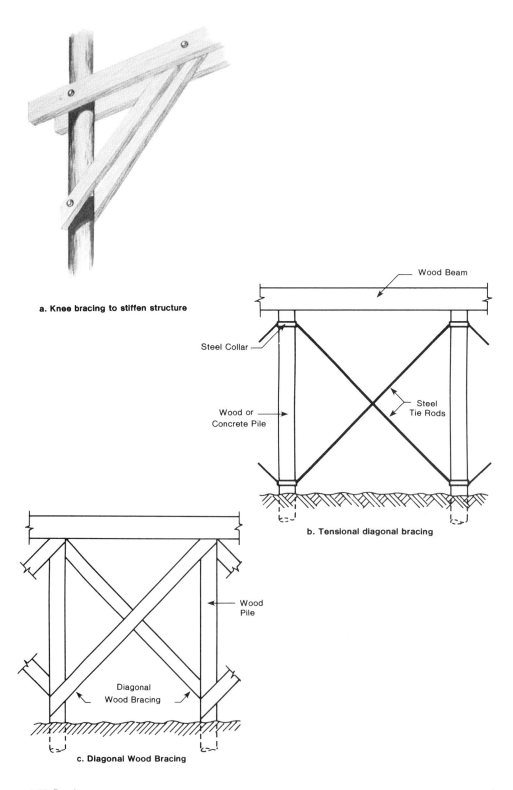

a. Knee bracing to stiffen structure

Wood Beam

Steel Collar

Wood or
Concrete Pile

Steel
Tie Rods

b. Tensional diagonal bracing

Wood
Pile

Diagonal
Wood Bracing

c. Diagonal Wood Bracing

3-27. Bracing.

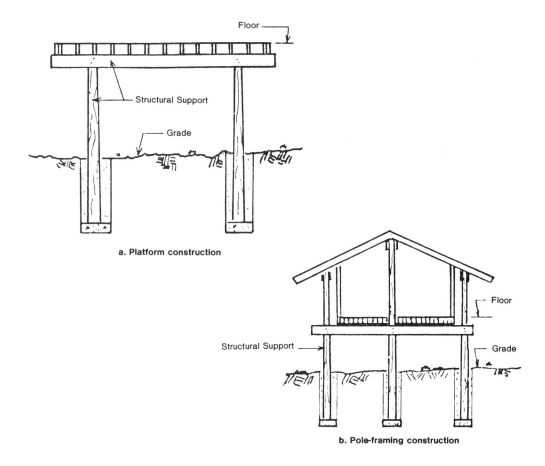

a. Platform construction

b. Pole-framing construction

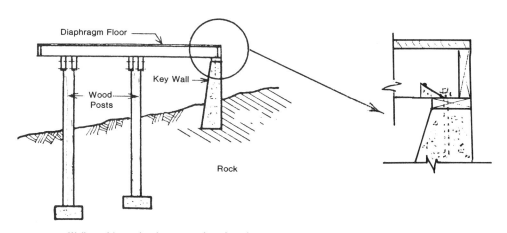

c. Wall used to anchor house on sloped, rocky site

3-28. Platform and pole-frame construction.

In *pole-frame construction* the piles or posts extend up to the roof and are rigidly tied into both the floor and the roof. Wood piles are generally driven butt first in this method because the narrower part of the pile is easier to frame. Construction is made easier if the piles are located either within or without the walls but not actually inside them. Standard house-framing techniques must be blended with heavy-timber-frame construction. At all joints involving heavy-timber-frame construction, bolting should be used. Nailed connections of structural elements may help somewhat in resisting lateral forces but are inadequate for severe storms. In a coastal high-hazard area, the method of connecting the structural members is critical; the conventional connections used in typical construction are not adequate to meet coastal forces and environmental conditions. Normal gravity loads in noncoastal areas are handled with standard methods of attachment (toe-nailing and anchor bolts), and the building holds together. The loads imposed on the structural system in a high-hazard coastal area are, however, far greater, and the framing and connections must be capable of withstanding these loads.

Figures 3-27a, 3-29, 3-30, and 3-31 illustrate good practice in connecting structural members. As shown, it is generally better to frame poles with pairs of beams, girders, rafters, or bracing—one on each side. One reason for this is that the load transmitted to the pole is then not eccentric (on one side); if it were, the pole would bend. Some connection details are illustrated in figure 3-32. A spike grid gives added support and avoids breaking into the surface layer of a treated pole more than necessary. The main beams, girders, and rafters should be spaced so that standard lengths and widths of lumber or plywood can be used. Joists on 16-inch (40-cm) centers with 1-inch-thick diagonal sheathing or plywood subfloor are widely used.

Some local building ordinances require that buildings erected within a certain distance (say 150 feet—45m) of the ocean be constructed on pilings or columns, and that the piles be driven no less than 10 feet (3m) below mean sea level. These regulations usually contain helpful details on the size, quality, and spacing of the piles, ties, and bracing, and the method of fastening the structure to them. Some ordinances assume that the piles will be sawed off smoothly along a horizontal plane, resulting in a platform-type construction. Building inspectors, however, are usually amenable to other designs that are equally or more effective, so builders need not necessarily avoid pole-type construction in which the poles extend to the roof. The area under the structure should be free of obstruction. Also keep in mind that building ordinances represent minimum standards.

To summarize, then, the pole house near the beach should have:

1. Floors high enough (sufficient elevation) to be above most storm waters (usually the 100-year flood).
2. Clearance under the house and between piles or posts for easy passage of water and debris.
3. Piles or posts, either of sufficient depth or embedded in concrete, to anchor the structure and to withstand erosion.
4. Well-braced piling or posts.
5. Roof tied to walls; walls tied to foundations; and foundations anchored to the earth.

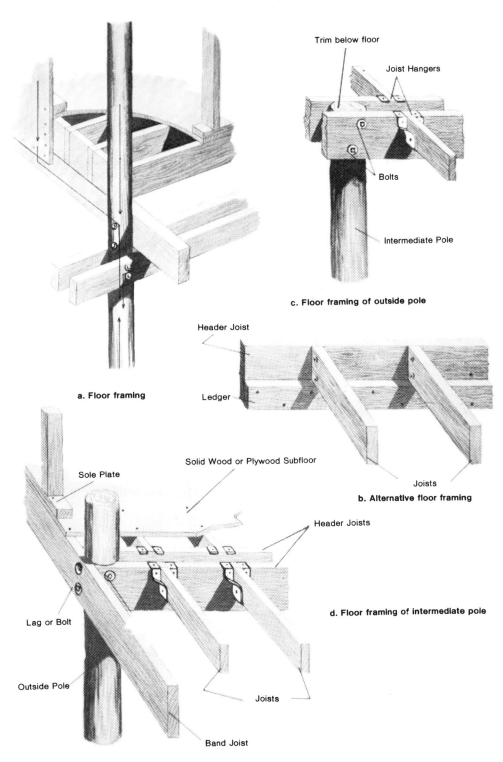

Trim below floor

Joist Hangers

Bolts

Intermediate Pole

c. Floor framing of outside pole

Header Joist

Ledger

a. Floor framing

Solid Wood or Plywood Subfloor

Joists

b. Alternative floor framing

Sole Plate

Header Joists

Lag or Bolt

d. Floor framing of intermediate pole

Outside Pole

Joists

Band Joist

3-29. Tying floors to poles.

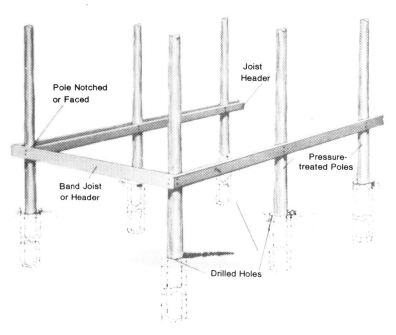

a. Embedment and alignment of poles. Depth of embedment depends on spacing and size of poles, wind loads, and so forth, and may vary from 5 to 8 feet (1.5 to 2.4 m).

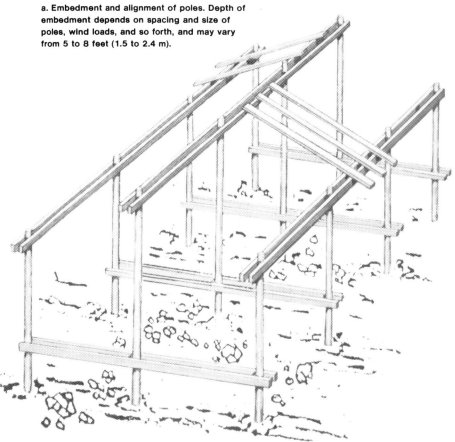

b. Isometric illustration of framing system.

3-30. Framing system for elevated house.

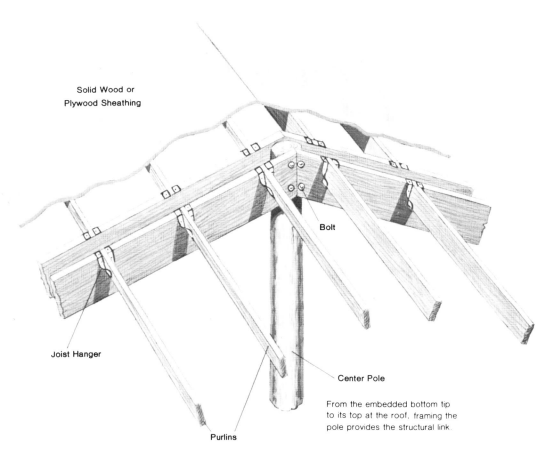

Solid Wood or
Plywood Sheathing

Bolt

Joist Hanger

Center Pole

From the embedded bottom tip
to its top at the roof, framing the
pole provides the structural link.

Purlins

3-31. Detail of roof framing at center pole and ridge.

Modular Unit Construction

The method of building a home by fabricating modular units in a shop and assembling them at the site (figure 3-33) seems to be gaining in popularity, especially on shoreline property. In some places these dwellings are termed ''sea cabins.'' These homes come in a wide variety of sizes, from a small single-family vacation cottage to multistory condominiums or apartment buildings. Some advertising literature indicates the availability of two- and three-story buildings with up to 20 living units.

There is nothing wrong with modular construction or shop fabrication as such. These methods have been used in the manufacturing of mobile homes for years, although final assembly of mobile homes is done in the shop rather than in the field. Doing as much of the work as possible in a shop is often recommended, as it can save considerable labor and cost. Workers are not affected by outside weather conditions, and they can be paid by piecework, enhancing their productivity. Shopwork also lends itself to labor-saving equipment such as pneumatic nailing guns and overhead cranes.

If the manufacturer desires it, shop fabrication can, in addition, permit higher quality. Inspection and control of the whole process are much easier. For instance, there is less hesitation about rejecting a poor piece of lumber when you have a nearby supply of it than if you are building a single dwelling and have just so much lumber on the site.

On the other hand, shopwork can have its drawbacks, too. Because so much of

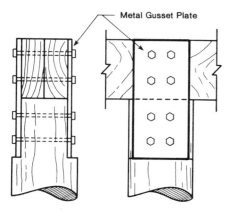

a. Dapped gusset plate connection

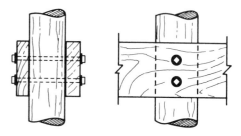

b. Bolted connection to round pole

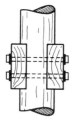

c. Dapped pole connection

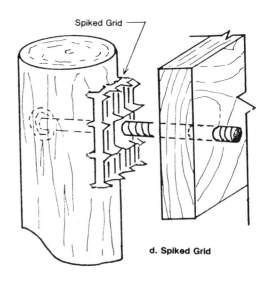

d. Spiked Grid

3-32. Some framing connections.

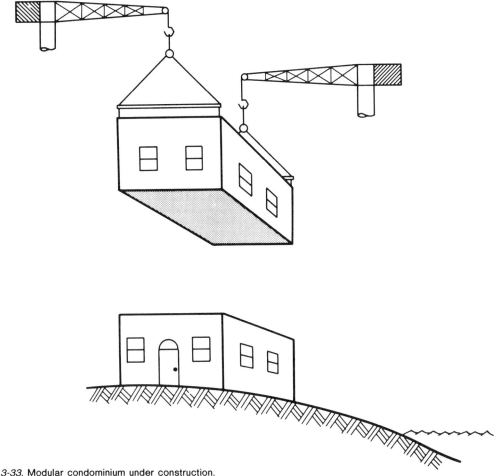

3-33. Modular condominium under construction.

the work is done out of sight of the buyer, there is opportunity to take shortcuts if the manufacturer is so inclined. It is quite possible that some modular dwelling units have their wiring, plumbing, heating, ventilating, and air conditioning installed at the factory by unqualified personnel, with the resulting inferior work either not being inspected or being inspected by an inept or unconscientious individual. Hence, the desirability of checking the reputation and integrity of the manufacturer, just as you would if you hired a contractor to build your individual house on the site.

The most important thing to be considered, viewed with caution, and checked out before buying a house of this type (as well as any other for that matter) is its suitability to conditions and forces encountered on the coast: hurricane winds, high water, waves, and salt air. It is also fundamental that such a house be built to provide safety in the event of fire, especially as many coastal homes are some distance from a fire department. Because of desire to keep prices competitive, a firm may manage to stay within the appropriate building code and yet make construction as light and as cheap as it can get away with. Again, do not forget that a building code specifies only *minimum* requirements. It is quite possible for a bouncy floor to be within a building code.

The prospective buyer should be especially cautious and investigate thoroughly a two- or three-level building. Are the levels fastened together or is there the prospect of the second and third levels blowing off the bottom level? Are metal clips and fasteners used to connect the structural members securely? Beware of a builder who places one unit on top of the other with minimal fastenings, relying on the weight of the material to hold the units in place and ignoring the possibility of high winds.

A perusal of the specifications for multifamily dwellings by one manufacturer shows its awareness of coastal conditions by the following: "1. Additional framing is required for structures in high wind areas. 2. All fasteners for coastal areas shall be galvanized. 3. Entry locksets for coastal areas shall be stainless steel." It does not follow, however, that all firms manufacturing modular unit buildings are conscious of the special coastal requirements.

Wind Forces

Wind is one of the most severe natural hazards, second only to fire in terms of lives lost and property damaged. Severe winds can tear light-framed houses apart, over-turn mobile homes, and destroy roofing. It is hoped this book will help the home owner and builder to achieve safer, wind-resistant housing.

Winds create pressures upon buildings on all surfaces: windward, leeward, on sidewalls, and on roofs. These pressures may be positive (pushing against the build-ing) or negative (suction, pulling away from the building). The pressures will vary considerably depending upon the shape of the building, its height, and its loca-tion.

In order to properly design a building—that is, to establish the required strength of construction in structural members, bracing, bolts, and nails—the magnitude of the wind pressure must be determined. The information in figures 3-34, 3-35, and 3-36 will aid in this determination. The use of these figures is recommended by *The Standard Building Code.* Determination of wind forces as prescribed by other build-ing codes is discussed in Chapter 9.

High wind velocities, particularly those above 50 to 60 miles per hour (80 to 100 km/h) will add another consideration to that of pressure—loading. This is impact loading from airborne debris in the form of tree limbs, loose boards, torn sheet metal, sheets of plywood, and loose objects lying in yards and lots. Both pressure loading and impact loading can occur simultaneously.

Figure 3-34 shows wind velocities for specific geographic locations. Use the basic wind velocity for your location, a prediction based on past wind histories. This basic wind speed must be modified by several factors, including personal judgment, aided by reliable local data if available. Elevation also affects wind speed in a particular location: the basic wind speeds in figure 3-34 are applicable to a height of 30 feet (9 m) above the ground.

Figure 3-35 provides data for wind force or pressure, as a function of basic wind velocity and height above the ground. Note that the wind pressure formula used in figure 3-35 indicates that the pressure increases with the square of the velocity and with the height of the building. The results obtained from figure 3-35 must then be modified by a shape factor to determine the design load. The pressure caused by wind that is felt by an object varies with its shape. A cylindrical object, for example, feels much less pressure than a flat surface does.

Figure 3-36 gives shape factors for a variety of conditions. The basic wind load

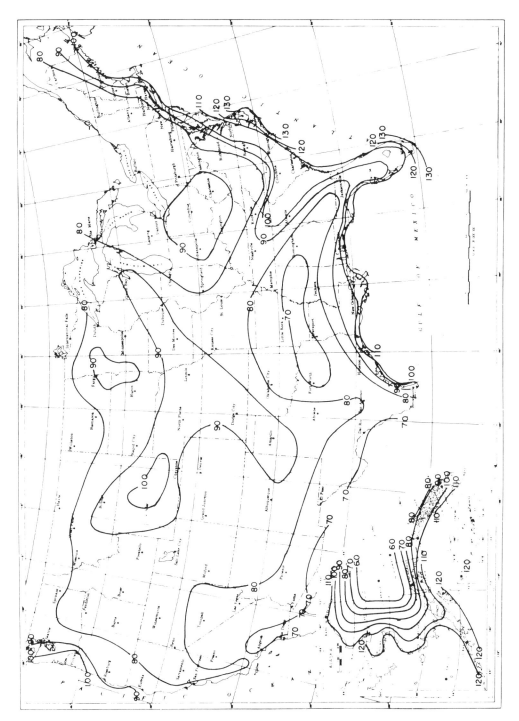

3-34. Basic wind speeds in miles per hour. This shows the annual extreme fastest mile speed 30 feet (9 m) above the ground for a 100-year mean recurrence interval. For extreme winds in severe storms in the United States, the unit of measure is the *fastest mile*—the highest speed at which one mile of wind passes the anemometer. Thus, in a hurricane the maximum sustained wind is the fastest mile. The *peak gust* is the highest instantaneous wind-speed value observed. (From the Southern Building Code Congress, *The Standard Building Code*)

Height above ground (feet)	100-Year recurrence of fastest mile of wind (mph, taken from figure 3-34)							
	70	*80*	*90*	*100*	*105*	*110*	*120*	*130*
0–30	10	13	16	20	23	24	29	34
31–50	14	18	22	28	31	34	40	47
51–100	16	21	27	33	37	40	48	56
101–200	20	26	33	40	45	49	58	68
201–300	23	30	38	47	52	57	67	79
301–400	25	33	42	52	57	62	74	87
401–500	27	36	45	55	61	67	80	94
501–800	30	39	50	62	68	74	89	104
801–1,000	33	43	55	68	75	82	97	114
over 1,000	34	45	56	70	77	84	100	117

Wind-load pressure in pounds per square foot

Heights are measured above the average level of ground adjacent to the structure. (The pressure should be modified by shape factors (fig. 3-36).

Wind-load pressures (P) are based on the following formula:
$$P = 0.00256 \times V^2 \times (H/30)^{2/7}$$
V = wind speed in mph
H = the height above grade (in feet) of the pressure being calculated.

This formula is applicable only to heights 30 feet or greater.

SOURCE: The Southern Building Code Congress, *The Standard Building Code*

3-36. Shape Factors

Shape factors for primary frames and systems—vertical surfaces

Vertical Surface	Factor
Rectangular prismatic structures[a]	1.3[b]
Cylinders (chimneys, tanks, etc.)	0.7
Flat surfaces with no appreciable depth, including signs and fences	1.4
Partially open surfaces (percent solid)[c]	
10%	0.35
20%	0.55
40%	0.80
60%	1.00
80%	1.20
100%	1.30

Shape factors for primary frames and systems—horizontal surfaces

Horizontal Surface[d]	Factor	
	Normal to windward $\frac{1}{3}$ of surface	Normal to leeward $\frac{2}{3}$ of surface
Enclosed buildings	−1.0[b]	−0.75
Buildings with one or more sides open	−1.5	−1.25
Overhangs and eaves[f]	−1.5	−1.50

Shape factors for primary frames and systems—inclined surfaces

Inclined Surface[e] Degree from horizontal	Factor	
	Normal to windward surface	Normal to leeward surface
70–90	+0.80[b]	−0.70
60–70	+0.65	−0.70
50–60	+0.55	−0.70
40–50	+0.25	−0.70
30–40	−0.25	−0.70
20–30	−0.75	−0.70
10–20	−0.93	−0.70
overhangs and eaves[f]	−1.50	−1.50

Shape factors for components transferring wind loads to the structural frame or system

Vertical Surface	Pressure Inward	Pressure Outward
Exterior walls of closed buildings, including fixed glass, glazing, and supporting members	+1.1[b]	−1.1
Operative windows and sliding glass doors, including parts	+1.1	−0.55
Exterior walls of buildings with one or more sides open	+1.1	−1.5

---

[a]Includes +0.8 on windward and −0.5 on leeward sides.
[b]Plus (+) indicates forces inward; minus (−) indicates forces outward.
[c]Shape factor to be applied to gross area of surface.
[d]Includes surfaces with less than 10° inclination to horizontal.
[e]For buildings with one or more sides open, add −1.0 to all negative factors.
[f]This factor is not additive and shall be treated as a separate load.

SOURCE: The Southern Building Code Congress, *The Standard Building Code*.

pressures from figure 3-35 should be multiplied by the shape factors to obtain the design pressure. This pressure is considered to be acting simultaneously with the vertical design loads.

Construction Checklists

Construction on the coastal shoreline presents many problems unique to the shore area. These are caused by the exposure to high winds, floodwaters, erosion, and subsidence, or sinking of soil to a lower level. The following checklists, which are taken from the Texas Coastal and Marine Council (*Building Construction Checklist for the Texas Coast and Shoreline*) and the University of Florida (*Checklist for Building Construction on Shore-Area Property*), are intended as a guide for those owners, designers, and builders concerned with these problems. Before you commit to a major expenditure, we recommend that a registered professional engineer be retained who is experienced and qualified in shore area design and construction. Ask him to supply satisfactory answers to the following checklists of questions.

Location Checklist

1. Local zoning regulations. *Does the building and building site conform to local city and county zoning regulations regarding the type of structure, its location with respect to dunes and water, and other code provisions?*
2. Beach access. *Does the structure block access to public beaches?*
3. Dune protection. *Has care been taken to protect any dunes and their vegetation? If dunes are located between the building and the beach, have elevated walkways for beach access been provided to prevent damage to the stabilizing vegetation on the dunes? These are especially necessary for multiple-unit dwellings or hotels.*
4. Check all jurisdictions. *The approval of one agency does not necessarily imply approval by other agencies. All applicable governmental regulations must be conformed to: local, state, and federal. Have requirements of local utility districts, if any, been met? If construction in wetlands or in navigable waters is involved, are permits required from the U.S. Army Corps of Engineers?*
5. Evacuation route. *Does the location have a suitable evacuation route to a safe inland refuge in case of severe storm tide and high wave conditions? Is the elevation of the evacuation route higher than the expected storm tide elevations? Road elevation information is available from city, county, and state departments of highways and public transportation.*
6. Insurability. *Have the requirements and recommendations of insurance companies been checked to assure that wind and flood insurance coverage can be obtained at reasonable rates?*
7. Site vegetation. *Is the finished site provided with natural or planned vegetation to protect against soil erosion from wind and surface-water runoff?*
8. Ownership. *Has attention been paid to boundaries between state-owned and privately owned land, especially on waterfront structures? If in doubt, check with the local government.*

Elevation, Erosion, and Subsidence Checklist

1. Storm tide elevation. *Has the elevation of the 100-year storm tide been determined and compared with the existing ground elevation at this building site? Call*

your local city or county engineer for information. Existing site elevation can be found by a registered local surveyor.

2. Floor above 100-year storm surge. *If this location is subject to flooding during a 100-year storm, is the lowest habitable floor raised above the top of the highest storm wave cresting on the 100-year storm tide?*
3. Local erosion rates. *Have local erosion rates been determined?*
4. Erosion prevention. *Have steps been taken to prevent erosion caused by wind and floodwater runoff, including provision for adequate natural or planted vegetation?*
5. When erosion occurs. *Should storm scour or erosion occur, is the foundation still adequate to support gravity and wind loads on the structures? (See the following foundation design checklist.)*
6. Subsidence. *Does the location have a history of ground subsidence or sinking? If so, has this been taken into account in design, access, and hurricane evacuation routes? Have measures been taken to prevent subsidence in likely areas?*

Wind Forces Checklist

1. *Has the effect of negative (suction) pressure been considered in the wind-load design? Consult city or county building department officials to determine minimum wind velocities and pressures for which the structure must be designed. Check this with the data in figures 3-34, 3-35, and 3-36.*
2. Building frame design. *Is the structural frame designed to withstand at least a 100-year storm wind with an adequate safety factor?*
3. Shape factor. *Have the effect of shape factors and roof slope been accounted for when calculating wind pressure and suction (see figures 3-2 and 3-36)?*
4. General building design. *Have all building elements (doors, siding, railings, and such) been designed to withstand both pressure and suction forces associated with at least a 100-year storm wind while remaining attached to the building?*
5. Adequacy of design. *Has the structure been designed by a registered professional engineer, qualified in this field? Do building drawings have the seal and signature of a registered professional engineer?*

Foundation Design Checklist

1. Wave forces. *If subject to wave attack during the 100-year storm, have the piles or other foundations been designed to withstand wave forces and battering action from floating debris?*
2. Erosion. *Has the foundation been designed to adequately withstand the effect of erosion or scour caused by wind and water runoff? A structure built on piling and properly anchored is generally much less susceptible to severe storm damage than a structure built on a slab foundation.*
3. Consider piles. *Are piles the best foundation in this case for raising the structure to the proper elevation and preventing any surface water flow from undermining the structure?*
4. Pile foundation. *If a pile foundation is used, are pilings driven deep enough below the scour zone to resist forces caused by wind pressures and wave forces after the scouring has taken place? Knowledge of the nature and character of the soil under the structure is necessary to make this determination.*
5. Post-scour ground elevation. *If subject to wave scour, has the elevation of*

stable soil after 100-year storm scour been determined for this site by a qualified consultant?

6. Post-scour pile loadings. *Have the piles or other foundations been designed to
sustain the horizontal and vertical loads associated with a 100-year storm after
the supporting soil has been scoured down to the 100-year storm scour elevation?*

7. Pile spacing. *Are the piles or other foundations spaced widely enough apart to
allow free flow of high-velocity floodwaters and to withstand the effects of storm
scour and erosion? Clearance between piles or other foundations is suggested
as 8 feet (2.4 m) or more where piles are subject to scouring action.*

8. Corrosion resistance. *Have pilings been properly treated to prevent damage
caused by constant moisture, salt water, marine borers, and rot?*

Wood-Frame Building Checklist

1. Sill plate. *Are sill plates securely attached to the foundation by means of anchor
bolts (or metal straps in the case of pile foundation) to resist uplift and lateral
forces caused by wind pressures?*

2. Wall connections. *Are wall studs securely attached to sill plates and top
plates?*

3. Roof. *Are rafters or trusses and joists fastened to top plates and studs with
metal straps or framing connections well enough to withstand a 100-year
storm?*

4. Hurricane straps. *Are metal hurricane straps required by governing building
codes? These straps are highly recommended on all coastal construction.*

5. Tie from roof to foundations. *Have metal straps been provided to ensure positive continuous connections, fastening all members together from the roof on
down through the foundations?*

6. Member design. *Have floor, roof, and wall members been designed to carry the
additional loads caused by higher wind pressure than is normal inland?*

7. Connection design. *Are member connections and fasteners adequate to carry
loads from high design wind velocities established for the area?*

8. Wall bracing. *Is diagonal wall bracing or properly attached plywood wall sheathing provided to resist high lateral loads on the structure?*

9. Corrosion. *Are bolts, straps, plates, nails, and all other metal fasteners hot
dipped galvanized or otherwise protected from corrosion?*

10. Secure cantilevers. *Are all cantilevered and other projecting members adequately supported and braced to withstand a 100-year storm?*

Concrete-Block Building Checklist

1. Masonry wall reinforcement. *Does the concrete-block wall contain vertical reinforcement firmly anchored into the beam on top and the footing on bottom?*

2. Reinforcement of corners and openings. *Is the reinforcement in the concrete
wall placed at all corners, all openings in the wall, and at periodic intervals
throughout the length of each wall?*

3. Tie beam. *Are the concrete-block walls topped with a reinforced concrete tie
beam that will resist uplift forces, extending continuously around the outside wall
of the building?*

4. Roof anchors. *Has the roof system (trusses or rafters) been firmly fastened to
the supporting concrete tie beam to resist uplift forces?*

5. Tie from roof to foundation. *Has vertical wall reinforcement been adequately tied to the foundation and to the bond beam to form a continuous tie from the foundation to the roof?*
6. Stacked bond. *Are the concrete blocks laid one directly above the other rather than the usual overlapping pattern? If so, avoid the building unless you have solid assurance that the wall has extra reinforcing to make up for the deficient design.*

Roofing, Siding, Shutters, and Trim Checklist
1. Roofing system. *Can you determine if the roofing system has been adequate in previous high-wind situations?*
2. Reduce shingle–tile exposure. *If the roof is shingle or tile, have the overlaps been increased and the fastening strengthened to account for 100-year storm pressures and suctions?*
3. Built-up roof. *Is each layer properly adhered to the previous layer and to the structural roof itself?*
4. No flying gravel. *Has gravel surfacing been eliminated to protect against pitting or cracking of finish and glass on nearby structures during high winds?*
5. Secure the corners. *Has particular attention been given to securing roof ridges, edges, eaves, corners, trim, and any other angular or irregular surfaces exposed to the wind to prevent loosening during high winds?*
6. Roof panels. *If roof panels are used, have they been securely fastened to the structural frame to withstand 100-year storm forces?*
7. Wall siding. *Has a type of wall siding been used that can be affixed to provide enough strength to withstand 100-year storm wind velocities?*
8. Reinforce the corners. *Has the fastening between siding and wall been reinforced at the corners of the building to account for the increased suction forces in these areas?*
9. Shutters. *Have shutters been provided for all glass openings and any other opening that may need protection from high winds?*
10. Fast, easy closure. *Are the shutters designed for quick, simple closure in time of need?*
11. Corrosion losses. *Will all the fastenings and hardware used in this building be able to withstand storm loadings after being corroded?*
12. Secure all parts. *Is this building with all its components adequately secured from roof through foundation and firmly anchored into the ground so as to safely withstand both wind and wave forces associated with at least a 100-year storm?*

Utilities Checklist
1. Storm-proof the telephone and electric lines. *Are telephone and electric lines located underground in waterproof conduit laid in protected areas not subject to erosion, flooding, and floating debris?*
2. Junction and breaker boxes. *Have junction boxes and breaker boxes been located above flood level and in a place not subjected to driving rain?*
3. Water and sewage facilities. *Are the water supply and sewerage facilities located in protected areas?*
4. Water and sewerage lines. *Are all water and sewerage lines constructed of a*

noncorrosive material and located to avoid damage and contamination caused by flooding, erosion, and floating debris?

Quality Assurance Checklist

1. Contractor qualifications. *Is the contractor experienced and qualified in shore area construction?*
2. Plans and specifications. *Does the contractor have fully detailed plans and specifications bearing the seal and signature of a registered professional engineer? Is the engineer experienced in the type of design proposed?*
3. Inspection. *Have arrangements been made to have a qualified registered professional engineer inspect the construction of the building? Have local building code regulations been checked for the necessity of required building inspections?*

The Older House

To Buy or Not to Buy

The principles involved in evaluating an existing house near the shore are similar to those in building a new house. Many of these are set forth in Chapter 3 and will not be duplicated in this chapter; hence, Chapters 3 and 4 should be read together to get a more complete picture.

In evaluating an existing house, consider three things:

- the location of the house;

- the type of house and how well it is built; and

- whether the house can be strengthened.

In general, the history of any given area should be checked with old-time residents and not real estate brokers, whose optimism must be taken with a grain of salt. A pictorial summary of some of the factors to consider in evaluating an existing house is provided in figure 3-2.

Location

While you may be able to strengthen a house after you buy it, you cannot reasonably change its location. Hence, location is the first item to investigate. Although this subject is treated more thoroughly in Chapter 2, the following will provide a good overview of what you will need to do:

1. Check the elevation of the ground above sea level and of the first habitable floor.
2. Find out the water level during a 100-year storm. Is the house eligible for the National Flood Insurance Program?
3. Check the elevation of the roads used for escape in the event of an emergency. If the house and the exit routes are at such an elevation as to be safe from high water, your main worry will be reduced to strong winds.

4. Look at the neighboring houses. Are they built so that portions can break loose and batter against and damage your house?
5. Use Chapter 2 as a guide to evaluating the location of the house with respect to migration of the land from erosion and other causes.
6. Visit prospective property after a hard rain to determine whether the lot drains. In some places the ground water table is close to the surface of the ground. This factor combined with a flat lot may cause the entire yard to become a pool in a hard rain and to remain so for some time. Also consider street drainage at this time. Some coastal areas are so flat that rainwater floods the street and does not drain off for a day or two.
7. Avoid a low site, vulnerable to flooding from high water, but keep in mind that a hilltop location is more vulnerable to wind forces. If the house is surrounded by woods or nearby homes, it will be partially protected from the wind. Damage may be caused by falling trees or limbs, but it is usually less than that caused by the full force of an unobstructed wind. Two or more rows of trees are better than a single row, and trees 30 feet (9 m) or more in height afford better protection than smaller ones.

The Type of House

You might as well put the odds in your favor by considering the type of house before you look at it in detail. A wood-frame house properly braced with well-fastened connections gives the best performance. Unreinforced masonry, that is, brick or hollow concrete block, is the most vulnerable to hurricane forces.

Masonry veneers—brick or stone facing on a wood frame—are easily torn away from the frame if poorly anchored. Poor-quality mortar also may make failure likely. Scrape a coin across the mortar. If weak, the material will come away easily and crumble between your fingers. Avoid a stuccoed house unless you can get reliable assurance that the stucco was properly applied and securely fastened to the walls.

Note the emphasis on proper reinforcing, fastenings, bracing, and anchorage in all the above cases. Without them, all types are vulnerable to storm forces.

If you are planning to move into a tall apartment building near the shore, consider that some buildings sustain motion and other effects in intense windstorms that can cause discomfort to the occupant. It is worth your while to check with tenants already living in the building to find out if it has motion characteristics that may be undesirable. Some buildings even make creaking noises that accompany the feeling of movement. Cases have been noted where people get motion sickness; in extreme cases people will vomit. Strange to say, in one study women felt the motion more than men, and a higher percentage of people under forty felt the motion more than those over forty. A higher percentage of women over forty became sick from the motion.

The shape of the house is important. A hip roof, which slopes in four directions, is better able to resist high winds than a gable roof, which slopes in two directions (see figure 3-2f). This was especially found to be true in Hurricane Camille, and later in Cyclone Tracy, which devastated Darwin, Australia, in December, 1974. The reason is twofold: the hip roof offers a smaller shape for the wind to blow against, and its structure is such that it is better braced in all directions.

Note also the plan of the house (the shape of the house as viewed from above).

The pressure exerted by a wind on a round or elliptical shape is about 60 percent of that exerted on the common square or rectangular shape; the pressure exerted on a hexagonal or octagonal cross section is about 80 percent of that exerted on a square or rectangular cross section (see figure 3-2g).

The design of a house or building in a coastal area should minimize structural discontinuities and irregularities such as nooks and crannies and offsets on the exterior, since damage to a structure tends to concentrate at these points. When irregularities are absent, the house can react to storm winds as a complete unit (see figure 3-2h).

How Well Built Is the House?

A number of factors will help determine how storm resistant a house is.

After reviewing figures 3-1, 3-2, and 3-3, you will no doubt want to know how well anchored to the ground the house is. If it simply rests on blocks, rising water could cause it to float off the foundations and drift against a neighboring house or into the middle of the street. If the house is built on a concrete slab, it will be difficult to discern if the structure has been properly bolted to the slab, as the inside and outside walls hide the bolts. But at least ask the builder if this was done. Best of all, it may be possible to ascertain if the wall is bolted to the slab by stripping away some of the bottom part of the inside wall and exposing the sill or plate and portions of the anchor bolts. The owner or real estate agent will hardly permit this without being certain of favorable results. If the building frame (walls and floor) is not anchored to the slab or to the foundation wall, it may be possible to achieve this anchorage by temporarily removing enough wall covering to add half-inch (1.3 cm) or larger expansion bolts (figure 4-1).

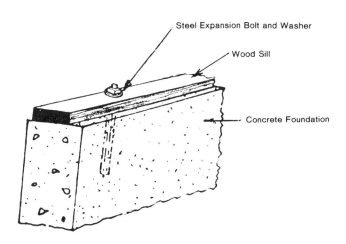

Steel Expansion Bolt and Washer

Wood Sill

Concrete Foundation

4-1. Additional connection of wood-frame building to foundation. Temporarily remove the wall covering enough to add half-inch (1.3 cm) or larger steel expansion bolts to gain additional anchorage.

Crawl under the house, if space permits, to see if the floor beams are securely connected to the foundations, whether they are piers or piles. If the floor system rests unanchored on piers, or on piles or stilts, do not buy the house unless it is practical to remedy this flaw.

The fundamental framing rule is that all structural elements should be anchored or fastened together in such a manner as to resist all forces, no matter which direction these forces may come from. Figure 4-2 provides an example of proper construction, as do figures 3-15, 3-16, and 3-17 in the previous chapter.

Be aware that many builders, carpenters, and building inspectors—particularly the older ones, who are accustomed to traditional construction—are apt to regard metal connectors, collar beams, and other such devices as newfangled and unnecessary. If consulted, they may assure you that a house is as solid as a rock when in fact it is far from it. Nevertheless, it is wise to consult the builder or knowledgeable neighbors when possible.

Also be aware that some builders and building inspectors may believe they are abiding by the building code when in fact they are not, because they do not understand the reasoning behind certain provisions and therefore interpret them incorrectly, often dangerously so. An example of this is the builder who, following a rule that alternate wall studs be fastened top and bottom with metal clips, used a top clip on one stud and a bottom clip on the next, so that no one stud was fastened both top and bottom (figure 4-3). Thus, if the roof were to try to lift up from the walls and foundations, the fastened studs would be useless. Half would go up with the roof and the other half would stay down with the floor and foundation. All this while the

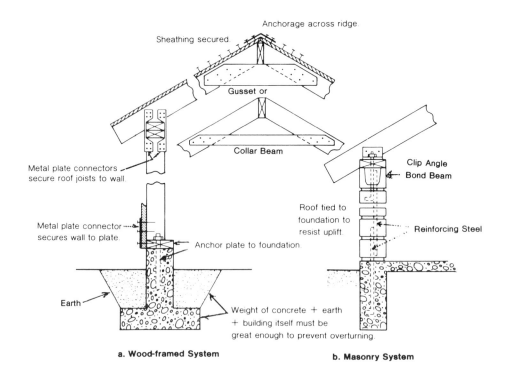

4-2. Where to strengthen a house.

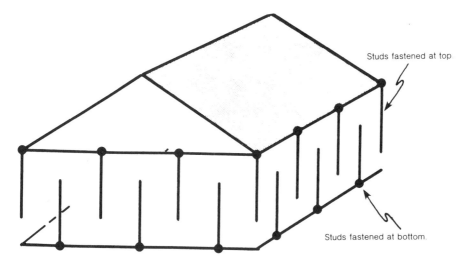

Studs fastened at top

Studs fastened at bottom.

a. Wrong Way to Fasten Studs

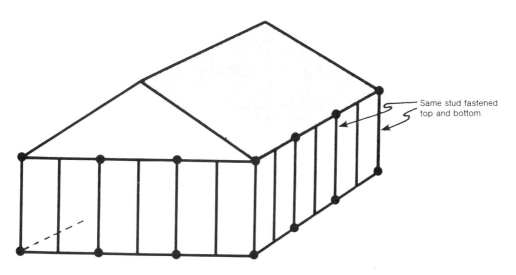

Same stud fastened top and bottom.

b. Correct Way to Fasten Alternate Studs

4-3. A wall stud should be fastened both top and bottom with metal clips.

builder and the building inspector both thought their interpretation of the rule was correct.

Be reasonably sure always that the roof is anchored to the walls, the walls to the floor, the floor to the foundation, and the foundation to the ground.

To determine if the roof is in fact anchored to the walls, visit the attic. Simple toe-nailing (nailing at an angle) is not sufficient; metal fasteners (see figure 3-17) are a must. It may not be easy to spot these fasteners, which may be obscured by insulation or the slope of the roof.

If roof trusses or braced rafters were used, look to see if the various members, such as the diagonals, are well fastened together. Some builders, unfortunately, nail together the parts of a roof truss just enough to hold it together to get it in place. A collar beam or gusset at the peak of the roof (figure 4-2) will provide some assurance of good construction.

Roofing Material

Be sure to look at the condition and composition of the roof. Quality roofing material should be used, and it should be well fastened to the sheathing. A poor roof covering can be destroyed by hurricane-force winds, allowing rain water to enter the house and damage ceilings, walls, and house contents.

Wood shingles and shakes, properly fastened, resist storm damage better than most roofing materials. For best performance in areas subject to storm, they should be connected to wood sheathing by two galvanized nails per shingle, long enough to penetrate the sheathing. If the sheathing is plywood, the nails should be threaded. For roof slopes that rise 1 foot or more for every 3 feet of horizontal distance, exposure of the shingles should be about one-fourth of each one's length—4 inches (10 cm) for a 16-inch-long (41 cm) shingle. If shakes (thicker and longer than shingles) are used, less than one-third of their length should be exposed—about 6½ to 7 inches (16 to 18 cm) for a 24-inch-long (61 cm) shake.

In hurricane areas, asphalt shingles should be exposed somewhat less than usual for inland regions. A mastic or seal-tab type or an interlocking shingle of heavy grade is recommended. Roof underlay of asphalt-saturated felt should be used with six galvanized roofing nails, or approved staples for each three-tab strip in a square-butt shingle. For low-pitch roofs, double coverage of the underlayment is preferred.

On built-up roofing consisting of layers of asphalt-saturated felt, the surfacing aggregate should be fully imbedded in the surface coating to minimize flying gravel and subsequent damage to adjacent windows, cars, and painted objects during high winds.

Corrugated metal and asbestos cement sheets are satisfactory if held down properly to the roof structure so they cannot detach themselves to become missiles. If a wood deck (closely spaced boards or plywood) is used, these sheets could be secured with drive screws of sufficient length to extend through the deck. If the sheets rest directly on purlins or other roof members, they should be secured with strap fasteners, bolts, or stud fasteners, or properly designed clip fasteners. In Darwin, Australia, since Cyclone Tracy, new construction utilizes battens or strips on top of the roof sheets to aid in holding them down in a high wind.

If the roofing sheets are aluminum, avoid iron nails or screws; the two materials are not compatible, and combining them results in corrosion. Aluminum nails are available and should be used. Likewise, aluminum roofing should be insulated when fastened to a steel-roof structure to prevent electrogalvanic action.

Brick, Concrete-Block, and Masonry-Wall Houses

Earlier in this chapter, we mentioned that unreinforced masonry, whether brick or concrete block, is most vulnerable to hurricane forces. Unfortunately, it is not easy to tell if masonry has in fact been strengthened, since the reinforcing is hidden from view; it is impossible to tell from the outside if reinforcing exists on the inside.

A poured concrete bond-beam at the top of a concrete-block wall just under the roof is one indication that a house is well built (see figure 3-19). However, most bond beams are formed by putting in reinforcing and pouring concrete in U-shaped concrete blocks. From the outside you cannot distinguish these U-shaped blocks from ordinary ones, and therefore cannot be certain that a bond beam exists. The wall should have vertical reinforcing, and this vertical reinforcing should penetrate the bond beam, but again this cannot be seen. Building codes applicable to high-wind areas specify the type of mortar, reinforcing, and anchoring to be used in construction. If you get assurance that the house was built in compliance with an appropriate building code, consider buying it.

Some architects and builders use a stacked bond—one block directly above another—rather than overlapped or staggered blocks, because they believe it affords a better appearance. The stacked bond is definitely weaker than the latter (see figure 3-20). Unless you have proof that the walls were adequately reinforced to overcome this lack of strength, avoid this type of construction.

In Hurricane Camille the brick veneer of many homes separated from the wood frames, even when the houses remained standing. Asbestos-type outer wall panels used on many houses in Darwin, Australia, were found to be brittle, and broke up under the impact of windborne debris in Cyclone Tracy. Both types of construction clearly should be avoided along the coast.

Consult a good architect or structural engineer who is familiar with construction on the coast for advice if you are in doubt about any aspects of the house. A few dollars spent for wise counsel may save you from later financial grief.

Can the House Be Strengthened (or, What Can Be Done to Improve an Existing House)?

If you already own a house or are contemplating buying one in a hurricane-prone area and this house needs strengthening, it may be practical to do so.

Does the House Need Anchoring to the Ground?

Suppose your house is resting on blocks but not fastened to them, and is thus not adequately anchored to the ground. Can anything be done? Yes, several solutions are possible. Perhaps the configuration of the house is such that piles can be driven deep into the ground at each corner, and then fastened to the house. This method of anchoring can apply to mobile homes as well as houses. Another solution is to treat the house like a mobile home, screwing ground anchors into the ground to a depth of 4 feet (1.2 m) or more and fastening them to the underside of the floor systems. Illustrations in Chapter 5 on mobile homes offer types of ground anchors and how they should be applied. The necessary number of ground anchors will differ, of course, between a house and mobile home, since one is affected differently than the other by the forces of wind and water. The dimensions of a house will usually differ from that of a mobile home in that the house may be wider and less likely to overturn. On the other hand, it may present more area against which the wind can blow, thus resulting in a greater force against the house. Note that recent practice is to put these commercial steel-rod anchors in at an angle so as to better align them with the direction of the pull. If a vertical anchor is used, the top 18 inches (45 cm) or so should be encased in a concrete cylinder about 12 inches (30 cm) in diameter. This prevents the top of the anchor rod from bending or slicing through the wet soil from the horizontal component of the pull.

Diagonal struts under the house—either timber or pipe—may also anchor a house that rests on blocks. This is done by fastening the upper ends of the struts to the floor system, and the lower ends to individual concrete footings substantially below the surface of the ground. These struts must be able to sustain both uplift (tension) and compression, and should therefore be tied into the concrete footing with anchoring devices such as metal straps or spikes.

Is the House Adequately Tied Together?

If the house has a porch with exposed columns or posts, it should be possible to install tie-down anchors on the tops and bottoms of them. Steel straps or clips should suffice in most cases.

Where accessible, roof rafters and trusses should be anchored to the wall system. On a completed house, the juncture of roof and wall is often very difficult to reach. Except where they meet the walls, the roof trusses or braced rafters are usually sufficiently exposed to make it possible to strengthen joints (where two or more members meet)—particularly at the peak of the roof—with collar beams or gussets (see figure 4-2).

A competent carpenter, architect, or structural engineer can review the house with you and help you decide what modifications are most practical and effective. Do not be misled by someone who is resistant to new ideas. One builder actually told a home owner, "You don't want all those newfangled straps and anchoring devices. If you use them the whole house will blow away, but if you build in the usual manner [with members lightly connected] you may lose only part of it."

In fact, of course, the very purpose of the straps is to prevent any or all of the house from blowing away. As the Standard Building Code states, "Lateral support securely anchored to all walls provides the best and only sound structural stability against horizontal thrusts, such as winds of exceptional velocity." And the cost of connecting all elements securely adds very little to the cost of the frame of the dwelling—under 10 percent—and a very much smaller percentage to the total cost of the house.

Consider bracing or strengthening the interior walls. Such reinforcement may require removing the surface covering and installing plywood sheathing or strap bracing to the extent possible. Where wall studs are exposed, bracing straps offer a simple way to achieve needed reinforcement against the wind. These straps are commercially produced and are made of 16-gauge galvanized metal with pre-punched holes for nailing. These should be secured to studs and wall plates as nail holes permit. Bear in mind that they are good only for tension. A 10d (tenpenny) nail is 3 inches (7.5 cm) long, and an 8d, 2½ inches (6.3 cm) long. Where compression forces are to be resisted, use 1 by 6 lumber with three 8d or 10d nails per stud and wall plate. If plywood is used it should be 4-feet by 8-feet by ½-inch thick (1.2 m x 2.4 m x 1.3 cm) for the full wall height. Secure plywood at the edges with 8d or 10d nails at 4-inch (10-cm) centers, and at inner studs with 8d or 10d nails at 8-inch (20-cm) centers. Bracing is not only important along the length of the wall, it should also be provided at right angles to the loaded surface of the wall at about 12-foot (3.7-m) centers to the extent possible. Remember that the wind force may come from any direction. Figure 4-4 illustrates bracing at right angles to a wall.

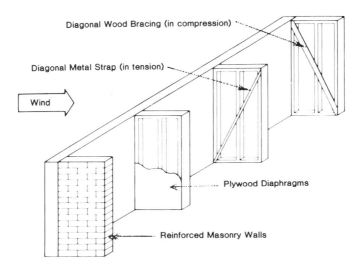

Diagonal Wood Bracing (in compression)

Diagonal Metal Strap (in tension)

Wind

Plywood Diaphragms

Reinforced Masonry Walls

4-4. Bracing walls at right angles to loaded surface. (From Defense Civil Preparedness Agency, Publication TR-83)

Will the House Leak Enough Air to Combat Changes in Barometric Pressure?

If the house has an overhanging eave and there are no openings on the underside of it, it may be quite feasible to cut openings and screen them. These openings keep the attic cooler (a plus in the summer) and help to equalize the pressure inside and outside during a storm with a low-pressure center.

How to Improve the Safety of the Occupants

If you wish to improve the protective capability of your house, several methods are available, even for the owner of an existing house, limited to modifications of in-place construction. One method is to strengthen the entire house. While this is easier to do when a house is being built, much can be done on an existing structure. If there are constraints, such as available budget or desire to leave the appearance unchanged, the owner may elect to strengthen only part of the house. A third option is to build within the house a shelter module in which to take refuge during a storm.

The advantages of such an in-house shelter module are that it is quickly accessible, it has a daily usefulness, and its protective features can be visually and functionally blended to fit the residence. To choose where it will be, examine the house and select the best room to stay in during a *wind storm*. Note the emphasis on *wind storm*. Such a shelter is *not* an alternative to evacuation prior to a hurricane. A small windowless room, such as a bathroom, utility room, den, hall, storage or mechanical equipment/laundry room space is usually stronger than one with windows (figure 4-5). A sturdy inner room with more than one wall between it and the outside is safest. The fewer the doors, the better; an adjoining wall or baffle or obstructing wall shielding the door adds to the protection.

The forces to be resisted are pressure and suction from the velocity of the wind,

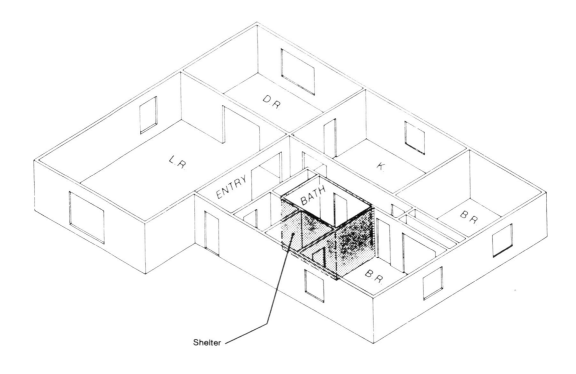

Shelter

4-5. Bathroom shelter module. (From Defense Civil Preparedness Agency, Publication TR-83)

the impact of flying debris, and the difference in air pressure between the inside and outside of the house from low atmospheric pressure caused by the passing of the center of the storm.

One would expect any prediction of the extent of impact from flying debris to be highly indeterminable. An interesting concurrence of opinion has developed, however, from two different sources. In a paper prepared for the Defense Civil Preparedness Agency, D.B. Ward recommends a 12-foot-long (3.7 m) 2 by 4 piece of lumber striking end first at 100 mph as the maximum force to be resisted. In Australia, since Cyclone Tracy hit Darwin, the recommended test has featured a 2 by 4 weighing 8 kilograms (17.6 lbs) (representing a length of approximately 12 feet—3.7 m) striking at 108 kilometers per hour (67 mph). Hence, both countries substantially agree on the airborne missile that might be expected to strike a house, which any house should be designed to resist.

Interior spaces are best because penetration of airborne debris is less likely. Small spaces are stronger than larger spaces with the same construction and are also less expensive to reinforce. Door openings into the shelter module should be shielded by adjoining or protecting walls, or else the door should be made heavier. Make the construction as independent as possible of other portions of the residence. Independent construction reduces the possibility that failure of other portions of the residence will cause failure of the shelter module. If the roof of the residence is torn off, for example, the roof or ceiling over the shelter module should be strong enough to prevent the occupants from being exposed to the elements.

Much good can be said for small protected spaces in yards or basements, at elevations above the flood zone, to which the residents can move when threatened with high winds. These types of facilities are inconvenient, however, and more important perhaps to shore dwellers, they are impractical, since few basements exist in coast-adjacent houses. Soil conditions simply are usually not favorable to the construction of an underground shelter (such as a cyclone or storm cellar). Some older coastal homes within the flood zone may have basements, and many have enclosed ground floors. Both of these areas are potential death traps during flooding and overwash.

A word as to minimum size: the Australian guidelines recommend that the residence shelter module have a minimum floor area of 52 square feet (5 sq m) with 11 square feet (1 sq m) per person.

Factors to be considered in the modification of existing space include:

1. Strength and rigidity to resist collapse should the surrounding residence fail.
2. Tie-down of overhead construction (roof, upper floor, or ceiling) above the protected space to the walls of the module. The floor above must be strengthened to prevent its possible inward collapse on the occupants below.
3. Sufficient wall strength to resist penetration of airborne debris.
4. Shielded openings into the space, or strengthening of door(s).
5. Adequate anchorage of all connections, including walls and floor to foundation.

From the above it can be seen that the choice of location in the interior of the house is very important.

There are several alternatives for wall construction, such as reinforced block masonry, reinforced poured concrete, and a wood-framed system with infill of concrete grout. The ceiling is best constructed with reinforced concrete infill between ceiling joists that are anchored to the walls.

The most likely type of existing construction that the tenant will confront when trying to provide a shelter module is a wood-framed roof, interior partitions of wood-stud construction covered with gypsum board, and exterior walls either of wood framing or wood sheathing, or of brick or block masonry. The shelter module can be vented by a ceiling fan that also provides ventilation for the bathroom.

If walls are not covered with gypsum board, it may be possible to add metal straps or connectors at exposed critical joints, such as studs to floor joists and studs to floor (sill) plates. The sill plate can be fastened to the slab with power-driven anchor bolts, if need be. Plywood can be added to the unfinished side of partitions and to the underside of ceiling joists. This provides added bracing for wind resistance and a bit more security from flying debris. The plywood should be secured to the studs, plates, and joists with 10d nails at 4-inch (10-cm) centers on edges and 8-inch (20-cm) centers at studs between edges.

Figure 4-4 shows several types of bracing that can strengthen the walls of a shelter module within a residence. As mentioned earlier in connection with strengthening the walls of the entire house, it may be necessary to remove the surface covering to expose the studs and joists to permit installing plywood sheathing or bracing in the shelter module.

If, after reading this chapter, you agree that something should be done to your house to make it safer to live in, do it now. Do not put it off until the next hurricane or tornado hits you. Do not be like the man (described by the French philosopher Montaigne) who, in his travels, came upon a river and stood on the bank, waiting for the river to flow past so he could cross with dry feet.

5

Mobile Homes in a Mobile Environment

Some 8 million Americans now live in mobile homes, but high winds damage or destroy over 20,000 mobile homes every year. This problem will surely become more severe as purchasing a house becomes more and more of an impossible dream for the younger generation of Americans. Today nearly one-third of all new single-family residences are mobile homes. Needless to say, the increasing popularity of mobile homes comes from their relatively low price, as well as the traditional desire of Americans to own their own place.

One might expect mobile homes to be the ideal way to go in a mobile environment such as a barrier island or a rapidly retreating sandy beach (figure 5-1). What better way to escape damage during a storm than to pick up one's entire home and immediately move it fifty miles inland? This does not work, of course, because mobile homes are not that mobile. Imagine the traffic jams if an entire mobile-home park picked up and left all at once to escape the storm! As a matter of fact, far from being able to escape storms, mobile homes are essentially the most vulnerable type of housing in coastal areas. Although moving them back quickly enough to save them from storm damage is not a likely possibility, they certainly can be moved back in response to gradual shoreline recession.

Mobile homes are vulnerable to high winds because they are of lightweight construction with flat sides and ends. Winds of speeds between fifty and seventy miles per hour routinely cause minor damage to mobile homes; higher windspeeds usually cause major damage. The winds of hurricanes, tornadoes, and severe storms can structurally damage mobile homes, toss unanchored ones around, overturn them, and smash them into neighboring mobile homes and other objects.

Mobile-home shortcomings that lead to wind damage include inadequate structural strength, vulnerable sites or orientation on a particular site, and improper footings or tiedowns. Mobile-home owners, park owners, and manufacturers seem aware of the damage winds can cause but often seem to be unwilling to take corrective measures or are uncertain as to what action is needed. In fact, because of the nature of the problem, what is most needed is a joint effort by all three parties. But, naturally, if too much money is required to give mobile homes the structural integrity

5-1. A large, densely packed trailer park on the backside of Ocean City on a Maryland barrier island. These trailers are extremely susceptible to flooding in a storm surge. (Photo: Evelyn Maurmeyer)

and proper tiedowns to truly resist hurricanes, they will become too expensive, and their raison d'etre will disappear.

Part of this several-pronged problem of shortcomings was alleviated on June 15, 1976, a most important date for mobile-home construction quality, when a federal code, which the industry refers to as the H.U.D. code, became law. This code, setting up minimum standards, insists that every mobile home built today pass certain H.U.D. requirements plus local building codes, resulting in many cases in standards tougher than those for site-built housing. It is interesting how mobile-home walls must now have 2 by 4 studs on 16-inch centers, the same as site-built homes. This represents an improvement over the lighter, flimsier construction often used in the past. In the mid-seventies many shoddy builders were put out of business because of these innovations. Unfortunately, their products often still survive.

From another standpoint, mobile homes truly make the ideal beach-front home. (They are, however, prohibited in the V zone of communities participating in the National Flood Insurance Program, unless they are located in already existing mobile-home parks.) Because the structures are relatively inexpensive, mobile-home owners are not likely to create a loud uproar for such costly shoreline stabilization projects as seawalls, jetties, and groins, processes that will eventually result in degradation of the beach. It is probably a fact of political life that the typical mobile-home park near a beach, for example, Indian Beach, North Carolina, is much less likely to generate a loud political voice than a shore lined with million-dollar homes such as in Westhampton Beach, New York, or La Jolla, California. Thus, while the mobile-home shoreline may suffer great environmental damage, it is not likely to be the cause of large tax expenditures relative to the rich man's shore-line.

Damage

As is to be expected from any natural disaster, hurricane-caused damage to mobile homes varies from year to year. The American Red Cross statistics for the cases referred to them during the years 1969 to 1975 indicate that an average of 343 mobile homes were destroyed by hurricanes each year, and an additional 321 per year were damaged. Included in these figures, however, are two damage-free years (1972 to 1974).

Unique to mobile homes is their vulnerable skin-type construction and pier-type foundations. The most common type of major damage is the tearing away of most or all of the roof. When this happens, the walls are no longer adequately supported at the top and are more prone to collapse. Total destruction of a mobile home commonly occurs when the roof blows off first, followed by the overturning of the complete structure.

Frequently, prior to overturning, the mobile home slides off its piers. In addition, wind can destroy an inadequately constructed mobile home by separating the walls from the floor system or by shearing off the entire superstructure from the underframe.

Poor siting of mobile homes makes them susceptible to rising water and storm overwash. In Chapter 2 the problem of site selection to avoid waves and rising water is discussed in more detail.

The potential damage to mobile homes at different wind speeds is summarized in figure 5-2. The windspeeds mentioned are the average speeds at a 30-foot (9-m) elevation in open terrain.

Last but not least of the myriad of ways by which mobile homes can be destroyed is destruction of one mobile home by another mobile home. It is not infrequent in major storms for a poorly anchored structure to be picked up and slammed into a neighboring one, resulting in demolition of both. In some coastal states, so-called travel trailers, some of which can be rather large, are not required to have the same tiedowns and anchorage as regular mobile homes because they are considered mobile and temporary. In fact, such trailers often become permanent. Since some mobile-home parks house both travel trailers and mobile homes, the resulting destruction from a storm should be something to behold.

Emergency Procedures

When alerted to an approaching hurricane, take certain precautions and emergency action. The following checklist is similar to the more detailed list in Chapter 8, but some emergency procedures are unique for mobile-home owners. The most important of these is the need to get away before the storm arrives—no matter what!

Checklist for Emergency Action if Heavy Weather Is Expected

1. Tie down awnings and other fixtures.
2. Prepare loose objects for indoor storage.
3. Tighten tiedowns.

5-2. Potential Mobile Home Damage at Different Windspeeds

Windspeed	*Potential Type and Extent of Damage*
Below 50 mph (80 km/h)	Minor damage, caused by weak attachments and accidents from missiles. Occasional minor damage because of poor roof-to-wall connections and sliding or overturning of very light, poorly supported homes without tiedowns.
50–70 mph (80–112 km/h)	More severe roof damage possible, but should not cause wall collapse or total loss of code-designed home. Sliding or overturning fairly likely for a lightweight mobile home that is not tied down. In this windspeed range, tiedowns very effective in preventing damage.
70–100 mph (112–160 km/h)	Severe damage and destruction common, most often by such major movement as overturning of homes not properly tied down. Proper preventative provisions: an adequate safety factor in the roof-to-wall connections and anchoring to prevent sliding or major movement. Without tiedowns, weight of the mobile home is the most important factor in preventing overall movement.
Above 100 mph (160 km/h)	Serious damage, unless home is tied down well and has a favorable combination of heavy, strong construction, a rough surrounding terrain, and effective shielding by nearby trees or building. Survival uncertain, since mobile homes simply not designed to resist windspeeds in this range, either structurally or in terms of tiedown systems. In fact, hurricane-resistant design pressures of current standards correspond only to 88 mph (140 km/h) windspeeds.

SOURCE: W. Pennington and J.R. McDonald, *An Engineering Analysis: Mobile Homes in Windstorms.*

Upon receiving the hurricane warning:
1. *Pack breakables.*
2. *Tape or board windows.*
3. *Disconnect electrical, sewer, and water lines.*
4. *Turn on faucets and drain out water. Leave the faucets open.*
5. *Continue to listen to a radio for information and instructions.*
6. *Depart for other shelter.*

Community Shelter

Although this chapter presents suggestions for protecting mobile homes from storms, the safest recourse in the event of an approaching hurricane or storm is to seek other shelter. Hazardous flooding often accompanies hurricanes, especially in low-lying coastal regions. Some mobile-home parks provide storm-secure shelters for residents. Local civil defense directors can supply information on the location of suitable shelters, including those operated by the Red Cross. *Never ride out even a minor storm in a mobile home.*

Site Selection and Orientation

Several lessons can be learned from past experiences in storms. One is that mobile homes should be properly located. After Hurricane Camille, it was observed that where mobile-home parks were surrounded by woods and homes were close together, damage to the homes was minimized, caused mainly by falling trees. In unprotected areas, however, many mobile homes were overturned and destroyed by the force of the wind. The best type of mobile-home park should not only be forested but should have altered original dune topography as little as possible.

Other rules of common sense should also be adhered to. For example, keep out of overwash passes and channels. Do not locate adjacent to a rapidly eroding beach. Do not locate where septic tanks won't drain properly.

Windbreaks

If possible, place your mobile home on a site with terrain protection from high winds. Locating your mobile home on a hilltop site will greatly increase your vulnerability to the wind but reduce your vulnerability to flooding. A lower, less exposed location that is still above storm-surge flood levels is safer from the wind.

In addition to protection by natural topography or vegetation, mobile homes can receive wind shielding from neighboring objects such as trees, buildings, and other mobile homes. Shielding by another mobile home is the least desirable of these. The potential protection afforded by upwind obstacles such as trees is greater than the possible damage from flying missiles from those obstacles, such as branches breaking off the trees. Even damage from falling trees is preferable to total loss in an unprotected area. Two or more rows of trees are better than a single row, and trees thirty feet in height afford better protection than shorter ones. Reasonably dense, narrow windbreaks can be as effective as wider barriers.

Positioning

It would of course be immensely helpful in laying out a mobile-home court or in positioning a particular home to have the psychic powers to ascertain the direction from which high winds will blow. In lieu of this, it is best to base positioning on prevailing strong winds. A phone call to the local weather office can provide information on the most likely direction of strong winds. In many regions, this information cannot be provided with much confidence. Hurricane directions are notoriously unpredictible, and rotational air flow patterns can lead to strong winds from all directions.

If possible, position a mobile home so that the narrow side faces the prevailing strong winds. For a home 12 by 60 feet (3.7 by 18.3 m), presenting the narrow side to the wind offers 80 percent less exposed wall area than facing the long side toward the wind would. This leads to a substantial difference in the odds in favor of survival of a mobile home, providing the wind cooperates and comes from the right direction.

In placing a mobile home in the vicinity of shielding objects, care must be taken that these objects do not channel or concentrate the wind. Position the long side of the mobile home to face the direction from which the neighboring objects provide the most protection and the least wind channeling.

The positioning of homes within a mobile-home park is also important, because the proper alignment of several homes increases the shielding afforded by neighboring homes. From the standpoint of maximum wind protection, homes should be closely spaced and lined up parallel to each other.

Last but not least, it should again be noted that proper positioning is a means of property protection. Do not be lulled into a sense of false security. Move your family members out of any mobile home at the first warning of an impending storm.

Anchoring Systems

For high-wind protection, mobile homes require a solid support system of embedded pilings, footings and piers, and a tiedown system to retard overturning and sliding off the piers. These anchoring systems are not the direct responsibility of the manufacturer. According to federal standards established by the American National Standards Institute and the Department of Housing and Urban Development, the manufacturer is responsible only for supplying tiedown straps and instructions for their installation. It is left to the owner or installer to see that the home is properly secured. As for existing older mobile homes, the National Fire Protection Association has issued a paper on standards for installation of mobile homes, providing guidelines for the installation of anchoring systems.

It should be noted that various coastal areas seem to have their own indigenously characteristic anchoring systems for mobile homes. Please remember that just because everyone else uses a certain system and has been doing so for years does not mean it is the best system, or even a good system. Be skeptical. Check it out.

A typical anchoring system is shown in figure 5-3. This consists of a concrete footing, concrete block piers, wood or concrete pier caps, hardwood shims, and ties connected to anchors set in the ground.

Piers and Footings

Pier foundations should be installed directly under the main frame of the mobile home. Normally there are two steel I-beams that run lengthwise under the mobile home and several smaller steel outrigger beams that are fastened at right angles to the main runner beams. The main members of the underframing are referred to as the *main frame* or *chassis*. Place the piers no farther apart than 10 feet (3 m) measured from center to center. Position the end piers no farther than 2 feet (60 cm) from the ends of the main frame of the mobile home. Build the piers on solid footings or foundations, placed level on stable soil. This should be undisturbed soil or controlled fill free of grass or organic material. If erosion potential is high, footings should be buried deep below grade.

Pier foundations should be a solid concrete pad at least 16 by 16 by 4 inches (41 × 41 × 10 cm), precast or poured in place. Alternatively, use an equivalent footing such as two 8- by 16- by 4-inch (20 × 41 × 10 cm) solid concrete blocks, with the joint between the blocks aligned parallel to the main frame.

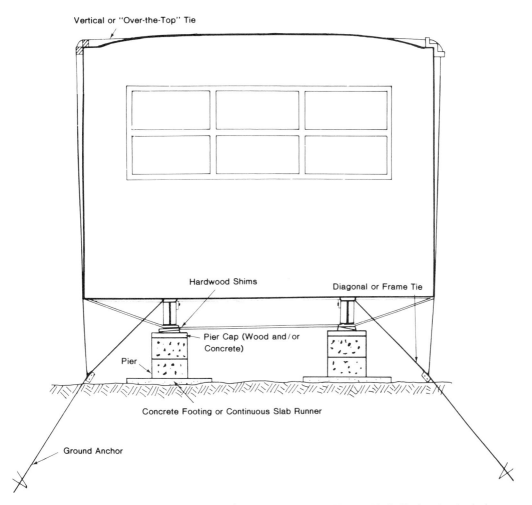

Vertical or "Over-the-Top" Tie

Hardwood Shims

Diagonal or Frame Tie

Pier Cap (Wood and/or Concrete)

Pier

Concrete Footing or Continuous Slab Runner

Ground Anchor

5-3. Typical mobile-home anchoring system. (From Pennington and McDonald, *An Engineering Analysis: Mobile Homes in Windstorms*)

Use piers designed and constructed to evenly distribute and adequately support the loads. Suitable pier designs of various heights constructed on the footings are shown in figures 5-4, 5-5, and 5-6 (all taken from the North Carolina Department of Insurance's *Regulations for Mobile Homes and Modular Housing*). In coastal areas, added anchoring strength can be obtained by using reinforcement in piers and tieing directly into footings.

Piers less than 40 inches (1 m) high should be constructed of open- or closed-cell concrete blocks measuring 8 by 8 by 16 inches (20 × 20 × 41 cm), with the open cells vertically placed. Install single-stacked block piers with the 16-inch dimension perpendicular to the main frame. Cover the piers with a pressure-treated wood or concrete cap measuring 2 by 8 by 16 inches (5 × 20 × 41 cm). If needed to provide uniform bearing, fit and drive tight treated wood shims between the cap and the supporting main frame. The shims should not occupy more than an inch (2.5 cm) of vertical space (see figure 5-4).

Special precautions need to be taken for piers more than 40 inches (1 m) high. Single tiers of concrete blocks are likely to collapse under wind loadings. Piers 40 to

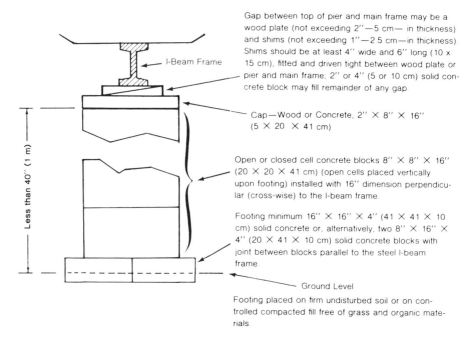

Gap between top of pier and main frame may be a wood plate (not exceeding 2"—5 cm— in thickness) and shims (not exceeding 1"—2.5 cm—in thickness). Shims should be at least 4" wide and 6" long (10 x 15 cm), fitted and driven tight between wood plate or pier and main frame; 2" or 4" (5 or 10 cm) solid concrete block may fill remainder of any gap.

I-Beam Frame

Cap—Wood or Concrete, 2" × 8" × 16" (5 × 20 × 41 cm)

Open or closed cell concrete blocks 8" × 8" × 16" (20 × 20 × 41 cm) (open cells placed vertically upon footing) installed with 16" dimension perpendicular (cross-wise) to the I-beam frame.

Footing minimum 16" × 16" × 4" (41 × 41 × 10 cm) solid concrete or, alternatively, two 8" × 16" × 4" (20 × 41 × 10 cm) solid concrete blocks with joint between blocks parallel to the steel I-beam frame.

Less than 40" (1 m)

Ground Level

Footing placed on firm undisturbed soil or on controlled compacted fill free of grass and organic materials.

5-4. Piers less than 40 inches (1 m) in height (except corner piers over three blocks high). Piers should be securely attached to the frame of the mobile home or should extend at least 6 inches (15 cm) from the center line of the frame member.

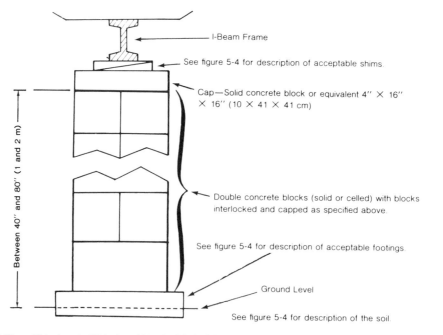

I-Beam Frame

See figure 5-4 for description of acceptable shims.

Cap—Solid concrete block or equivalent 4" × 16" × 16" (10 × 41 × 41 cm)

Double concrete blocks (solid or celled) with blocks interlocked and capped as specified above.

See figure 5-4 for description of acceptable footings.

Between 40" and 80" (1 and 2 m)

Ground Level

See figure 5-4 for description of the soil.

5-5. Piers 40 inches to 80 inches (1 to 2 m) in height and all corner piers over three blocks high. Piers should be securely attached to the frame of the mobile home or should extend at least 6 inches (15 cm) from the center line of the frame member.

80 inches (1 to 2 m) high and all corner piers over three blocks high can be made more stable by using double tiers with interlocking blocks. They should be capped by a 4- by 16- by 16-inch (10 × 41 × 41 cm) solid concrete block or pressure-treated wood plate (see figure 5-5).

If the height of the pier exceeds 80 inches (2 m), construct as shown in figure 5-6. Lay the blocks in concrete mortar, with steel reinforcing bars inserted in the block cells. Fill the block cells with concrete (figure 5-7).

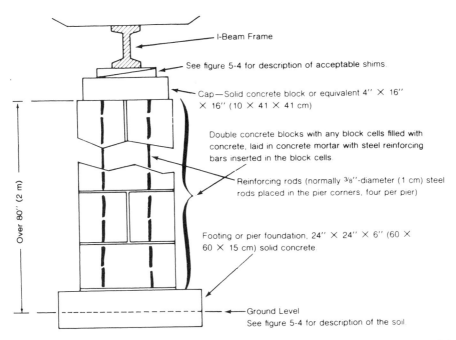

I-Beam Frame

See figure 5-4 for description of acceptable shims

Cap—Solid concrete block or equivalent 4″ × 16″ × 16″ (10 × 41 × 41 cm)

Double concrete blocks with any block cells filled with concrete, laid in concrete mortar with steel reinforcing bars inserted in the block cells

Reinforcing rods (normally ⅜″-diameter (1 cm) steel rods placed in the pier corners, four per pier)

Footing or pier foundation, 24″ × 24″ × 6″ (60 × 60 × 15 cm) solid concrete

Over 80″ (2 m)

Ground Level
See figure 5-4 for description of the soil

5-6. Piers exceeding 80 inches (2 m) in height. Piers should be securely attached to the frame of the mobile home or extend at least 6 inches (15 cm) from the center line of the frame member.

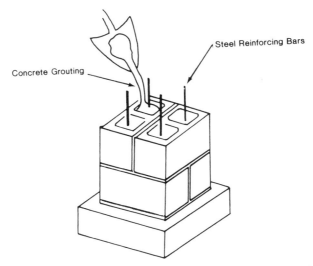

Steel Reinforcing Bars

Concrete Grouting

5-7. Piers exceeding 80 inches (2 m) in height. The concrete blocks must be filled with concrete grouting, with steel reinforcing rods.

Wood-Post Foundation Systems

Much of the past damage to mobile homes could have been avoided by anchoring them to a wood-post foundation system. By this means they can be firmly attached to the ground and raised to a desired height above the ground (above sea level).

The posts or piles should be pressure treated and either set or driven deeply into the ground. (For more information, see in Chapter 3 the discussion on pole houses.) The mobile home must be securely fastened to these poles, or to cross beams attached to the poles. As in the case of immobile homes, poor connection of mobile homes to piles has been a major cause of damage.

Because of the narrowness of a mobile home compared with a conventional home, the support structure will need to be stronger than usual to resist lateral forces. One can intuitively visualize that the narrow structure will be more easily overturned. If the mobile home is set at any great height above the ground, there should be lateral or diagonal bracing between the poles. The poles should be adequately embedded in the ground. If the design flood level is above grade, it is preferable to use cable-type cross-bracing to minimize the forces from water or wave on the structural framing. Such cables, however, will require higher maintenance due to corrosion.

Two basic types of pole construction exist. On one type, the poles are cut off at the floor level; on the other, the poles extend to the roof level. Either type can be used with mobile homes. In both cases the poles and the home must be securely tied together. Poles extending to the roof level make a much more secure and wind-resistant support system than floor-level poles.

Of course it is possible to place a mobile home at any height above the ground, but it is not practical. From the standpoint of stairs as well as the supporting structure, it is advantageous to keep the distance between floor and ground as small as possible, consistent with safety. The height of the floor above sea level should be somewhat above the 100-year storm; the height above the ground, then, depends upon that minus the ground elevation.

Tiedowns

Simple prudence dictates that when buying a mobile home it is best to give preference to one with built-in tiedown straps. Most mobile homes available in coastal areas will be equipped with such a built-in system. The built-in straps are usually concealed under the skin and thus are more attractive than exposed straps (figure 5-8a). One problem with hidden straps, however, is that their corrosion from salt spray may go unnoticed. A casual walk through almost any coastal mobile-home park will reveal corroded straps, loose straps, and sometimes no straps at all. Perhaps having tiedown straps clearly visible has the advantage of letting individuals know the status of their safety precautions, as well as those of their neighbors.

The tiedown straps must be secured to ground anchors to assure that the mobile home is firmly attached to the ground. An alert mobile-home court would provide permanent concrete anchors or piers to which hold-down ties could be fastened. Not only are tiedown systems good common sense and matters of self-interest, in many communities ordinances and regulations actually require them. Furthermore, many insurance companies will not insure a mobile home unless it is adequately anchored with tiedowns. Tiedown systems generally will not exceed a nominal cost per home. But it is essential that tiedown systems be installed on *all* mobile homes in a community. Unsecured homes will present hazards to neighboring homes from blowing debris.

Two forms of ties are needed: over-the-top ties (including concealed straps) attached to ground anchors, which prevent the home from overturning; and frame ties, connecting the steel underframe to the anchors, which keep the unit from sliding off the supports (figure 5-8). Frame ties also serve to reduce overturning, but many mobile homes are not structurally strong enough for the unit to remain intact with frame ties only. Thus, although frame ties will secure the underframe, the rest of the home may be blown away.

An exception to the two-form tie requirement would be a double mobile-home unit, which at approximately 24 feet (7.3 m) wide, is sufficiently stable to bypass the over-the-top ties. A double unit would still, however, require the frame ties.

Remember, tiedowns need tightening from time to time and, in the corrosive salt air of the beach community, occasionally may need complete replacement.

Types of Tiedowns

Over-the-top and frame ties are both shown in figure 5-8. As mentioned above, both types of tiedowns are necessary. Either type 1 (figure 5-8c) or type 2 (figure 5-8d) can be used for the frame ties. Since the ties (not the anchors) of type 2 are more horizontal, they can resist a greater horizontal load than can the type 1 ties, and hence fewer of them are required.

Tie Material

Ties should be made of rust-resistant steel in the form of cables or flat straps. Cables should be galvanized or stainless steel with a breaking strength greater than 4,800 pounds (21.4 kN). Suitable commercially available cables are at least $7/32$-inch-diameter (0.56-cm) 7×7 cable or $1/4$-inch (0.64-cm) 7×19 aircraft cable. The figures 7×7 and 7×19 define the type of cable: a 7×7 steel cable has seven strands, each of which contain seven wires; a 7×19 cable has seven strands, each of which has nineteen wires.

The alternate type of tie, a rust-resistant steel flat strap, should have a breaking strength of at least 4,750 pounds (21.1 kN). This strength can be achieved with a cold-rolled, heat-treated, galvanized flat strap $1 1/4$ inches (3.2 cm) wide by 0.035 inches (0.09 cm) thick, conforming to Federal Specifications QQ-S-781G, Type 1, Class B, Grade 1. It is important that the breaking strength be included in the purchase specifications.

The supplier will understand the requirements of both cables and straps, as these items are commercially available. Use of the wrong or poor-quality material will weaken the tiedown system. The protection provided by high-quality components is well worth the cost.

Number of Ties

Each mobile home should be secured with the number of over-the-top and frame ties listed in figure 5-9. This number is a function of the length and width of the home, as well as expected windspeed. It is assumed not only that the home is constructed with firm connections to the steel-supporting frame, but also that the tie material and anchoring requirements specified in this chapter are observed.

For coastal regions subject to hurricanes, it is recommended that anchorage

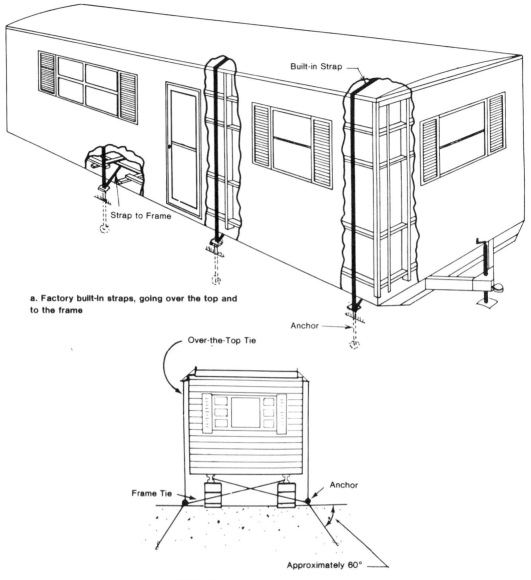

Built-in Strap

Strap to Frame

a. Factory built-in straps, going over the top and to the frame

Anchor

Over-the-Top Tie

Frame Tie

Anchor

Approximately 60°

b. Over-the-top ties connected to the same anchors as frame ties

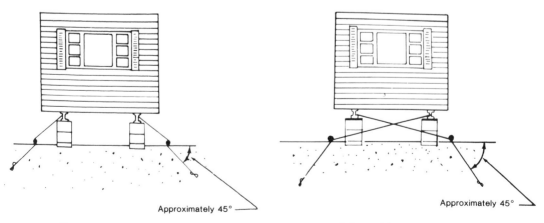

Approximately 45°

c. Diagonal frame tie, type 1

Approximately 45°

d. Crossed frame tie, type 2

5-8. Types of tiedowns.

Mobile Homes 10 and 12 Feet (3 and 3.6 m) Wide — **Mobile Homes 12 and 14 Feet (3.6 and 4.3 m) Wide**

Wind Velocity (mph)	30 to 50 Feet (9 to 15 m) Long			50 to 60 Feet (15 to 18 m) Long			60 to 70 Feet (18 to 21 m) Long		
	No. of Frame Ties		No. of Over-the-Top Ties	No. of Frame Ties		No. of Over-the-Top Ties	No. of Frame Ties		No. of Over-the-Top Ties
	Type 1	Type 2		Type 1	Type 2		Type 1	Type 2	
70 (112 km)	4	3	2	5	4	2	5	4	2
80 (128 km)	5	4	3	6	5	3	6	5	3
90 (144 km)	6	5	4	7	6	4	8	7	4
100 (160 km)	7	6	5	8	7	5	9	8	6
110 (176 km)	8	7	6	10	9	6	11	10	7

SOURCE: Defense Civil Preparedness Agency. Reports TR-75 and TR-73-1.

5-9. Number of Ties Required

systems capable of resisting winds of at least 110 mph (177 km/h) be installed.

Location and Mounting of Ties

An over-the-top tiedown should be positioned at stud and rafter locations close to each end of the unit. The other over-the-top ties should be spaced evenly between these two end ties. Frame ties can be placed directly beneath the over-the-top ties and can use the same anchors.

The ties should be mounted on the corners between wall and roof so as to prevent them from being cut by or cutting into the mobile home. Special commercial adapters or mounting brackets are available for this purpose, but a homemade system can do as well (figure 5-10).

Connections

Failure commonly occurs at a tie connection because a carelessly constructed connection will be weaker than the tie itself. As described below, ground anchors are integral parts of the tiedown system. The ties should be drawn tight to the anchors with galvanized steel turnbuckles as yoke-type fasteners and tensioning devices. Turnbuckles should end with jaws or forged or welded eyes as in figure 5-11, and not with hooks, which may become unhooked or straightened out by gusting wind.

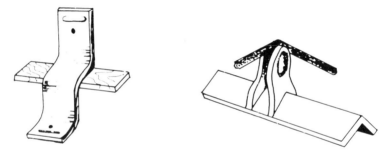

a. Commercial adapter for strap   b. Commercial adapter for cable

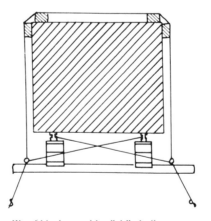

c. Wood blocks used to distribute the pressure of
the tie, should commercial adapter be unavailable

5-10. Mounting adapters protect ties from being cut and the home from being damaged.

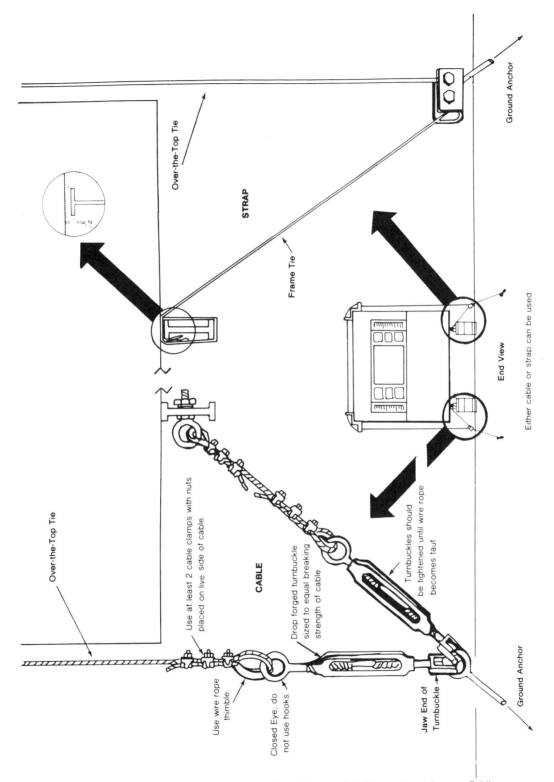

5-11. Suitable connections for cables and straps. (From Defense Civil Preparedness Agency, Publication TR-75)

All cable ends should be secured with at least two U-bolt-type cable clamps or other equally strong fastening devices (see figure 5-11). An insufficient number of clamps or improperly installed clamps are common causes of failure.

Frame ties should be attached to the main frame of the mobile home. Under no circumstances should the frame ties be connected to one of the steel outrigger beams fastened at right angles to the main frame. These cross-beams may not have adequate strength to resist the tie loadings during high winds.

The cable frame tie should be connected to one of the main runner members of the underframing using a ⅝-inch (1.6-cm) drop-forged closed eye bolted through a hole drilled in the center of the web of the member (see figure 5-11). The web should be sufficiently reinforced around the hole to maintain the strength of the member. Alternatively, the cable can be wrapped around the main runner beam and carefully clamped.

Strap ties should be wrapped around the main runner beam, with the buckle on the upper inside, also shown in figure 5-11. Care should be exercised to make sure the minimum bending radius is maintained so as not to lower the breaking strength of the strap.

Periodically, straps and cables should be checked to assure that they are tight. Overtightening can be counterproductive, however, as this reduces the ties' capability of withstanding the abruptly varying loadings of severe, gusting winds.

Anchors

Ties should be attached to anchors on both sides of the mobile home. Several types of anchors can be used. These include soil or screw anchors that are screwed into the ground; metal devices seated at the bottom of a hole; "deadmen," or heavy concrete blocks placed or poured in the ground and covered up; rock or hard ground anchors; and anchors fixed in a concrete slab. Several types of ground anchors are illustrated in figure 5-12.

As mentioned earlier, wooden piles or posts driven deeply into the ground can be used to form a splendid foundation and anchorage if the mobile home is securely attached to them.

Anchors must be matched with the soil conditions. Obviously, soil conditions vary widely, but on a barrier island and many other beach areas, sand will most likely be encountered. Each type of anchor will provide a range of different holding capacities, depending on the soil in which it lies.

Anchors should be installed to withstand 5,700 pounds (25.4 kN) of pull in a vertical or diagonal direction. This criterion can be achieved by many types of anchors in most kinds of soil. It is advisable to have anchor-pull tests performed to assure that the desired capacity of 5,700 pounds is feasible. The local mobile-home dealer should be able to advise you as to who should perform the tests. If you have already decided on a certain mobile-home park, ask the management for results of any tests they may already have performed.

There is a tendency for the top of the anchor rod to move or bend and "slice" through the soil when connected to a frame tie. This is especially true when the soil is saturated with moisture, as is likely in a hurricane. This movement of the rods is disastrous, since it may permit the mobile home to slide off its piers. The piers can punch through the floor and damage the bottom of the home or the heating and

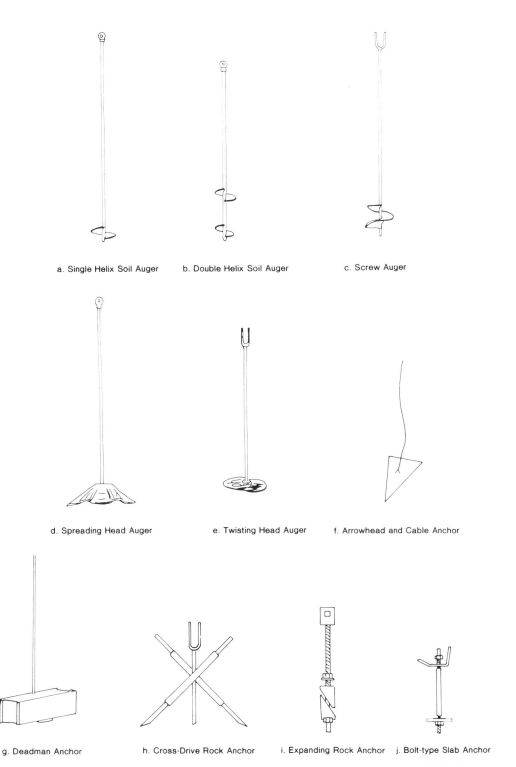

a. Single Helix Soil Auger   b. Double Helix Soil Auger   c. Screw Auger

d. Spreading Head Auger   e. Twisting Head Auger   f. Arrowhead and Cable Anchor

g. Deadman Anchor   h. Cross-Drive Rock Anchor   i. Expanding Rock Anchor   j. Bolt-type Slab Anchor

5-12. Typical ground anchors. (From Pennington and McDonald, *An Engineering Analysis: Mobile Homes in Windstorms*)

ventilating ducts and other utility lines. If the desired capacity load is applied to the anchor rod in an anchor pull test, the horizontal movement should be less than 3 inches (8 cm). To limit possible horizontal displacements, auger-type anchors and other anchors using steel rods should be placed at an angle so that they are more in line with the direction of pull (shown in figure 5-8). This can best be accomplished by installing the anchors prior to placement of the mobile home on the lot.

If a vertical anchor is desired, excavate a cylindrical section 10 to 12 inches (25 to 30 cm) in diameter and 18 to 24 inches (45 to 61 cm) deep around the anchor shaft. Fill the hole with concrete as shown in figure 5-13. Commercial anchors usually come with installation instructions, which should be followed precisely, especially when choosing the proper anchor for a particular soil type.

Align anchors with the edge of the piers. Moreover, place them just below the outer wall of the home so that over-the-top as well as frame ties can be accommodated.

Soil Auger

The most common type of ground anchor is the soil auger. It should have a steel shaft at least 5/8 inches (1.6 cm) in diameter and 4 feet (1.2 m) in length. It can usually be installed by one person twisting the shaft by hand with a lever or using a hand-held motor mounted on the head of the shaft. The mechanical driver can be braced against the side of the home as it screws the auger into the ground. The anchor should be sunk to its full depth; do not compromise.

At the top of the shaft should be a forged or welded eye for attaching one or more cables or shafts. Alternatively, a yoke-type fastening and tensioning device or a threaded connector and tensioning device can be placed at the top.

Typically, a circular plate that is cut, bent, and welded to the shaft in the form of a helix is at the lower end of the shaft (see figure 5-12a). It should have a diameter of at least 6 inches (15 cm).

As mentioned earlier, an anchor must be chosen to match the soil. An anchor cannot be driven in a soil that is too stiff, and the required load capacity cannot be

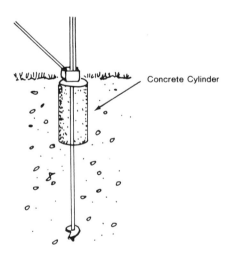

Concrete Cylinder

5-13. Vertical anchor with cylindrical concrete sleeve needed to prevent horizontal movement of the anchor and consequent sliding of the home off its piers.

achieved in a soil that is too soft. A larger plate, perhaps 8 inches (20 cm), is more suitable for soft soils, and a shaft with two plates of the minimum acceptable diameter may be more appropriate for a stiff soil (see figure 5-12b). A screw auger that has a longer plate with a greater pitch and wraps more than once around the shaft, such as that in figure 5-12c, may also be suitable for a stiff soil.

Seated Anchors

Sometimes adjustments in the type of soil auger will not produce an adequate anchor. This is often the case when stratified soils are involved. One solution is to seat the anchor in a predrilled hole. The augers of figures 5-12a, b, and c should not be used for this purpose. Some ground anchors have been specially developed to insert a plate into undisturbed soil at the bottom of a predrilled hole. The anchor in figure 5-12d spreads out at the bottom under a vertical force, whereas the one in figure 5-12e has two circular plates that are inserted in the undisturbed soil by twisting the shaft.

The cost of installing these seated anchors is greater than that of the simple soil augers because of the need to drill a hole. Another type of seated anchor that avoids the predrilled hole is the arrowhead-plate cable system in figure 5-12f. This plate can be driven into the ground and positioned horizontally without digging a hole. The arrowhead should be at least 8 inches (20 cm) along each side.

Deadman Anchors

The deadman anchor (seen in figure 5-12g) also requires the costly digging of a hole. This anchor should be sunk to a depth of at least 5 feet (1.5 m). The steel shaft should be at least 5/8 inches (1.6 cm) in diameter and hooked into the concrete deadman. The exposed surface of the deadman should be at least 2 feet by 6 inches (61 × 15 cm). Hollow concrete blocks are not acceptable, although the concrete deadman can be poured in place. Deadman anchor systems are usually more expensive than seating a fabricated metal anchor. The deadman anchor is, however, easier to design to hold a greater load than a typical metal anchor.

Hard-Ground Anchors

Special devices and techniques are necessary to assure that anchor systems in hard ground or rock have a reliable load capacity. Two frequently employed hard-ground anchors are shown in figures 5-12h and i. In the first case, crisscrossed rods are driven in at opposing angles. The rods tend to be difficult to drive in. The second type of anchor has an expanding element that grips the side of the hole when the bolt is tightened. For proper installation, the hole must be drilled with a bit the correct size.

Concrete Slab

Some mobile-home parks provide concrete slabs on which mobile homes can be placed. As shown in figure 5-14, the ties can be safely connected to anchors, assuming the slab is equipped with attachments and that the concrete slab and anchor system are properly designed.

In designing such a system, the goal is to achieve the same strength as with other anchor systems. Since the weight of the concrete slab must provide all of the resistance to the wind forces, care must be taken to make sure that the weight is sufficient to accept the required pull of 5,700 pounds (25.4 kN) per anchor. The con-

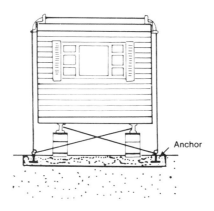

5-14. Placement of a mobile home on a concrete slab. Anchors embedded in the slab can be connected to both frame and over-the-top ties.

crete can be assumed to weigh 144 pounds (2,308 kg/m³) per cubic foot unless it is heavily reinforced, in which case 150 pounds (2,404 kg) can be used. To achieve the desired 5,700-pound pull will require approximately 40 cubic feet (1.13 m³) of concrete. Bolts can be cast in place in the slab with a washer and nut underneath to prevent pulling out (see figure 5-12j). Alternatively, an expanding device whose elements grip the side of a drilled hole can be used (see figure 5-12i).

The important thing, however, is to make sure that the concrete slab is heavy enough so it will not lift up. In most cases you are basically at the mercy of the mobile-home park management concerning the type and quality of slabs. It may pay to know your manager.

Mobile Home Checklist

Use this checklist in conjunction with those in Chapter 2.
1. Escape route: *Is it readily accessible?*
2. Shelter: *Does the park provide a storm-secure shelter for park residents?*
3. Site: *Look at the site in general. Does its location make it especially vulnerable to storms?*
4. Elevation: *The higher, the better. It certainly should be above the 100-year flood elevation (storm surge plus waves).*
5. Vegetation: *The more trees and the larger, the better.*
6. Dunes: *The more dunes and the less dune flattening, the better.*
7. Anchoring systems: *Are they of good quality? Do your neighbors have good-quality ones as well? Are they maintained?*
8. Park: *Does the park have permanent foundations and anchors for tiedowns, as well as utility services?*
9. Insurance: *Do your policies cover rising water as well as wind damage? If not, is federal flood insurance available?*
10. Structural integrity: *Can you get from the manufacturers assurance that the mobile home is structurally sound against moderately high winds?*

Example Designs

Some examples of typical tiedown arrangements are shown in figure 5-15. Note the special accommodations that should be given appendages to the basic single-width mobile home.

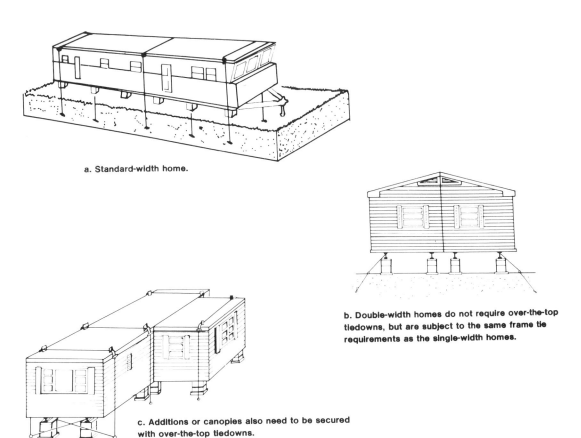

a. Standard-width home.

b. Double-width homes do not require over-the-top tiedowns, but are subject to the same frame tie requirements as the single-width homes.

c. Additions or canopies also need to be secured with over-the-top tiedowns.

d. Clerestory roof requires over-the-top ties at each end of the raised portion in addition to the other ties.

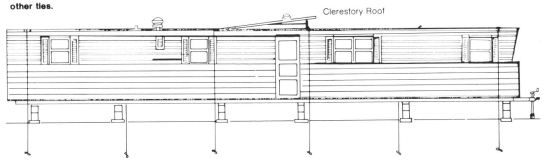

Clerestory Roof

5-15. Typical tiedown configurations. (From Defense Civil Preparedness Agency, Publication TR-75)

Figure 5-16 illustrates the design of a tiedown system for a mobile home 12 feet wide by 55 feet long (3.7 by 16.8 m), to resist 110-mph (177 km/h) winds. Type-2 frame ties are chosen. (If type-1 frame ties were desired, ten frame ties would need to be employed.)

Problem: Select a tiedown system for a 12' × 55' (3.7 × 17 m) mobile home to resist 110 mph (177 km/h) winds. Assume type-2 frame ties will be installed.

Solution: Using figure 5-9 as a guide, 9 type-2 frame ties and 6 over-the-top ties are required; 6 of the frame ties can be connected to the same anchors as the over-the-top ties; therefore, 18 ground anchors (9 on each side) are required, each anchor having a capacity greater than 5,700 pounds (25.4 kN).

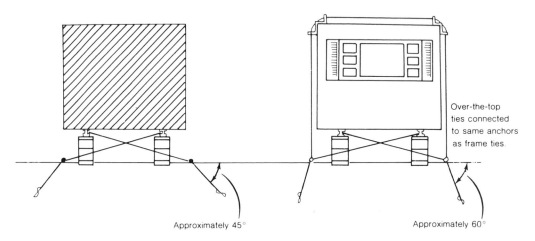

Approximately 45°

a. Three type-2 frame ties like this are required.

Over-the-top ties connected to same anchors as frame ties.

Approximately 60°

b. Six combined over-the-top and type-2 frame ties like this are required.

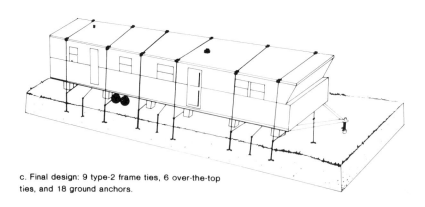

c. Final design: 9 type-2 frame ties, 6 over-the-top ties, and 18 ground anchors.

5-16. Example design of a mobile home tiedown system. (From Defense Civil Preparedness Agency, Publication TR-75)

5-17. This is how a New Jersey barrier island looked after the 1962 Ash Wednesday storm, which beached the small U.S. Navy vessel in the upper part of the photo. Note that trailers fared much worse than houses on this island; most of them ended up in a "log jam" in one corner of the trailer park. (Photo: courtesy, U.S. Army Corps of Engineers)

A Final Word

The photo in figure 5-17 was taken by the Corps of Engineers on an island in New Jersey after the 1962 Ash Wednesday storm. The mobile homes are scattered about like matchsticks. "Normal" housing did not fare well either in this massive storm, although except for the front row or two such houses were largely in one piece and still in place. We recently visited this same mobile-home park to see what effect the sad lessons of 1962 had on the present-day outlook on mobile homes. The answer is apparently none! The mobile homes we observed were not tied down or anchored in any way suitable for even moderate winds.

6

Multistory Buildings

High Rise—High Risk?

John D. MacDonald's novel *Condominium* culminates with a hurricane and storm surge striking a fictional barrier island on the South Florida Gulf Coast. A high-rise condominium is undermined and collapses into the surging sea. His description of the wave attack on the fictional seawalls and buildings could as easily be a page of fact were an eyewitness able to survive in a beachfront observation post during a hurricane:

> The waves had plucked away the riprap, revetments, seawalls and backfill in front of Azure Breeze and the Surf Club. It was thudding against the very heavy reinforced wall that was a part of the seaward foundations of the Surf Club. At Azure Breeze the waves dug into the spaces between the support pilings. They smashed the thick slab between the pilings once they had undermined it. They pulled out pieces of the slab, and once they had reached far enough back under the building, they began the same process on the pilings that was used to bury the heaviest pieces of slab. The water, rushing back out, scoured sand away from the sides of the pilings, making deeper and deeper furrows which extended farther and farther down the beach slope.

MacDonald continues with an imaginative description of the effects of wind and waves as the maximum storm surge strikes, topped by hurricane waves. In the aftermath the island is swept clean of small structures and is truncated, its causeway lost, and four high-rise condominiums are destroyed.

One can find real examples of all the events and impacts described in this fictional novel. Hurricane Allen repeatedly washed over South Padre Island, Texas, in 1980, causing fifty-eight major "breaks," according to newspaper reports. Hurricane Frederick wiped out the causeway to Dauphin Island, Alabama, in 1979. After Hurricane Hazel struck the North Carolina coast in 1954, some cottage owners could find neither the remains of their houses nor any trace of driveway slabs or other structures to mark the former position of their property, and two new inlets cut through Bogue Island.

Hurricane Camille, the strongest of them all, totally removed the three-story Richelieu apartments in Pass Christian, Mississippi. Unfortunately, the now-famous hurricane party involving two dozen participants was going full blast when it happened.

6-1. A high-rise building on the beach at Myrtle Beach, South Carolina. (Photo: Bill Neal)

Only one survived. Another resident of the same apartment building who was smart enough to leave before the storm was never able to collect insurance for the loss of his Volkswagen Beetle. The car disappeared without a trace and the insurance company insisted it must be found before payment for its destruction could be made. The 1962 Ash Wednesday storm destroyed a four-story hotel on a Delaware beach (figure 6-2). The structure was left standing but nothing was left inside.

Large buildings have problems along the Pacific shore, too. The Self-Realization Fellowship Temple in Southern California slipped down a cliff and into the sea after a storm. Tillamook Spit, a large sand bar on the Oregon coast, began to migrate landward after Tillamook inlet was jettied. Paved roads, streetlights, swimming pools, cottages, and a large hotel, all in the community of Bay Ocean, eventually went out to sea.

In 1975 Hurricane Eloise struck the Florida panhandle with 120 mph (190 km/h) winds and 16.2-foot (5-m) waves. In Panama City the now-infamous Peppertree condominium, then under construction, sat just back of the beach. Waves scoured sand from around the foundation and exposed it, bringing to light what future residents neither would have known nor could have checked, until disaster struck: some thirty pilings beneath the structure had no concrete around them whatsoever, and there was no connection with the overlying slab. Of course, the Peppertree now

6-2. Large buildings can be destroyed in storms. The 1962 Ash Wednesday storm severely damaged the seaward-most portion of the Henlopen Hotel, Henlopen, Delaware. (Photo: Delaware State Highway Department, furnished by John C. Kraft)

stands abandoned, unfinished, and without tenants. But suppose nature had not exposed the contractor's shortcomings? How many other Peppertrees exist?

As coastal developments evolve, lateral space becomes exhausted: the price of land skyrockets, and the growth turns upward in the form of multistoried buildings. Included are medium-rise buildings, which have two to three stories, as well as high-rise buildings or tall buildings, variously defined as having four or more stories, being high enough from ground level to require elevators, or a building whose height is greater than twice its width.

Building the first multistoried structure on a barrier island is analogous to building the first seawall or groin. A beach cottage can be moved back in the face of shoreline retreat. But a high-rise cannot be moved back; it can only be destroyed.

Unfortunately, since the cost of lots with a sea view is higher than for those set farther back from the shoreline, it is most profitable from a developer's point of view to use such sites for multistory buildings. The high-rise is an immediate source of increased political pressure to have the shoreline stabilized. As pointed out in Chapter 7, such stabilization will definitely lead to increasing tax bills for the local community and very likely will result in beach degradation as well. The additional highways, pipelines, utility lines, and other trappings of dense development increase the community's susceptibility to natural hazards. Thus, the high-rise building creates a permanent conflict with nature and pressure to follow the course of New Jerseyization.

Condominiums built near the edge of sea cliffs create essentially the same problem as those built next to a sandy beach (figure 6-3). In Encinitas, California, multistory condominiums stand perched a few feet from a cliff edge that has a history of falling in from time to time. Needless to say, a number of stabilization techniques are being carried out (none very successful so far). Cliff stabilization will ultimately be detrimental to the public beach at the base of the cliff.

The inescapable conclusion: The American shoreline would be in much better shape if no multistory buildings were built near the shoreline.

Fortunately, high-rise buildings are generally designed by architects and structural engineers who presumably are well qualified and aware of the unique requirements for building on the shoreline. Tenants of such a building should not, however, assume that the building is therefore invulnerable. Despite the assurances that come with a professionally designed structure, a prospective tenant should always take certain factors into consideration about a multistory building. The chief problems stem from high wind, high water, poor foundations, and the occasional less-than-respectable contractor or building inspector. Perhaps the best advice we can give is to consult a structural engineer before you buy. Consideration should also be given to the future impact of such development on the coastal environment that you came to enjoy. Usually this is the beach. Wouldn't it be nice if your grandchildren could enjoy the same terrain?

Older multistoried apartment complexes and motels should be regarded with

6-3. Condominium construction on the bluff edge at Solana Beach, California. The rapid erosion by rain runoff on the bluff face exemplifies the extreme hazard in this type of bluff edge construction. (Photo: G.G. Kuhn)

particular concern. Following the balanced risk concept, such structures may have been of marginal design to begin with because of previous intended uses, or they may have predated stricter building codes. People living in such structures have been killed when the buildings were ravaged by such storms as Hurricane Camille.

The great demand for condominium space has led to the reworking of buildings such as those noted above, in what are termed condo-conversions. Because some of these buildings were not designed originally as multiple dwellings, there may be inherent safety shortcomings when they are modified to become condominiums.

Wind

Significantly, collapse of a tall building caused solely by the wind has never been documented. Several cases of severe damage have been recorded, and a few have been studied from an engineering point of view. One of the earliest known cases is that of the fifteen-story Meyer-Kiser building, whose outside wall was severely damaged and structural frame permanently deformed during the Miami hurricane of 1926.

Knowledge of tall-building response to high winds also was gained from the damage inflicted by the 1970 Lubbock, Texas, tornado and associated windstorm. The seventeen-story Great Plains Life Building experienced extensive glass breakage and had its structural frame permanently deformed. Tenants had to vacate the building during its extensive repairs. The fourteen-story First National Bank–Pioneer Gas Building sustained window failures that resulted in over $1 million damage to interior furnishings and partitions. Lubbock, Texas, is a long way from the coast, but the 1970 storm provides a lesson that is applicable to hurricane-prone coasts.

Wind pressure is greater near the shore than at inland locations (with the exception of tornadoes), and increases upward from ground level. A high-rise building constructed near the shore will be subjected to both of these effects, and so wind force must be considered in building design. The Uniform Building Code specifies that at most inland locations a structure up to 30 feet (90 m) high (two or three stories) should withstand 15 pounds of wind pressure per square foot (718 N/m² — 718 Newtons per square meter), whereas the same structure on a shore with a hurricane history should withstand 40 pounds per square foot (1.9 kN/m²). This 2½-times increase trend applies for higher buildings: for example, at 100 feet (30 m, ten stories) the design pressure needs to be 30 psf (1.4 kN/m²) inland, as opposed to 75 psf (3.6 kN/m²) on the shore. This figure means that if you are living inland in a two-story house and move to the eleventh floor of a high-rise on the shore, you should expect five times more wind pressure than you are accustomed to. This can be a great—and possibly devastating—surprise.

As mentioned in Chapter 4, high wind pressure can create unpleasant motion of the building, to the point of causing motion sickness in the tenants. Newer buildings are now lighter and more flexible than older buildings were, through the use of less masonry for both exterior and interior walls, higher-strength structural steel, welding, prestressing, larger glass areas, and new design methods. Older skyscrapers with heavy masonry construction were not as susceptible to wind-induced sway because their considerable mass reduced the motion. In the last two decades the density of tall buildings has dropped to about half their earlier value. This reduction in building weight is accompanied by a reduction in stiffness and damping. The increase in flexibility and sway and the decrease in damping are undesirable side effects of modern construction, permitting as it does more windows to pop out, walls to crack, and discomfort to be felt by inhabitants.

More serious, of course, is the destructive power of a high wind, which can break windows, let in torrential storm rains, and harm property and people. Airborne debris is a major threat. Some design engineers and architects seem to regard window failures caused by high winds and missile impacts as nonpreventable. But this does not have to be the case. The adequacy of your exterior windows to support hurricane-level winds may be investigated by consulting figure 6-4. The tabled data assumes that all windows have sufficient four-sided support. A prospective resident can inquire of the builder or owner about the type of glass used. Certainly, such measures as shutters, smaller panes, and stronger glass can decrease wind damage. Inside drapes can lessen injury from shattered glass, and especially that caused by small flying objects. The heavier the drapes, the better suited they are for this purpose.

As a final word on wind, note the precautions about various types of construction discussed in Chapters 3 and 4. For example, a multistory building (or for that matter a single-story building) faced with concrete block should be avoided unless the concrete block is reinforced. Recently we watched a four-story condominium being built with unreinforced concrete block adjacent to a North Carolina beach. Although the frame of the building may survive the next storm, the occupants may find themselves in rooms without outside walls. Concrete block without substantial reinforcement has little more strength than uncemented blocks simply placed against the building's frame.

How do you tell whether a concrete block building has been reinforced? Basically you are once again at the mercy of the developer's/builder's statements. It is sometimes possible to tell if reinforcing is present by breaking into a few of the blocks. Very likely the building owner would frown on this, however.

In modular-constructed buildings the Achilles heel seems to be the connecting systems. Even if individual apartment modules are constructed well, where the whole system is not connected strongly it will blow apart readily. The connecting system must be checked continuously for corrosion, as materials such as connecting straps and bolts that are quite suitable for inland areas may be unsuitable for the corrosive salt air conditions of the beach. Do not be too dignified to crawl around, over, and under the modular building you may live in.

Water

A high-rise building on the beach, just as any other dwelling or structure, can be subjected to high water. The wise designer and owner will make the first floor, and possibly the second floor, sacrificial, on the assumption that sooner or later water will sweep through it. The design will be such that essential services will not be interrupted. Machinery for elevators, stand-by generators, boilers, and air conditioning will be located above the predicted high water. From the tenant's standpoint, having the machinery located on the first floor insures that there is much potential for a complete and prolonged breakdown of essential services. On the other hand, if the machinery is located higher, unpleasant vibration and perhaps noise could occur. From the owner's standpoint, locating machinery higher in the building requires stronger framework and added expense, so he or she may elect to take a chance on flooding to the detriment of the tenant.

6-4. Glass Size Limits for Exterior Walls (Regular Plate and Sheet Glass)

Maximum Area of Glass in Square Feet

Wind Velocity Taken as 140 MPH at 30 Feet Above Grade

Height Above Grade	S.S.	1/8 & D.S.	3/16 & 13/64	7/32	1/4	5/16	3/8	1/2	5/8	3/4
0'–5'	7.3	11.4	22.0	27.2	33.8	47.0	60.1	88.2	119.8	150.6
5'–15'	6.0	9.2	17.6	22.0	27.2	38.2	49.2	72.0	97.7	124.2
15'–25'	5.0	7.6	15.4	17.6	22.8	31.6	41.1	60.0	80.8	101.4
25'–35'	4.3	6.8	13.2	16.2	19.8	27.9	36.0	52.9	71.3	89.6
35'–55'	3.9	6.1	11.8	14.0	17.6	25.0	32.3	47.0	63.9	81.6
55'–75'	3.5	5.4	10.7	12.9	16.1	22.8	28.7	41.9	57.3	72.7
75'–100'	3.2	4.9	9.7	11.8	14.7	20.6	26.4	38.9	52.9	66.9
100'–150'	3.0	4.6	8.8	10.8	13.2	19.1	24.2	35.3	48.5	61.0
150'–250'	2.6	4.0	7.7	9.4	11.8	16.2	21.3	30.9	41.9	52.9
250'–350'	2.3	3.5	6.8	8.3	10.4	14.0	19.1	27.2	37.5	47.0
350'–550'	2.1	3.1	6.1	7.4	9.2	12.9	16.9	24.2	33.1	41.9
550'–750'	1.8	2.8	5.4	6.6	8.3	11.6	15.4	22.0	30.1	38.9
750'–1000'	1.7	2.6	5.0	6.1	7.6	10.7	14.0	19.8	27.2	34.5
over 1000'	1.6	2.5	4.8	5.9	7.3	10.3	13.2	19.1	26.5	33.8

S.S. = Single Strength
D.S. = Double Strength

Source: Dade County, *The South Florida Building Code.*

Note: For glass types other than regular plate or sheet, the size limits for exterior walls should not exceed the areas obtained by multiplying the figure found above by the following factors:

Tempered safety glass ....4.0 factor
Insulating (double glazed) ....1.5 factor
Rough rolled plate ....1.0 factor
Laminated ....0.6 factor
Wired glass ....0.5 factor
Sandblasted or etched ....0.4 factor

In summary, if the building is at such an elevation above sea level that the prospective tenant can assume that the water will flood the first floor, it should be determined if the building is designed to take this into account; otherwise, a new inhabitant should prepare to suffer a long interruption of service and livability.

An interesting sidelight on the unexpected effect of moving water on a high-rise came about in Hurricane Eloise, which struck the Florida Panhandle in 1975. There were cases of cantilevered slabs for overhangs in which the reinforcing was positioned for the usual downward gravity loads. Unfortunately, when waves dashed against the building they splashed *upward*, imposing an upward force against the slabs for which they were not reinforced, and causing them to crack and fail.

Foundations

Proper foundations are critical for buildings built adjacent to a shoreline. This is especially true for high-rise buildings on barrier islands. Major storms or gradual erosion responding to the sea level rise may undercut buildings. Pilings are the first line of defense against such an occurrence. In theory, any large high-rise in a beach area should be capable of withstanding complete removal by waves of several feet of sand from beneath it and still stand firmly on deeply rooted pilings. For safety's sake and to test the soundness of one's investment, the prospective tenant should make some inquiries about the foundation. Specifically, the number of pilings and the depth of their penetration is critical. Just as important as driving the piling deep enough to resist scouring and to support the loads they must carry is the need to fasten them securely to the structure above them that they are supporting. The connections must resist both horizontal and uplift forces from wind and wave during a storm. In some cases, knowing the building code in force and the integrity of the inspectors will be sufficient to discern likely construction quality. The bottom line, however, is usually that the tenant is at the mercy of the integrity of the developer.

Condomania and Its Repercussions

Condominum developments at the shoreline lead to problems that go far beyond the structures themselves. The potential tenant will do well to consider the following coastal impacts before making a significant investment in a multistory structure.

High-rises encourage dense populations that almost always overwhelm the carrying capacity of coastal environments, particularly on barrier islands. Any decision to locate should include some knowledge of the quality and adequacy of water supply, capacity of the waste treatment system, and future development plans for the area. If the water supply and septic systems are likely to be overwhelmed, the prospective tenant should find out who will pay for a sewage plant and piped water, and what this will do to property taxes.

The aesthetics, including the beach, the natural scenic environments such as marsh and maritime forest, and the dunes, may be destroyed as a result of structures interfering with the natural system or through removal for additional development. Even your view can be lost should other high-rise buildings be constructed in line with your structure, and a scenery of sameness is likely to evolve. Water, waste, road, shoreline "protection," and other man-made systems are likely to fail or must be continually enlarged to bear the traffic. The latter will require either an expanding tax base (more people) or higher taxes. Quality of life will change, for better or worse depending on one's priorities, as condominium density and population density of the beach community grow.

The greatest external repercussion of such dense development is the possibility of an evacuation crisis, a major safety consideration. The more people, the more difficulty in getting away.

Safety Considerations

The prospective tenant of a multistory building should assume that such a building is vulnerable to hazards just as a smaller ordinary building would be. Although the size of a high-rise condominium provides a picture of security, resistance, and immobility not shared by the beach cottage, this image should not diminish the assumption of vulnerability. One must not forget that the higher the structure, the stronger the wind forces it must resist.

One cannot personally inspect a high-rise structure the same way one would a beach cottage. You cannot walk beneath it as with a stilt house and inspect the pilings and connections to the building frame, or crawl through the attic to inspect roof trusses, rafters, and joist hangers. Your safety rests with the building's design, the building code, and building code enforcement.

One way to determine safety of construction is to ask the realtor or developer if the building was designed to withstand expected wave and wind forces. Do not stop there, however. Ask to see the plans. Has the structure been designed by a certified engineer? Do the building drawings have his seal and signature? Take the plans to an architect engineer and ask his opinion.

An effective, "storm smart" building code that takes all of the natural forces into account is the first essential requirement for building safety (see Chapter 9 for a discussion of building codes). According to a recent article in *Smithsonian Magazine*, Miami, Florida, has one of the better building codes, but it still does not require proper protection against storm surge. Furthermore, in Miami Beach the code was frequently violated and variances were granted at the drop of a hat. When not enforced, such building codes are close to no building codes.

The safety implied by even the best building codes is only as real as the enforcement of that code. Code enforcement should include frequent inspection during construction to see that the structure is indeed being built to specifications. The Peppertree condominium is an example of where closer inspection by both the supervising contractor and building inspector would have averted the potential loss to future tenants had the problem not been accidentally exposed.

Community regulations should require inspection for high-rise building maintenance throughout each structure's useful life. A casual stroll along the Ocean City, Maryland, beach might serve as an example as to why this is needed. High-rise condominiums and multistory buildings have been built here on the edge of a retreating beach, without the benefit of a protective dune line. Some of the buildings have already sustained frontal damage during storms. Such structures warrant close watching for serious damage, which may occur behind a cosmetic front. The undermining of high-rise structures in Ocean City by storms is quickly repaired by a fleet of city-owned bulldozers. This, however, is not an open-ended process. Evidence, which can be applied universally, has developed on the Ocean City beach that indicates the simple moving of sand from the low-tide to the high-tide line actually increases the rate of beach erosion. Chances are that the city's bulldozers will be increasingly busy in the future. Other structures in the area show badly corroded metal connectors, so even though the initial strength may have been high, time and salt spray have weakened the connections and hence the structures as well.

Corrosion may be a serious unrecognized problem in many old multistory buildings. High-rise buildings whose construction was interrupted, such that plumbing or wiring systems sat exposed, may have suffered corrosion damage. A good example is the unsightly skeleton of an abandoned high-rise on the beach at Monmouth Beach, New Jersey. Undoubtedly someone will come along with refinancing money and construction will commence again.

The bottom line: Since quality of construction of high-rise buildings is difficult to determine, we recommend that you assume the worst. Play it safe and evacuate your beach-front high-rise when storms threaten.

Evacuation

It is essential, if you are considering a high-rise building as your residence, to be sure that the location provides a ready egress or escape route. The number of people to be evacuated, transported, and housed elsewhere in the event of a major storm will be greatly increased if high-rise buildings are added to the more modest dwellings along the shore.

The confusion of escaping a multistory building will be multiplied many times over that of a single dwelling. Not only will cars crash into each other in the parking lot trying to get out, but once they do exit, the escape road will be more crowded with closely spaced cars.

The major safety consideration for any Atlantic and Gulf coastal community is evacuation, the only real and absolutely certain preventive medicine in the face of a hurricane. Both residents and visitors should be aware of evacuation procedures and routes. In the face of an impeding major storm, any type of evacuation other than leaving the area of expected impact is a compromise. Your best alternative *always* is to leave the location of expected impact.

In some areas there may be too many people to attempt late evacuation. More people would be lost while escaping on roads, bridges, and causeways than if they had remained in their homes. Where such critical conditions exist, an untested safety procedure called *vertical evacuation* is being considered (see Chapter 2). Designated hurricane-resistant high-rise structures known to be well built will serve as emergency storm shelters with evacuees using the upper corridors for last-chance protection. New Orleans, a city with much of its area below sea level, is developing a large-scale vertical evacuation plan. In those cases where vertical evacuation is a possibility, the structural integrity of the high-rise building is especially significant. Keep in mind that civil defense experts have grave doubts about such evacuation plans.

Galveston Island, the nation's first barrier island city, was also the first to be wiped out in a hurricane (a loss of 6,000 lives). Today, not far from the east end of the island is the University of Texas Medical School, complete with several high-rise buildings packed to the brim with hospital patients. Are University of Texas officials insane, one is inclined to ask? There is a method in their madness, however. These buildings are specifically designed for vertical evacuation. The lower floors of these "hurricane-proof" buildings are devoted to storage, office space, and other nonpatient uses. Patients are restricted to floors above the expected flood level of a major hurricane. Time will tell whether the buildings are truly hurricane-proof or not.

Vertical evacuation is an example of the corner we have backed into with respect to beach community safety. In some communities and islands where vertical evacuation is proposed by local officials, the carrying capacity of suitable high-rises may have been exceeded. Somewhere in an untried high-rise in the Florida Keys, Sanibel Island, or Miami Beach, or in southern New Jersey or on Cape Cod, this procedure will be put to the strongest test. Real people will be involved, and they may well be just like John MacDonald's fictional characters—the victims.

7

The Retreating Shoreline

Vanishing American Dreams

Preparing for natural catastrophes is nothing new to mankind. Most civilizations record the legend of an immense flood that caused the death of all but a few of the human race. The best known of these accounts are the Gilgamesh myth and the Biblical account of the deluge in the Old Testament. The Gilgamesh account originated in about 2000 B.C., the earliest version being from a Babylonian cuneiform tablet. It told how the gods decided to send a flood to destroy the human race, but the king was saved in a giant ship that he had built in accordance with instructions from a god who took pity on him. There are several versions of this, some of which are strikingly similar to the story of the flood in Genesis 6 through 9, which dates back to about the eighth century B.C. In this account God decided to destroy the human race except for one just man named Noah, who was saved by building a ship or ark, which held Noah, his family, and certain animals until the water subsided.

The story of the flood in Greek mythology dates back to about the fifth century B.C. In the version by Pindar, Zeus, the supreme deity of the ancient Greeks, decided to destroy the human race. But King Deucalion, advised by his father, Prometheus, built an ark in which he and his wife, Pyrrha, took refuge with provisions. The ark floated for nine days, after which it came to rest on a mountaintop, and Deucalion and his family were saved. When the rain ceased, King Deucalion came out of the ark and made a sacrifice. Zeus, thus appeased, offered Deucalion anything he wanted. Deucalion chose to increase the human race. To accomplish this he threw stones over his shoulder which then turned into men. Pyrrha threw stones over her shoulder which became women. Thus, the world was repopulated.

Other legends about floods abound in all parts of the world, including India, China, Australia, and the American continents. Strangely, Africa, including Egypt, seems to be the exception. Most of these stories feature the saving of a few people in a vessel, often with the help of a god, and the subsequent repeopling of the earth. The moral is that we are not dealing with a recent phenomenon but one that mankind has faced since the beginning of time.

Recognizing the Enemy

Nature's threat at the shoreline is like that of a boxer with a one-two punch. Shoreline retreat can be compared to a constant rain of left-hand jabs. The storm is the right-hand knockout punch. Big right-hand punches in recent memory include the East Coast's Ash Wednesday storm of 1962, the 1983 winter storms of Southern California, and Mississippi's Hurricane Camille of 1969.

The jab or the gradual shoreline retreat is less spectacular than the knockout punch, but it is probably a far more deadly enemy of the shoreline dweller. The jab is the sea level rise. The most common mistake made by beach community leaders is to ignore the jab and to concentrate only on the powerful right hand of the storm.

Sea Level Rise: The Left Jab

The rise in sea level discussed in Chapter 1 is probably responsible for many houses ending up in the surf as well as for most of the beach erosion problem in this country. Evidence that the sea level is rising includes the records of tide gauges in various harbors around the world, field observations such as widespread drowning of trees along salt marsh coasts (as shown in figure 1-12), and the strongest evidence of all, the very widespread erosion problem along America's coasts (figure 7-1). Even Texas oil wells are going to sea (figure 7-2).

7-1. One would not have to be an outstanding scientist to know that trees do not grow naturally on open ocean beaches. Hence a scene such as the above on an undeveloped Georgia barrier island indicates that the ocean is reclaiming some of the land, and the water level has risen relative to the land in very recent years. (Photo: Bob Frey)

7-2. An oil well, still producing but going to sea as Padre Island, Texas, migrates. (Photo: Bob Morton)

Recent studies by the National Academy of Science indicate that there is a strong likelihood that in the coming decades the sea level rise will continue and even accelerate. The underlying cause of the rise is melting polar ice, and National Academy scientists point out that melting may well accelerate because the earth's surface is warming up. The warming is caused by increased carbon dioxide in the atmosphere from burning of the so-called fossil fuels, coal and oil. This is referred to as the greenhouse effect. In particular, scientists concerned with sea level rise are watching the west Antarctic ice sheet closely. If this ice sheet, much of which sits over water, begins to deteriorate, the sea level rise will accelerate tremendously.

Estimates vary as to the magnitude of this sea level rise, but the common figure agreed upon is that the present rise is somewhat greater than one foot (30 cm) per century. The rate of rise is highly variable from place to place because in some areas the land is sinking or rising also, and this will cause apparent if not real sea level changes. Dr. Ken Emery of the Woods Hole Oceanographic Institute believes that the sea level rise began a significant acceleration about 10 to 15 years ago.

In December, 1981, Edward Epstein and Robert Etkins, both of the National Atmospheric and Oceanic Administration, reported the startling news that the sea level may have risen four inches during the decade of the 1970s. At the same time indirect evidence indicates that the critical over-water portion of the west Antarctic ice sheet has indeed shrunk during the last hundred years. If these observations are true, and they are very preliminary at this point, we could be having major inundations of land areas within the next three to ten decades. Beyond a shadow of a doubt, if a rise of considerable magnitude occurs, protection of the recreational areas along our coasts will take a distant back seat in national priorities to protection of major coastal cities.

Whatever the cause of the sea level rise, the safest and most intelligent assumption that a coastal dweller can make is that the rise will continue into the foreseeable future and is likely to accelerate. More important and more to the point is the fact that this means American shoreline retreat should continue into the future and should be expected to accelerate. Coastal zone planning based on any other assumption is foolhardy in the extreme.

The direct impact of sea level rise on coastal retreat is much more important along our low-lying coastal plain coasts (the Gulf Coast and the Atlantic Coast south of New York) than on the more steeply sloping bluffed Pacific shoreline. As discussed in Chapter 1, the horizontal retreat of a shoreline is very large, relative to the actual rise in sea level. Along coastal plains the retreat should be of the order of 1,000 times the rise. This means that during the 1970s the shoreline should have retreated (theoretically) 1000 × 4 inches or 330 feet (100 m). This, of course, has not happened except in a few places, probably because the response of a shoreline to a change in rate of sea level rise is not instantaneous and also because a lot of other short-range factors are involved in shoreline erosion.

Storms: The Knockout Punch

Storms are superimposed on the sea level rise. As the sea rises, damage from storms pushes farther inland (figure 7-3). Storms are a natural and expected part of the dynamic equilibrium of the shoreline, but it is difficult for those who live with a view of the sea to consider storms anything but a "tragic act of God" or a natural disaster.

For all practical purposes we can recognize two types of storms: hurricanes and the so-called nontropical storms, that is, storms not derived from the tropics as hurricanes are.

Hurricanes are large, violent disturbances with winds rotating about a low-pressure center. They begin as low-pressure areas over tropical ocean regions. A hurricane evolves from a tropical disturbance through a tropical depression into a tropical storm, which then becomes a genuine hurricane. A *tropical disturbance* is a moving area of thunderstorms. A *tropical depression* is a low-pressure area with winds up to 38 miles per hour (61 kilometers per hour) and rotary circulation. A *tropical storm* has winds from 39 to 73 miles per hour (63 to 117 km/h) and counterclockwise circulation. A *hurricane* is a tropical storm whose winds equal or surpass 74 miles per hour (119 km/h).

Hurricanes are spectacular whirling maelstroms, 60 to 1,000 miles (100 to 1,600 km) in diameter. In the center of the hurricane is the much-heralded eye, a region of calm and cloudlessness, 10 to 20 miles (16 to 32 km) in diameter. As the eye passes, the calm may last anywhere from a few minutes to an hour.

Hurricanes in the northern hemisphere always rotate to the left, or counterclockwise. The reason for this is complex and has to do with the rotation of the earth. These huge tropical storms begin when air currents begin to flow into a low-pressure area from a surrounding higher-pressure zone, much as air rushes into a released vacuum. Anything that follows a trajectory along the surface of the earth, be it an artillery shell, an oceanic current, or a wind current, is deflected to the right in the northern hemisphere. The force causing this deflection is the earth's rotation and it is referred to as the Coriolis force. The net effect is a counterclockwise flowing circulation.

Immediately surrounding the eye are the wall clouds where maximum rainfall and wind velocities occur. By definition, such maximum velocities must be more than 74 miles per hour (119 km/h); in major storms velocities reach 150 miles per hour (240 km/h) and more. Statistics indicate that these storms will most likely occur in the late summer and early fall months of August, September, and October.

Hurricanes gain energy from the evaporation of warm ocean water. They quickly lose energy when they reach land because the sea, their source of energy, no longer is available. Heavy rainfall is a major source of damage from hurricanes. Hurricane Camille, which struck Mississippi in 1969, may have been the greatest coastal hurricane of the century, but it killed more rural Virginians in floods than coastal Mississippians, who bore the main brunt of the high winds and storm surge.

Hurricanes are called typhoons in the Pacific and cyclones in the Indian Ocean. Pacific typhoons are rarely a problem for coastal dwellers of American Pacific shores. Typhoons usually form in tropical waters of the north Pacific, move northwest, and then turn northeast. They strike the shores of Asia rather than America. Japan is particularly vulnerable to damage from these Pacific "hurricanes."

Associated with hurricanes are the smaller, more violent storms called tornadoes. The most violent winds on earth are found in tornadoes—up to 300 miles per hour

7-3. The house at One Pennsylvania Avenue, Rehobeth Beach, Delaware, after the 1962 storm. (Photo: Delaware State Highway Department, furnished by John C. Kraft)

(480 km/h). After the passage of a hurricane, strips of particularly heavy damage are often in evidence. Such high-damage areas are assumed to have been victimized by hurricane-generated tornadoes.

Figure 7-4 lists the costliest hurricanes in the United States, 1900–1982, as measured by the damage in dollars. Those that caused more than $50 million damage are included. Figure 7-5 lists the deadliest hurricanes in the United States, 1900–1982, measured by the number of deaths. Only those that caused twenty-five or more deaths are included.

The hurricanes that strike the eastern United States and Gulf coasts are born in the tropical and subtropical North Atlantic Ocean, the Caribbean Sea, and the Gulf

7-4. Costliest Hurricanes in the United States, 1900–1982 (more than $50 million damage)

HURRICANE	YEAR	SAFFIR–SIMPSON CLASS	DAMAGE (U.S.)
1. FREDERICK (Miss./Ala.)	1979	3	$2,300,000,000
2. AGNES (Northeast U.S.)	1972	1	2,100,000,000
3. CAMILLE (Miss./La.)	1969	5	1,420,700,000
4. BETSY (Fla./La.)	1965	3	1,420,500,000
5. DIANE (Northeast U.S.)	1955	1	831,700,000
6. ELOISE (Northwest Fla.)	1975	3	550,000,000*
7. CAROL (Northeast U.S.)	1954	3	461,000,000
8. CELIA (S. Texas)	1970	3	453,000,000
9. CARLA (Texas)	1961	4	408,000,000
10. DONNA (Fla./Eastern U.S.)	1960	4	387,000,000
11. DAVID (Fla./Eastern U.S.)	1979	1	320,000,000
12. New England	1938	3	306,000,000
13. HAZEL (S.C./N.C.)	1954	4	281,000,000
14. DORA (Northeast Fla.)	1964	2	250,000,000
15. BEULAH (S. Texas)	1967	3	200,000,000
16. AUDREY (La./Tex.)	1957	4	150,000,000
17. CARMEN (Louisiana)	1974	3	150,000,000
18. CLEO (Southeast Fla.)	1964	2	128,500,000
19. HILDA (Louisiana)	1964	3	125,000,000
20. Florida (Miami)	1926	4	112,000,000
21. Southeast Fla./La.–Miss.	1947	4	110,000,000
22. Northeast U.S.	1944	3	100,000,000
23. BELLE (Northeast U.S.)	1976	1	100,000,000
24. IONE (N. Carolina)	1955	3	88,000,000
25. Southwest and Northeast Fla.	1944	3	63,000,000
26. Southeast Florida	1945	3	60,000,000
27. Southeast Florida	1949	3	52,000,000

SOURCE: National Hurricane Center, Miami, FL.

*Includes $60,000,000 in Puerto Rico.

7-5. Deadliest Hurricanes in the United States, 1900-1982

HURRICANE	YEAR	SAFFIR–SIMPSON CLASS	DEATHS
1. Texas (Galveston)	1900	4	6,000
2. Florida (Lake Okeechobee)	1928	4	1,836
3. Florida (Keys/S. Texas)	1919	4	600–900**
4. New England	1938	3*	600
5. Florida (Keys)	1935	5	408
6. AUDREY (Louisiana/Texas)	1957	4	390
7. Northeast U.S.	1944	3*	390***
8. Louisiana (Grand Isle)	1909	4	350
9. Louisiana (New Orleans)	1915	4	275
10. Texas (Galveston)	1915	4	275
11. CAMILLE (Miss./La.)	1969	5	256
12. Florida (Miami)	1926	4	243
13. DIANE (Northeast U.S.)	1955	1	184
14. Florida (Southeast)	1906	2	164
15. Mississippi/Alabama/Pensacola	1906	3	134
16. AGNES (Northeast U.S.)	1972	1	122
17. HAZEL (South Carolina/N.C.)	1954	4*	95
18. BETSY (Fla./La.)	1965	3	75
19. CAROL (Northeast U.S.)	1954	3*	60
20. Southeast Florida/La.–Miss.	1947	4	51
21. DONNA (Fla./Eastern U.S.)	1960	4	50
22. Georgia/Carolinas	1940	2	50
23. CARLA (Texas)	1961	4	46
24. Texas (Velasco)	1909	3	41
25. Texas (Freeport)	1932	4	40
26. South Texas	1933	3	40
27. HILDA (Louisiana)	1964	3	38
28. Louisiana (Southwest)	1918	3	34
29. Florida (Southwest)	1910	3	30
30. CONNIE (North Carolina)	1955	3	25
31. Louisiana (Central)	1926	3	25

*Moved more than 30 miles per hour.
**Over 500 of these lost on ships at sea.
***Some 344 of these lost on ships at sea.

ADDENDUM

Louisiana	1893		2,000
South Carolina/Georgia	1893		1,000–2,000
Georgia/South Carolina	1881		700

SOURCE: National Hurricane Center, Miami, FL.

of Mexico. On the average, six occur off our coasts each year. Most, but not all, occur in August, September, and October. To play it safe, the hurricane season is considered to be the six-month period from June 1 to December 1.

A truly remarkable calm has settled upon our Atlantic Coast. It has been over twenty years since a major storm has struck. Meanwhile, the Gulf Coast seems to be making up for the Atlantic calm period. Hurricane Camille (1969) and Hurricane Frederick (1979) are two major examples of the recent problems besetting Gulf Coast residents.

The reasons for the cyclical changes of hurricane paths from our Atlantic Coast to the Gulf and back again are not well known. It is believed that slight changes in oceanic and atmospheric circulation patterns in low latitudes of the North Atlantic Ocean are responsible for the changing paths of hurricanes. In the late 1970s, oceanographers began predicting that the hurricanes should once again begin striking in the Atlantic Coast. The twenty-year gap in major hurricanes along our Atlantic shores is unprecedented in historical times. The storms will return.

Hurricanes cause damage in four ways: high winds, sudden changes in barometric pressure, storm surges, and river flooding. Taking these characteristics into account in building design was discussed in Chapter 3. We have more to say about all of these forces in the next chapter. Wind velocity, storm surge, and pressure changes are three factors that form the basis for classification of hurricanes. In describing a hurricane or storm, today's television narrators use such adjectives as violent, intense, severe, and terrific, with waves that are "mountain high." This is all very imprecise, as such words are very much subject to interpretation and vary with the individual. Furthermore, it has been noted that eyewitnesses tend to believe that the last storm was always the worst ever. In response to this, a numerical scale has been devised, called the Saffir–Simpson Scale (figure 7-6) that takes much of the vagueness out of storm descriptions and is gaining in use. It is hoped that the scale will find as wide an acceptance as the Richter earthquake scale.

A scale for tornadoes developed by T. T. Fugita (figure 7-7), naturally called the Fugita Scale, is useful but has not yet received the attention accorded the Saffir–Simpson hurricane scale.

In any scale it is difficult to take into account all of the variables. For instance, in a tornado the wind velocity is important, but so is the track (path, length, and width). The longest track recorded in 1971 was 198 miles (320 km) long and 0.6 miles (1 km) wide, while the smallest one was only 10 yards (9 m) long and one yard (1 m) wide.

Winter storms, rather than hurricanes, are the bane of the existence of Pacific Coast beach dwellers, and the damage wreaked is principally through beach and cliff erosion (figure 7-8). Unlike the case with the Gulf and Atlantic coasts, storm damage by flooding and direct wind effects is relatively minor. There are two reasons for this: Pacific shores are rarely struck by hurricanes (typhoons), and relatively few towns or communities are built in such low-elevation and extremely vulnerable locations as Galveston. Texas; Miami Beach, Florida; Ocean City, Maryland; or Atlantic City, New Jersey. Many of the winter storms that do serious damage to Pacific beach dwellings are not accompanied by significant winds at all. The waves that strike the beaches are sometimes generated hundreds and even thousands of miles offshore. Big waves that strike the beaches of San Diego are sometimes generated in the Gulf of Alaska.

7-6. Saffir-Simpson Hurricane Scale

Class	Pressure (millibars)	Pressure (inches)	Velocity (mph)	Storm Surge (feet)	Classification
1	980	28.94	74–95	4–5	minimal
2	965–979	28.50–28.91	96–110	6–8	moderate
3	945–964	27.91–28.47	111-130	9–12	extensive
4	920–944	27.17–27.87	131–155	13–18	extreme
5	less than 920	less than 27.17	155	greater than 18	catastrophic

SOURCE: National Oceanic and Atmospheric Administration, NWS Southern Regional Technical Report 2.

7-7. Fugita Tornado Scale

Classification	Maximum Pressure Drop (psf)	Winds Speeds (mph)	
F0	1–7	40–72	
F1	7–27	72–112	moderate
F2	27–65	113–157	
F3	65–125	158–206	
F4	125–214	207–260	severe
F5	214–336	261–318	

SOURCE: T. T. Fujita, "Proposed Characterization of Tornadoes and Hurricanes by Area and Intensity."

Nontropical storms are important on the Atlantic and Gulf coasts too. Consider the granddaddy of them all, the 1962 Ash Wednesday storm. Few hurricanes did as much property damage as this storm, and no hurricane spread damage over such a wide area. The Ash Wednesday storm caused property damage from New England to Georgia.

The Ash Wednesday storm was unusual in many ways. It occurred during spring tides (the highest tides of the month corresponding to the full moon), the worst possible time for a storm to strike. The level of the tide adds to the effective height of the storm surge and increases the damage potential. Also, the Ash Wednesday storm stayed in one place, pounding the shoreline for almost three straight days before moving out to sea, whereas most storms pass on within a few hours. A similar unusual storm in the Netherlands, striking at spring tide in 1953 and hanging around for three days, broke dikes and killed hundreds of Dutchmen living on land below sea level.

7-8. South Salina Beach, California, bluff top development. The bluff top was graded to enhance the view. Prior to the grading, drainage was directed away from the bluff face. Now rainwater drains down the bluff and has hastened erosion. (Photo: G. G. Kuhn)

The value of natural dune defense systems was dramatically illustrated by the Ash Wednesday storm. Several New Jersey beach communities were not damaged by the storm until day three. The reason: it took the storm two days to batter its way past the natural dune-line between the beach and the ocean. In a more ordinary storm of shorter duration, the dunes would have done their job well and the communities would have remained unscathed.

Confronting the Enemy: At What Price Victory?

When a coastal community is faced with the threat of an eroding shoreline, it has two choices: move back or confront the sea. This is true whether the erosion is caused by a big storm or more gradual processes such as sea level rise and loss of sand supply. The choice is not an easy one, but in the "old days," the second choice would not have been available. This is why if one wants to visit the old beach communities of Cove Point, Washington; Bay Ocean, Oregon; Edingsville Beach, South Carolina; and Hog Island, Virginia, one must put on scuba gear. These communities fell in as shoreline retreat caught up with them, and they are now offshore on the continental shelf.

To confront the sea at the shoreline inevitably means stabilization; that is, holding the sea back against erosion and the rising sea level. But stabilizing an open ocean shoreline will almost always result, ultimately, in the narrowing and destruction of the beach (figure 7-9). The beach, of course, is the raison d'etre for most shoreline communities to begin with. On the other hand, to make the choice of nonstabilization

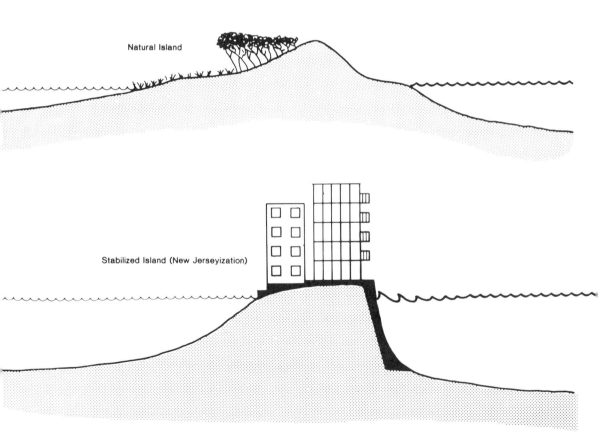

Natural Island

Stabilized Island (New Jerseyization)

7-9. The long-range effect of stabilization, or what we call the process of New Jerseyization.

means that houses, highways, and utility lines will fall into the sea. Stabilization has been highly successful in prolonging the life of buildings adjacent to all kinds of shorelines.

Stabilization costs large amounts of money, which usually comes from taxpayers; partly local, but mostly federal money is involved. Hence, from the standpoint of the overall national interest, it can be strongly argued that the halting of shoreline erosion is bad. And because stabilization costs much in tax money and ultimately results in degradation of the public's beach (figure 7-10), the argument can even be made that private beachfront property owners have no right to protect their own homes. As an example, homeowners on private Sea Island, Georgia, erected a privately funded seawall over much of the length of the island in response to Hurricane David in 1979. Average cost of the wall was $350 per foot and each owner purchased the section in front of his or her house. The seawall is calculated to save the houses for a while, but the wall will also destroy the beach. Already there is no beach at high tide on Sea Island, and someday there will be only a narrow beach at low tide, covered with boulders torn from the seawall. Should these people have the right to destroy their beach in order to save their houses?

Most American beach community dwellers are protected (by taxpayers) from the rising sea level in two ways. If their houses are threatened, they have the option, depending upon their political clout, of calling in the Corps of Engineers to halt shoreline retreat. If the corps fails to respond or fails to halt the forces of the sea, the shoreline citizen could be reimbursed for his or her fallen house by federal flood insurance if they are covered and if the damage is caused by flooding, not erosion. From the standpoint of the coastal dweller, this double safety net is a major plus in shoreline living. From the standpoint of the citizen of Topeka, Kansas, the shoreline dweller is given a degree of protection with tax money unavailable to other American citizens. Additional post-storm aid adds even more to the federal cost.

7-10. Miami "Beach," 1972, before the 15-mile $65-million replenishment project was emplaced. (Photo: Orrin Pilkey, Jr)

Sometimes shoreline stabilization is carried out to protect harbors important to the commerce of major ports. In such cases, damage to adjacent beaches may be considered acceptable. Much local erosion, for example, has been caused by off-shore harbor breakwater construction in the California communities of Redondo Beach and Santa Barbara, and the jetties protecting the harbor entrance to Charleston, South Carolina, have accelerated the erosion of nearby Morris and Folly islands. A seawall has caused most of the beach to disappear in front of Galveston, Texas. But the Galveston wall was placed there after 6,000 people died in the 1900 hurricane, long before we began to address the problem of long-range effects of shoreline stabilization.

The questions that need to be asked by a community before stabilization of a shoreline are:

1. What damage will the proposed structures cause in the long run?
2. Are there less costly alternative approaches (figure 7-11)?
3. Is the cost of the structure worth it?
4. How long will the structure be effective if the sea level is rising?

These questions are frequently asked, but seldom answered in more than a fifteen-year context. If you are thirty years old, think of what the planned development will leave for your grandchildren.

7-11. The community of South Seaside. New Jersey, chose to move back as the shoreline eroded. Adjacent communities confronted the sea. South Seaside now has a very wide beach; the adjacent communities have little beach at all, though they did save their houses with seawalls. (Photo: Orrin Pilkey, Jr.)

Harbor Design, or How to Tell Breakwaters from Elephants

The following vignette was written anonymously at Scripps Institution of Oceanography in the 1950s. There are two morals to this story. One concerns elephant warfare and is probably not relevant to modern times. The second concerns the breakwater form of stabilization and is highly pertinent to modern times.

In history one reads of man's interference with nature and of the disastrous results that follow. One such interference has been the building of harbors and breakwaters, of one form or another, along the coastlines of the world. These structures interfere with the wave action and with the drifting of beach sands. So nature crushes the structure or fills the harbor with sand and seeks a new equilibrium. Man, struggling as he may, never quite succeeds with his meddling.

In early history, men without machines built crude structures easily damaged by the forces of the sea. Today, through the use of steel, concrete, and cranes that can handle forty-ton stones, the structures destroyed by the sea are well built. Modern design has also improved harbors; the efficiency at which they trap sand has been increased many fold.

Our own Southern California coast provides fine examples of modern design and construction, the best of which is a small sport and fishing boat harbor at Redondo Beach.[1] A rubble breakwater was constructed 1,000 feet long perpendicular to the beach which was attached to an 800-foot leg parallel with the beach to the south. Sand was trapped on the north side of the breakwater and the south shore eroded. The erosion was one of the finest ever. All the sand disappeared, the boardwalk with its hot-dog stands and shooting houses disappeared. No telling how great the erosion might have been if the property owners hadn't insisted on a retaining wall to protect their land. The sand then flowed around the end of the breakwater and was deposited in the boat anchorage. Naturally, the sand wouldn't deposit on the denuded southerly beach until the boat anchorage was filled. Another similar harbor was soon built at Santa Barbara.[2] The property damage along the southern beach was much less than at Redondo Beach because there wasn't as much property to be damaged.

Sand again was deposited on the northerly side of the harbor and this made a fine beach. Since sand has deposited on the northerly side at Crescent City, Hueneme, El Segundo, Santa Barbara, Santa Monica, Redondo Beach, San Pedro, Seal Beach, Newport, Oceanside, and San Diego, many people have concluded that sand drifts from the north to the south along this coast. The sand also drifted around the end of the dog-legged breakwater, was deposited in the harbor,[3] and proved a vantage point from which the boats could be viewed from the other side. This deposit became so extensive

---

1. By the time of Hamilcar (275 B.C.) history taught us never to use elephants in war. Hamilcar, however, didn't believe this and stuck to his elephants to the end. The elephants were trained to rush forward and trample the Romans, but on many occasions would rush backward and trample Hamilcar's Carthaginians. He always felt that his elephants would have won the first war if it hadn't developed into a naval affair.

2. Hamilcar was drowned in 228 B.C. while crossing a stream with a herd of elephants, but not before his son, Hannibal, was well versed in the strategy of elephant warfare. Hannibal crossed the Alps in 218 B.C. with a large army and thirty-seven elephants to start the Second Punic War, but everything went badly until all thirty-seven had died. Hannibal then defeated the Romans in the Battle of Trasimene. Again at Cannae, fresh out of elephants, another great victory was won. He lost a chance of complete victory, however, through his inactivity for the next few years. He was waiting for more elephants.

3. The final showdown of the Second Punic War, fought near Carthage in 203 B.C., ended when Hannibal's eighty front-line elephants turned and trampled his army. Hannibal tried to stir up another war with a scheme involving elephants, but no one seemed interested.

the entire harbor was threatened. The late Will Rogers, when asked what he thought of the problem, remarked, "I don't believe the harbor will be of much value unless we can devise a way of irrigating it." Besides protecting the boats from southwest seas (most bad weather is from the southeast) the harbor also provides an excellent opportunity to study the sand movement along the coast. The amount of sand moving along the coast can be determined by measuring sand deposited in the harbor. Santa Barbara harbor might better be called the prototype sand-trap.

With the information gained at Santa Barbara and Redondo Beach, a harbor was built at Santa Monica. The harbor comprised only a 1,000-foot breakwater parallel to the beach, behind which small boats could seek shelter in heavy seas. Eliminating the section perpendicular to the beach was intended to allow the sand drifting along the coast to continue without interruption. Again the sand was deposited behind the breakwater in the anchorage area.[4] Boats were found high on the beach following each storm after being torn from their anchors by waves in the harbor. This can all be explained, of course, by considering the [wave] refraction pattern around the breakwater.[5]

Since World War II the problem of harbor design has been studied with more vigor than ever. No telling what may be accomplished in the years to come. The trend is for bigger and better breakwaters.[6]

The Hows, Whys, and Wherefores of Preventing Shoreline Erosion _____

Most of America's open ocean shorelines are retreating. When a house is built near a retreating shoreline, retreat becomes erosion. It is possible to halt shoreline erosion on any oceanic shoreline, given enough money and a willingness to accept severe environmental damage. The job is much easier on quieter lagoon shores, however, in comparison to open ocean conditions.

Shoreline stabilization techniques for preventing erosion fall into three categories: replacing sand, trapping sand, and blocking wave energy. The first solution is considered to be a nonstructural approach; the second two are structural, in that they involve construction of some fixed object. The nonstructural approach is always preferrable whenever feasible or available.

Replacing Sand

Replacing sand, or beach replenishment, is the gentlest approach to shoreline stabilization. At one end of the spectrum, it may consist of a homeowner hiring a dump truck or two to unload sand in front of a house, or a bulldozer pushing sand from the lower beach to the upper beach (figure 7-12). At the other end of the spectrum is the Miami Beach replenishment project: $64 million for fifteen miles of new beach. Between these two extremes is the city of Virginia Beach, Virginia, which each summer hauls thousands of dump-truck loads of sand to her beaches.

In general, it is reasonable to assume a minimum cost of replenishment of an open ocean beach of $1 million per mile (1.6 km). Cost is often a function of the location

---

4. Hannibal's greatness, of what there may have been, was found in his strategy of drawing his enemy into a trap and killing them. He might also have been known for his elephant tactics but then elephants didn't understand.

5. When Hannibal crossed the Alps many of his men died of hunger and cold, but he encouraged those that survived by saying, "Cheer up, the elephants are all right."

6. To the end Hannibal knew everything would still come out right if he just had a few thousand more you-know-whats.

7-12. Bulldozing sand in Topsoil Beach, North Carolina, after a 1977 storm that threatend to undermine the hotel. In 1981 the hotel once again was almost undermined by storm waves, and the beach was once again bulldozed. In 1982 this precariously perched hotel was sold off as condominium units. (Photo: Duncan Heron)

of the supply of sand that is to be pumped or trucked to the beach. In past years, sand for replenishment of barrier island beaches (or Pacific barrier spit beaches crossing the mouths of lagoons) usually came from lagoons or sounds behind the beaches. This is generally the cheapest way to go. A dredge in the lagoon digs sand from the lagoon floor and then pipes it to the beach. Because this method causes environmental damage through muddying of waters and destruction of important biological habitats, however, it is not likely to be a future option for many communities.

A much better and larger source of sand is usually available offshore from beaches. Offshore dredging is, however, more costly than lagoon dredging because heavier equipment is required. Also, care must be taken to choose the offshore site of the dredging. Very recent research has indicated that the wrong choice may actually result in an increased rate of erosion for the new beach. The hole dug out on the shoreface to get beach sand may cause the waves to bend on their way ashore and to concentrate more waves on particular stretches of shoreline, hence increasing the rate of erosion.

Replenished beaches generally erode much faster than natural beaches. Although surprisingly few studies of this effect have been carried out, we believe a good *minimum* figure for an artificial beach is an erosion rate 10 times that of the natural system.

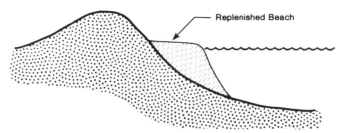

The Immediate Problem: Oversteepened Beach

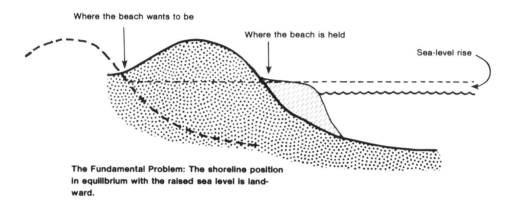

The Fundamental Problem: The shoreline position in equilibrium with the raised sea level is landward.

7-13. The two reasons why a replenished beach disappears much faster than its natural predecessors.

There is good reason for this increased rate of erosion (figure 7-13). Replenished sand is pumped up only onto the upper beach; the part we swim on. The cost of replenishing the entire beach system to a depth of 30 feet (10 m) is absolutely prohibitive. In effect, then, a replenished beach is a pile of sand perched atop a sloping surface.

The grain size of the replenishing sand also is an important factor to consider. Fine sand, typical of lagoon sources, makes gently sloping beaches suitable for small children. Coarse-sand beaches are steeper and more likely to be appreciated by surfers. Coarse sand is typical of continental shelf sources. Beaches in Corpus Christi, Texas; Wrightsville Beach, North Carolina; and Oceanside, California, were replenished by sand coarser than the original sand, creating steep beaches and a change in the average age and type of people attracted to these communities.

Replenishment, like other forms of beach stabilization, does not respond to sea level rise. It holds the island or beach in place where it does not want to be rather than allowing it to retreat as it wants to do. The practical ramifications of this increasing disequilibrium with time is that (in theory) each time a beach is replenished, it is likely to erode away faster than the previously replenished beach. Typically, beaches must be replenished every three to ten years after a major replenishment project. Of course, if a major storm strikes soon after renourishment, the beach would need repair in a shorter time.

Replenished beaches have an important effect on the community. Confidence in the future and real estate prices both rise after replenishment. Light development tends to be replaced by heavier development; beach cottages give way to condominiums. One beach cottage owner told us that his property value jumped by $20,000 in six months following beach replenishment at Wrightsville Beach, North Carolina.

When the replenished beach disappears once again, a denser, more politically powerful community is standing next to the surf zone. Lots of clout is available to bring in the Corps of Engineers. Very likely, replenishment will occur. The phenomenon of New Jerseyization, however, tells us that over the years, sand supplies tend to diminish, costs accelerate, and seawalls are likely to replace replenished beaches. Replenishment should be viewed as a stopgap effort before structural measures will have to be taken to protect houses. It is a political and economic truth that the relatively gentle procedure of beach replenishment usually leads to the less gentle solutions.

There is a fundamantal reason for beach replenishment other than furnishing a community with a beach. A wide beach and especially a row or two of dunes is excellent protection from hurricane damage. Basically, a beach must be chewed away by the storm waves before the waves can start chewing away at the buildings. Of course, in major hurricanes with 10- to 20-foot (3- to 6-m) storm surges, nothing can help the first row of beach structures.

Frequently storm protection is used as a justification by a community for beach replenishment. The political truth is usually that the pressure to replenish the beach is not the threat of storm but the fact that the house of the mayor, the local senator, or other prominent persons is about to fall into the sea.

Sand Trapping

The beach is like a river of sand. Slowly but surely, millions of cubic yards of sand are moving from one place to another. The volume, the direction of transport, and the speed of transport of sand is quite variable from beach to beach. On many beaches the direction of sand movement reverses from one season to another.

The sand moves because the waves coming in at an angle form longshore currents that push the sand along in the surf zone. Anything that stops the waves also stops the current, which stops the sand flow.

In the discussion above, comparing breakwaters and elephants, the sand-trapping effect of breakwaters was pointed out. Usually, offshore breakwaters, as in the California examples, are built to furnish shelter for boats. They may, however, also be used specifically to build up sand on a beach. A special type of breakwater that received considerable attention was constructed in front of the Cape Hatteras lighthouse in North Carolina. Rows of plastic seaweed were placed in the surf zone in 1982, and the beach immediately grew seaward. Anything that blocks waves may cause at least temporary deposition on beaches—even sunken ships have been considered for use as breakwaters.

The more common way to trap beach sand is with groins. Groins are walls of steel, wood, concrete, or plastic sandbags built out from the beach and perpendicular to it. These obstructions trap the sand flowing along a beach and result in the building out of the beach (figure 7-14). The other side of the coin is that they cause erosion in a downstream direction. One beach's salvation can be another beach's destruction.

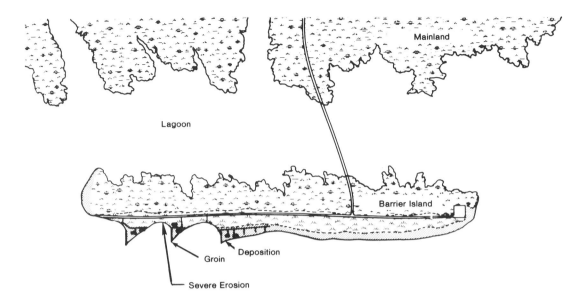

Mainland

Lagoon

Barrier Island

Deposition

Groin

Severe Erosion

7-14. The "downstream" erosive effect of groins.

The deleterious effects of groins on beaches has been documented on all of our shoreline types. No coastal state is without numerous examples of groin- or jetty-related beach erosion problems. Jetties, by the way, are similar to groins in principle, except they are usually much longer and they are used to prevent sand from flowing into shipping or boating channels.

Environmental problems aside, groins can be tricky. Many times groins have been placed on beaches where sand is not moving laterally. Instead the loss of sand from the beach was occurring in an offshore direction. In such cases, groins sit there doing nothing useful. Careful study of a beach system is required before groin emplacement.

Sometimes groins are used simultaneously with beach replenishment. The idea is to hold the beach sand in place a bit longer than would be possible without such structures.

There are many types of groins. *Short groins* do not extend beyond the surf zone and thus allow some sand to migrate around the structure. *Long groins* extend through the normal surf zone and trap sand efficiently and totally. Therefore, long groins are more likely to cause problems downstream. *High groins* are built above the zone of breaking waves, even for minor storms. *Low groins* allow high tide waves to slop over the top, and thus some sand to make it through. The *permeable groin* is designed to allow some wave energy and sand to pass right through the structure.

Groins generally can be assumed to cost somewhere between $200 and $500 per foot of shoreline that is to be protected. Costs may be much lower than this on quiet lagoon shores, however.

Besides interrupting the sand flow, groins also may cause problems to pedestrian and vehicular traffic. Small plastic sandbag groins on Atlantic and Gulf beaches seem to have a high rate of sabotage, possibly by kids with pen knives or beach buggy drivers with hunting knives. But what appears to be sabotage may also be the result of tree trunks and limbs or other flotsam ripping the bags during storms.

Groins may serve still another function. Before the massive beach replenishment job in Miami Beach was carried out, plastic sandbag groins offered virtually the only beach surface on which to sun oneself.

Blocking Wave Energy

The absolute last resort for shoreline stabilization should be to build a structure parallel to the beach to absorb the impact of waves. Such structures fall into the *sea-wall* family. They consist of various types of walls designed to take the daily impact of waves and are built on the lower beach. *Bulkheads* by one definition are vertical walls built on the upper beach, perhaps fronting or replacing the first dune row. They are designed to be struck only by storm waves. A second definition of bulkheads is that they are simply weak seawalls; we will not use this definition. *Revetments* are usually boulders armoring the sloped first dune bluff but can be made of other materials (figures 7-15, 7-16, 7-17, and 7-18). Bulkheads and revetments are supposed to see action only during a storm.

Bulkheads and revetments cost from $100 to $300 and higher per foot of shoreline. Seawalls cost $300 to $800 and higher per foot of shoreline. It takes a wealthy community indeed to construct a seawall on an open ocean beach without federal aid. Such a community is the previously mentioned Sea Island, Georgia, as is, not surprisingly, Palm Beach, Florida.

7-15. Casey Key, Florida. Four methods of shoreline erosion control can be seen here, including the small groins extending offshore. All four methods failed. (Photo: Dinesh Sharma)

7-16. Yankee ingenuity at work, West Coast style. This La Jolla, California, bluff was temporarily saved by buying used cars and driving them to the beach during a storm. (Photo: G. G. Kuhn)

7-17. A unique type of revetment on Vero Beach, Florida. (Photo: Dinesh Sharma)

7-18. A lagoon or backside beach on Bogue Bank, North Carolina, a barrier island. Everything including the kitchen sink has been thrown in to halt (unsuccessfully) shoreline erosion. (Photo: Al Hine)

Seawalls destroy or narrow the beach by reflection of wave energy from the steep front face (figure 7-19). Destruction or drastic narrowing of a beach may take anywhere from one to twenty years or more. But a yet more fundamental and insidious thing other than beach narrowing also happens in front of seawalls. The shoreface, down to a depth of about 30 feet (10 m) gets steeper and steeper. On a normal beach, big waves coming ashore may be tripped by offshore bars and slowed down

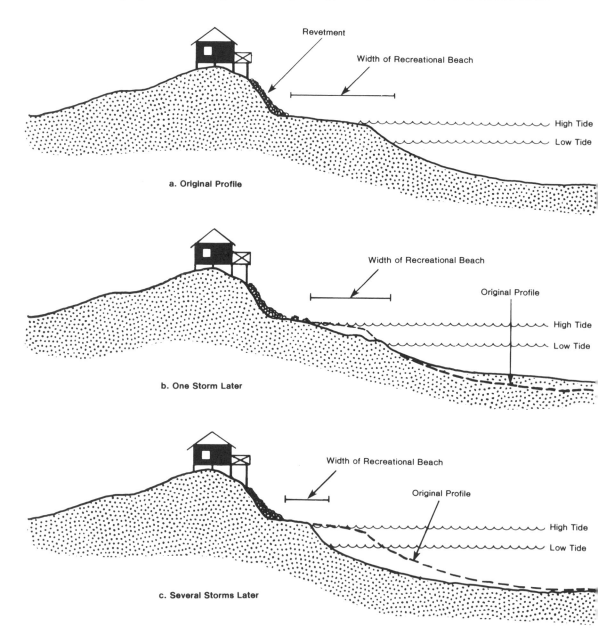

7-19. The response of a stabilized beach to a storm. Each storm may cause permanent loss of a portion of the recreational beach and a steepening of the offshore portions of the beach. Compare this with figure 1-2, which illustrates the response of the natural beach to a storm.

through friction with the bottom. On a seawall-steepened shoreface, all waves, big and small, strike the seawall head on. Storm damage is likely to be great. Seawalls are replaced by bigger and better walls. We have personally observed that a 25-mile-per-hour (40-km/h) onshore wind produces waves that can top over the giant wall of Seabright, New Jersey (figure 7-20).

An excellent illustration of this problem is the seawall in Galveston, Texas, built in response to the 1900 hurricane that killed 6,000 people. Over the years the beach in front of the wall narrowed, and as the shoreface steepened the base of the seawall was threatened with undermining. Along the southern portion of the wall, the Corps of Engineers emplaced a row of boulders, called rip-rap, to stop the undermining. The shoreface continued to steepen and soon a second row of rip-rap was emplaced to protect the first row of rip-rap. Plans are now afoot for the third row of rip-rap to protect the second row of rip-rap, which protects the first row of rip-rap which protects the seawall footings. Someday there may well be a fourth row of rip-rap which will . . .

Once the shoreface is steepened, other alternatives such as beach replenishment are economically out of the question. Sand pumped up on a steepened beach will rapidly disappear offshore. The seawalled beach is the end of the line.

Revetments are often held out as a less environmentally damaging alternative to seawalls. The reason is that waves striking revetments lose much of their water into the interstices between boulders and thus less water is available to be reflected back onto the beach. This may be true, but revetments cause other problems. For one thing, the presence of a revetment (or a seawall or bulkhead) prevents the beach system from responding properly to a storm. The revetment seals off the beach's storm supply of sand. No longer can the walled-in beach obtain sand from the first dune row and use it to flatten the beach profile. The effect of a storm on a revetted beach is to steepen the shoreface, which is cut off from its sources of sand. Each storm in theory should produce higher waves than the last one as the shore-face steepens.

The only good thing that can be said about seawalls is that they are quite successful in saving buildings. But as our shores becomed walled in and our islands and beaches become walled fortresses, what do we do for beaches?

Facts Worth Pondering

It is apparent that the decision whether or not to halt coastal erosion on a shoreline stretch facing the open ocean is a complex one. Sooner or later every coastal dweller will be involved in such decisions. Decision makers and citizens alike should keep in mind the following facts:

There is no erosion problem until someone builds next to the beach. Many stretches of American shoreline are moving back at a rapid rate, but no one notices until the trappings of man are involved.

The beach is in no danger from nature. No matter how the shoreline is moving, some sort of beach will always be present. The beach may be in a different location from year to year, but there will always *be* a beach, unless the hand of man intervenes.

Stabilization of retreating shorelines is carried out to save buildings, not beaches. Political rhetoric to the contrary, it is the endangered structures owned by influential people that always generate the clout for stabilization.

7-20. Effect of a seawall-topping wave produced by a 25-mph (40-km/h) wind, Seabright, New Jersey. Such large waves from such small winds reflect shoreface steepening. (Photo: Bill Neal)

*Stabilization is successful in **temporarily** saving buildings.* No amount of stabilization will protect structures in the Big Storm.

Stabilization in the long run degrades or drastically narrows beaches. Beaches are the reason a beach community was built.

When viewed in the long run, stabilization of shorelines is extremely costly. Government estimates concerning long-range costs almost always come in far below the real cost. Often stabilization costs are greater than the value of the structures to be saved.

The rates of shoreline retreat can be expected to accelerate in coming decades. The perceived need for stabilization can be expected to accelerate. The cost to coastal dwellers will accelerate in proportion. The narrowing and loss of American beaches will also accelerate in proportion.

8

The Storm

What to Expect, How to Prepare

All kinds of storms strike American beaches. The big nontropical storms along the East Coast are generally the northeasters, storms with winds blowing *from* the northeast. The Gulf Coast is most affected, of course, by storms from the south. A northeaster blowing off the beaches of Biloxi, Mississippi, for example, would actually beat down the waves rather than build them up. Perhaps the strangest storms to cause coastal damage occur during the winter in Southern California. Huge waves come crashing ashore on bright sunny days with no sea breeze at all. These waves may have travelled many hundreds of miles and were formed by storms far out at sea. The Pacific coastal resident must depend on local weather forecasts for warning about these events. For all practical purposes, Pacific residents need not worry about hurricanes. The 1982 hurricane that struck Hawaii clearly demonstrates, however, that the fiftieth state does not share this immunity. Oceanographers studying water temperatures in regions south of Hawaii predict that hurricanes may strike the islands with increasing frequency in the future.

Wind

In Chapter 7 we discussed the Saffir–Simpson hurricane scale and the associated wind velocities. Gusts of wind can be expected to be 25 to 50 percent higher than the sustained wind velocity. Thus, a 150-mile-per-hour (240-km/h) hurricane may produce gusts exceeding 200 miles per hour (320 km/h). These gusts are responsible for the many recorded incidents of wind-measuring devices disappearing from weather bureau roofs in midstorm. They are also responsible for much of the storm damage by wind.

Hurricanes may produce significant and damaging winds for periods of up to twenty-four hours. If the storm stalls, there may be an even longer period of strong wind. Other types of storms such as the winter Pacific storms may remain in the area for several days. The Ash Wednesday storm, a 1962 northeaster, affected the East Coast for three long days.

The effect of a storm's wind is best evaluated in terms of the force or pressure it exerts. The pressure varies with the square of the velocity, meaning that pressure increases very rapidly with increasing wind velocity. For example, a 100-mile-per-hour (160-km/h) wind exerts a pressure of about 40 pounds per square foot (1.9 kN/m^2) on a flat surface. On the other hand, a wind of 190 miles per hour (300 km/h) exerts a force of 144 pounds per square foot (6.9 kN/m^2). The pressure effect on a round surface such as that of a sphere or cylinder is less than the effect on a flat surface. Also, winds increase with height above the ground level, so a tall structure is subject to greater pressure than a low structure. The best types of sites to reduce wind damage are, as common sense would dictate, those sheltered from the wind's direct onslaught. Shelter may be furnished by vegetation, dunes, other houses, and particularly forests.

Barometric Pressure

As the low-pressure center of a hurricane—and to a greater extent, a tornado—suddenly passes by, its effects on structures can be very dramatic. If a house is sealed at a normal barometric pressure of 30 inches (1016 millibars, or mb) of mercury, and the external pressure suddenly drops to 26.61 inches (901 mb) of mercury, the pressure exerted within the house would be 245 pounds per square foot (11.7 kN/m^2). An ordinary house would explode if it were leakproof. Fortunately, most houses leak, but they must leak fast enough to prevent damage. The pressure differential problem can be alleviated by leaving windows slightly open during storms.

A difference of opinion exists on the matter of opening windows, but experts agree that windows should be closed on the windward side and open on the leeward side. This should help relieve pressure differential. A question arises because open windows can lead to wind or water damage. In a tornado the direction of the wind can change so rapidly that it may be prudent to keep all of the windows closed. At the most, open them only a crack. In hurricanes, if you remain in the house, you can keep up with the wind direction, and so control the window opening and closing. If you evacuate, it is better to leave windows slightly ajar. The cracks, of course, furnish avenues for water to be blown into the house.

One civil defense coordinator has suggested an alternative to opening windows. This is to open the entrance hatch to the attic, on the theory that the internal pressure will equalize with the external pressure via vents in the attic. Venting the underside of the roof at the eaves also helps to equalize internal and external pressure. This alternative may reduce the amount of water blown into the house, compared to the open window approach. One square foot of venting area per 1,000 cubic feet of building volume should be adequate. This conclusion is based on certain reasonable conditions, including the assumption that three seconds are available for the pressures to equalize.

Several authorities assess barometric pressure change as a minor phenomenon in causing damage on the theory that the time it takes for the storm to approach and the pressure to change will permit the indoor and outdoor pressures to equalize through leaks and openings through air conditioners, attic doors, and the like. A word of warning is in order, however. The present-day energy crisis is causing people to seal up the cracks, to cover windows with plastic, and in other ways to tighten up a house and reduce the leaks. As a result, a house that previously had sufficient venting area may now be sufficiently leakproof to pose a problem from atmospheric pressure changes. Furthermore, many of the suggestions we make in this chapter for storm preparation will further seal a house.

Certainly more damage is caused by wind effects than by changes in barometric pressure, but it would be unwise to ignore pressure changes when preparing for a hurricane and its associated tornadoes. For other types of coastal storms, it is a reasonable gamble to ignore the possibility of extensive damage from pressure changes.

Waves

Waves can cause severe damage not only in forcing water onshore to flood buildings, but also in throwing boats, barges, piers, houses and other floating debris inland against standing structures. In addition, waves can destroy coastal structures by undermining the sand dunes that lie under them (figure 8-1), causing the structures to collapse. It is possible, however, to design buildings for survival in crashing storm surf. Many lighthouses, for example, have survived storm surges. From a cost-benefit standpoint, it usually is not economically feasible to build ordinary cottages to resist such forces. They must be constructed above the flood level and elevated on pilings or columns to allow waves to pass under the structure.

The force of a wave may be visualized when one considers that a cubic yard of water weighs over three-fourths of a ton; hence, a breaking wave moving shoreward at high velocity can be one of the most destructive elements of a hurricane. Breaking waves may move shoreward at about half the sustained wind velocity of the storm, hence the advisibility of leaving the area under the structure free of obstructions.

Some guidelines as to the extent of the forces caused by floating objects carried shoreward by moving waves are offered by the Texas Coastal and Marine Council in their paper on minimum hurricane-resistant building standards (see reference section for details). For ordinary buildings and structures vulnerable to being struck by floating objects, the normal battering load is considered to be the impact force produced by a 1,000-pound (450-kg) mass travelling at a velocity of 10 feet (3 m) per second and acting horizontally on a one-square-foot (0.09-m²) surface of the structure. If a building is designated as a "safe refuge," it should be designed for special battering loads. The intensity of that load is taken as 500 pounds (250 kg) per square foot acting horizontally over a one-foot-wide (30-cm) horizontal strip. This special battering load assumes a large conglomerate of floating objects striking or resting against the structure. The battering load may be ignored when natural or artificial barriers exist to prevent its occurrence.

Storm Surge or Rising Water

A storm surge is a rise in sea level above normal water level on the open coast. Storm surges occur when wind pushes water ashore while the water level rises because of lowered atmospheric pressure. Although sometimes incorrectly called a "tidal wave," it is not associated with the tide-producing forces of the moon and sun.

In most hurricanes it is the inundation of the coast by the storm surge that causes most of the property damage and loss of life. Superimposed on this high water and adding to the misery of coastal residents are storm waves.

The storm surge develops off the coast over deep water where the low pressure

December 28, 1972

January 19, 1973

8-1. Before and after the storm on an Oregon beach. (Photo: Paul Komar)

in the center of the storm causes the surface of the sea to bulge upward. In a perfect vacuum (zero pressure) a column of water will be raised 34 feet (10.4 m). This is why a suction pump on a well is limited to a rise of 20 feet (6 m) or so, and when the depth of the well is greater, the propelling part of the pump must be at the bottom of the well to "push" the water up. Barometric pressures as low as 26.35 inches (892 mb) of mercury have been recorded in the center of a hurricane. In Hurricane Camille the pressure was measured at 26.61 inches (901 mb). Normal barometric pressure is around 30 inches (1016 mb). The drop in atmospheric pressure of 3.5 inches (119 mb) of mercury should by itself cause a rise in sea level of 4 feet (1.2 m).

Simultaneous with the creation of the upward bulge by the drop in air pressure at the center of the storm is a second phenomenon. The counterclockwise swirl of the hurricane winds causes a similar swirling movement of the water, which may eventually extend downward to a depth of about 300 feet (90 m). The highest wind speeds are to the right of the hurricane's path, that is, to the east if the hurricane is travelling north; hence, the maximum swirl is likewise to the right of the path (figure 8-2).

Storms vary, but let's take a typical one. The maximum wind speeds usually occur 10 to 20 miles (16 to 30 km) to the right of the storm track. Similarly, the maximum water swirl usually occurs about 15 miles (24 km) to the right of the track. This, the so-called *northeast quadrant*, is the point of greatest danger from the storm.

So long as the water is deeper than about 300 feet (90 m), this swirl does not appreciably raise the sea level at this distance—about 15 miles (24 km)—from the center. But as the hurricane approaches land and the water becomes shallower, the swirling water mass scrapes bottom and begins to pile up in a mound to a height considerably above the sea level rise aided by the drop in air pressure. When the coastline is reached, the moving water piles up to its greatest height and the total surge may reach a level of 15 to 20 feet (4.6 to 6.1 m) or more above sea level. In Camille the surge was about 25 feet (7.6 m) above mean sea level in some locations. On top of this 25-foot (7 6-m) storm surge were waves whipped up by winds of nearly 200 mph (320 km/h).

Often the pressure of the wind backs water into streams or estuaries already swollen from the exceptionally high rainfall brought by the hurricane. On a barrier island shore, water is piled into the sounds between an island and the mainland. When the storm moves inland, the sound water suddenly flows back seaward much faster than it flowed into the sound. The result is that a home may be flooded from the sound side of the island. In fact, on many narrow barrier islands the damage from flooding from the backside or lagoonside can be greater than the danger from the frontside (figure 8-3).

Storms that strike at high tide will cause the most extensive flooding of all. Both the great European storm of 1953 that killed hundreds of Dutch and the Ash Wednesday storm of 1962 that caused great destruction on the Atlantic Coast from New England to Georgia struck the coast during the highest spring tides.

Flooding can cause an unanchored house to float off its foundation and come to rest against another house, severely damaging both. Even if the house itself is left structurally intact, flooding may destroy its contents. People who have cleaned out the mud from a house that was subjected to rising water will retain vivid memories of the effects of flooding.

A word of caution: the term 100-year flood can be misleading. The 100-year flood is commonly defined as a flood that has a 1 percent chance of being equaled or

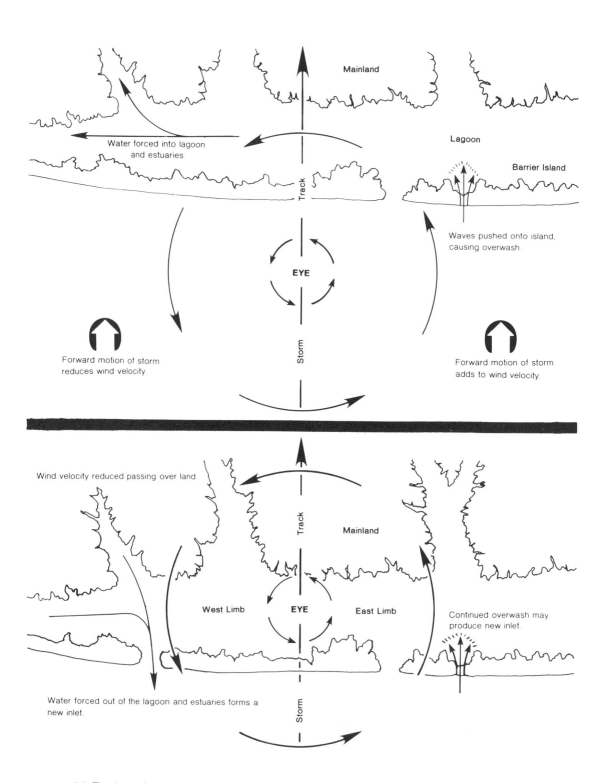

Mainland

Water forced into lagoon
and estuaries

Lagoon

Barrier Island

Track

Waves pushed onto island,
causing overwash.

EYE

Storm

Forward motion of storm
reduces wind velocity.

Forward motion of storm
adds to wind velocity.

Wind velocity reduced passing over land.

Track

Mainland

West Limb   EYE   East Limb

Continued overwash may
produce new inlet.

Water forced out of the lagoon and estuaries forms a
new inlet.

Storm

8-2. The forward progress of a typical hurricane across a hypothetical barrier island chain.

8-3. A narrow portion of a New Jersey island with a new inlet formed during the 1962 Ash Wednesday storm, probably from the sudden seaward rush of water pushed into a lagoon by the storm (see figure 8-2). The bulkhead on the backside of the island controlled the location of the new inlet. (Photo: courtesy U.S. Army Corps of Engineers)

exceeded in any given year. Over a long period of time such as 10,000 years, one would expect floods of 100-year magnitude or greater to occur one hundred times. During a shorter period of time, such as the life of a mortgage, several 100-year or greater floods could occur. There are even reported instances of two or more 100-year floods hitting an area in a single year. In addition, much more severe storms can and do occur. Storms such as the 1962 Ash Wednesday storm, Hurricane Camille in 1969, and Hurricane Frederick in 1979 produced flood levels in some areas that were far greater than those calculated for the 100-year flood. In addition, smaller, more frequent floods can cause extensive damage to poorly constructed buildings even if those buildings are elevated to above the 100-year flood level. Finally, the methods used to calculate the 100-year flood levels assume a basically stable system. The combination of sea level rise and erosion fo beach and dunes could in the long run result in 100-year flood levels far in excess of those that are now in effect for a specific location.

Proper coastal development takes into account the expected level and frequency of storm surge for the area. In general, building standards for coastal high-hazard areas require that the bottom of the horizontal structural members supporting the lowest floor of the building be above the 100-year storm surge level. The space below the elevation must be free of obstruction or built with breakaway walls. In coastal high-hazard areas (V zones), the National Flood Insurance Program has been adding 2 to 6 feet (0.6 to 1.8 m) to the elevation of the 100-year flood level to account for wave action.

To avoid storm-surge damage, property owners should build well-constructed houses in carefully chosen locations. Elevation is the number-one consideration for storm-surge safety; the higher the better (figure 8-4). Depending on location, 2 to 6 feet (0.6 to 1.8 m) above the 100-year flood level should be considered a minimum elevation. Higher elevations are recommended. If the site is on a wide barrier island or on the mainland, the distance from the beach is important. The greater the distance, the less the flood potential. Other site considerations include avoidance of obvious channels or low areas where water may flood or wash over the island (figure 8-5). On many coasts and islands, roads built straight through dunes directly to the beach afford natural paths for storm surge to reach and flood residences. There is a time factor here as well. If a hurricane moves ashore slowly, there is more time for the storm surge to move farther inland, relative to a fast-moving storm.

River Flooding

Once the hurricane hits land it begins to die. Cut off from the warm ocean, it is starved for water and heat energy, and dragged apart by friction on the land surface. Long after the storm is no longer recognizable as a hurricane, however, it may continue to dump large amounts of rain on inland residents. This rain, of course, will eventually cause flooding of the rivers in the coastal zone, adding several more days of problems for coastal residents just digging out from the storm.

Twenty-four-hour rainfall ranging from 5 to 30 inches (13 to 76 cm) may fall during a hurricane. Roads are frequently severed by local rivers flooding just when the storm recovery effort gets under way. Know the local drainage pattern and stream locations. If you live on a river flood plain, evacuation may be prudent, even if your homesite is way above expected storm-surge levels.

How to Survive a Hurricane

The weather service will issue information on potential hurricane problems. It helps to be familiar with the terms they will use.

A *hurricane watch* means that hurricane conditions are a real possibility for a specific and usually large coastal segment; it does *not* mean that they are imminent. You should listen for further advisories and begin preliminary preparations immediately.

A *hurricane warning* means that hurricane conditions are expected within twenty-four hours. The coastal areas will be identified where winds of at least 74 miles per hour (118 km/h) are expected to occur, and where dangerously high water or exceptionally high waves are forecast, even though winds may be less than hurricane force. When a hurricane warning is issued, your precautions to protect life and property should be in full gear.

What to Watch For

In the old days, Caribbean fishermen were experts on the signs of nature that indicated a hurricane was coming. They had to be, or they would not have survived for long. But just as modern weather forecasters sometimes err, so did Caribbean fishermen. As recently as the early 1950s, over fifty fishermen from the Bahamian island of Caicos perished in a hurricane that seemed to come from nowhere.

8-4. This house in Truro, Massachusetts (February 8, 1978), would not be in trouble if it had been built at a higher elevation. (Photo: Graham Geise)

8-5. Washovers formed by Hurricane Allen (1980) across South Padre Island, Texas. If houses had been built on these overwash passes, they would have disappeared. (Photo: courtesy *National Oceanic and Atmospheric Administration*)

Typically, the day before a hurricane strikes will be bright and sunny, with atmospheric pressure slightly above normal. The first visible sign of a hurricane is usually a change in the pattern of waves breaking on shore. Waves larger than usual begin to break on the beach more frequently than usual. These are waves that were formed far offshore in the still invisible hurricane. At about the same time, feathery high-altitude cirrus clouds begin to form in the sky. From this point on, everything is downhill. Waves, wind, cloud cover, and rain gradually pick up. Sometimes the actual hurricane can be seen as a massive bank of almost black clouds moving ominously ashore.

To Leave or Not to Leave

If your property is on high ground and your home is sturdy, you may be as safe at home as in a shelter. If this is the case, consider inviting a neighboring family to use your house as an emergency shelter if they are more poorly situated. If you live in a low-lying area that may be swept by high water or storm waves, leave. Remember, storm and hurricane winds do much damage but drowning in low areas is the greatest cause of hurricane deaths. A well-built high-rise above the third floor may provide adequate shelter. If in doubt about possible flood levels in your community, do not stay in your house if it is lower than 15 feet (4.6 m) in elevation. Twenty feet (6 m) is usually a safer minimum elevation (although it was not in Hurricane Camille). Do not ride out a big storm if you are within three rows of buildings of the beach, no matter what the elevation.

Never ride out a hurricane in a mobile home; if you live in a mobile home, leave for more substantial shelter. A newspaper reporter who lived through Hurricane Frederick in a trailer that was overturned by the wind in spite of (probably insufficient) anchor ties said, among other things: "It was my misfortune to live in a house trailer. Trailers are not the most desired dwellings in hurricane country. . . . Another inconvenient fringe benefit of hurricanes is tornadoes; and everybody knows a tornado will go ten miles out of its way to hit a trailer park. That's just what happened in my trailer park." After describing some of the damage, including trouble with looters, he philosophized, "I learned one thing: people who live in flimsy houses shouldn't have hurricanes."

Before you leave your mobile home, follow precautions used for houses. Turn off the electricity, water, and propane gas. Disconnect the sewer, remove awnings, and tape windows.

If in doubt as to the safety of your house, move invalids in the family to a safer place. Better yet, move everybody!

Once you decide to leave or are asked by the authorities to leave (which will be done only if your life is seriously threatened), GO! Do not procrastinate, as travel is extremely dangerous when winds and tides are whipping through your area. Such winds and tides may arrive as much as five hours before the hurricane center reaches the coast.

As you depart, lock up. Do everything possible to protect your property from damage. Bring such survival supplies as a first-aid kit, canned or dried provisions, bottled water, medication, and spare eyeglasses. Take with you important papers such as driver's license, insurance policies, and medical information. Also, take at least one change of warm, protective clothing.

If you decide to stay at home, remain indoors. Do not venture out during a lull that might well be the arrival of the eye of the hurricane. A lull can end abruptly with winds in the opposite direction. Winds can return to hurricane level in a few seconds.

While indoors stay away from exposed windows and glass doors. Remain on the leeward or downwind side of the house. As the wind changes, move to another room. If your home has an interior room, stay there during the height of the storm. Of course, if you have a strengthened interior room, remain there throughout the hurricane.

Listen frequently to your battery-powered radio or television for hurricane information from official sources. Unexpected changes can lead to a call for last-minute evacuations or relocations.

Prepare Ahead of Time
General Precautions
If you plan to stay or live in the house immediately after a hurricane, it is wise to assume that electricity, gas, water, and telephone will be cut off, and you should provide yourself with the things that are essential to living, including canned (not frozen) foods.

Store drinking water in clean bathtubs, jugs, bottles, and cooking utensils. Have sufficient water for several days. Even if not cut off, your water supply may be contaminated. If in doubt, boil the water for thirty minutes.

You will have to provide some way for cooking and lighting, such as bottled gas, canned heat, or kerosene. There should be flashlights, extra batteries, and battery radios, as your radio may be your only link with the world outside during the hurricane. Have enough batteries to last several days. Essential also are canned foods, dry ice if refrigeration fails, rope, nails, tools for emergency repairs, and a first-aid kit for injuries.

If the electricity fails, turn off the electricity at the supply panel. Food in the refrigerator and freezer will keep for a reasonable length of time. It is good sense to keep perishable food to a minimum when a storm is imminent. The potential loss from the fire hazard of connected electricity is greater than the loss from spoiled food.

Every reasonable step should be taken to prevent fires. Lowered or no water pressure, debris-laden streets, unavailable fire-fighting personnel all may contribute to making fire-fighting impossible after a storm.

Valuable and personal papers should be placed in waterproof containers and moved to high locations.

Your Car
The gas tank should be full in case you decide to escape. If you choose to stay, set the parking brake to keep the car in place and slightly open the windows to reduce the effects of low barometric pressure. If you have a garage so well built that the roof or walls will not collapse, put the car in the garage.

Your Yard
Dead trees should have been taken down. Even old trees that might blow over when the ground is saturated should be topped. Do not wait for a hurricane warning to trim your trees. All loose things should be put away, anchored, or stored inside before the storm strikes. Garbage cans, garden tools, toys, ladders, porch furniture, and pails can become missiles of destruction in hurricane winds. Lower the water

level of your swimming pool to about two feet below normal. Brace your garage doors.

Your House

Whether you go or stay, board up windows or protect them with storm shutters or tape. Danger to small windows is mainly from wind-driven debris; larger windows may be broken by wind pressure. Draw drapes across patio doors and windows to protect against flying glass if shattering occurs. Although personal observation indicates that this is rarely done, houses in a hurricane area would benefit from heavy wooden or steel shutters that can be easily attached or are fastened permanently and swung into place. Heavy branches, boards, or other debris can blow through the air and crash through unshuttered panes of glass and let in torrents of rain. Last, lower television antennas, if possible.

Your Apartment/Condo

Know your building ahead of time. Can it withstand the storm battering? Each building should have a building captain who is well read on the subject of storms and who can advise or instruct occupants and supervise the storm preparation measures. Remove all loose items from terraces, making sure they are removed from unoccupied apartments as well. Wedge terrace doors and close and lock all windows. Presumably you already know well the emergency exits; do not forget, you may be evacuating in total blackness. Count the stairs ahead of time. The building captain should assign individuals to remove loose items from adjacent grounds.

Your Boat

Moor your boat securely before the storm arrives or move it to a designated safe area. Safe anchorage should be chosen and arranged a long time before trouble arises. Where possible, take the boat far up inland rivers. In the shelter harbor, secure the boat fore and aft to pilings on lines long enough to ride the high water. If possible, anchor boats in groups. Anchor or tie boats separately, but also tie boats together with bow and stern lines. If small enough, take your boat out of the water to a sheltered place. Fill a small boat on a trailer close to the house with water or sand to weigh it down. Lash it to the trailer with deflated tires which in turn are tied securely to the ground or to the house. Pull small open boats to high ground and fill them with sand. Whatever you do with your boat, once you have left it and the winds and waves are up, do not return. *Que sera, sera!*

Your Business

The businessman located next to a shoreline has a special problem. Because it is particularly difficult to secure a building full of merchandise at the last minute, it is thus most important for any owner to be prepared far ahead of time. For one thing, the employees of a business may well be busy protecting their own property and family as the storm approaches.

Most prestorm precautions are the same as one would take for any other structure. All utilities should be disconnected, windows boarded up or taped, loose signs and display racks moved indoors, and antennas removed from the roof. The stock or merchandise of a store should be moved as high as possible and away from windows. Covering the shelves with plastic may reduce damage from water leaks and flooding. Special care must be taken to protect financial records and insurance policies.

Toxic and water-reactive chemicals pose a special problem. If time does not permit removal, they should be stored in the safest part of the building, appropriately packaged and covered.

The prudent store-owner will take lots of photographs of the building and the stock. The kind store-owner will make arrangements to pay off employees in cash before the storm; banks, like other businesses, may be closed for some time afterwards. As the storekeeper leaves, the building should be securely locked.

After the Hurricane

Listen for an official announcement that the danger has passed. If telephones are working, contact appropriate relatives to inform them of your safe survival of the storm.

Check refrigerated food for spoilage if the power was off during the storm.

Disinfect all cans and utensils before use if they were in contact with the floodwaters. Dispose of mattresses, pillows, and cushions that have been in floodwaters. These may be contaminated and cannot be dried and cleaned in the same way as rugs and other items of furniture.

When possible, report broken sewer or water mains to the water department. Avoid loose or dangling wires; if your phone works, report them to your power company or law enforcement officer.

Drive carefully along debris-filled streets. Roads may be undermined and may collapse under the weight of a car. Walk cautiously, as snakes may be a hazard. Stay out of disaster areas unless you are qualified to help. Your presence might hamper first-aid and rescue work. Do not visit to sightsee. You will be a nuisance and may even be arrested.

People tape their windows because they realize the taping helps prevent breakage of the glass by damping the vibrations caused by gusting winds, and also because, if the window should break, the masking tape will help prevent shattering. A nasty problem is removing the tape itself—or the tape marks—after the storm. This should be done as soon as possible; every time the sun heats up the glass, the adhesive bakes harder into it. Hard work is required. First try rubbing alcohol. If that does not work, try household ammonia, full strength. Acetone, available from hardware and paint stores, is effective, but must be used with extreme caution as it is dangerous if the fumes are inhaled, and it is also flammable. Liquid cleaning fluids such as Energine or Carbona available from drug stores will work. If all else fails, very carefully scrape off the tape with a razor blade. Since any scratch in the glass may cause the glass to break from future pressure along the scratch line, use special care.

For some good commonsense advice, we refer you to the H.U.D. booklet *When You Return to a Storm Damaged Home*, which offers such suggestions as: "Move wooden furniture outdoors and take out as many drawers, slides, or other working parts as possible. Do not force stuck drawers with a screwdriver or chisel from the front. Remove the back by cutting out if necessary, and push out the drawers." Three of the authors of the book you are now reading learned the wisdom of this advice the hard way after Hurricane Camille.

If Your Property Is Damaged

Make temporary repairs to protect your property from further damage. Board up broken windows and otherwise try to cover anything that might suffer further wind or water damage or even looting.

Make a detailed inventory of all damaged items. Take lots of photographs. Do not dispose of items that appear to be a complete loss until they are examined by an insurance adjuster. If water entered your home, leave it well ventilated to allow for drying. Clean and dry your rugs and wood furniture as soon as possible. To prevent corrosion, dry and oil metal objects. Dry but do not oil radios, televisions, and other electrical equipment. Have water-exposed electrical devices professionally serviced before use.

Notify your insurance representative about all losses. Be patient. Hardship cases may be settled first. Because of policy and company differences, your settlement may vary from your neighbor's.

If at all possible, use local, reputable contractors for repairs. A disaster always attracts fly-by-night as well as reputable contractors from out of town. Check out the firm before employing it. Your local lumberyard, building supplier, or hardware dealer may be able to help, if you do not have access to a chamber of commerce or division of the Better Business Bureau. Above all, do not pay for a job before completion or before checking to be sure the contractor has paid for the material and labor used on your job. Your insurance adjuster will provide guidelines on getting started, such as how to get estimates. Get and keep all receipts for materials and labor.

Hurricane Checklist

When a hurricane threatens, keep this checklist handy for protection of your family and property. This duplicates some previous discussions, but should provide a quick, thorough review. The list has been compiled from several publications from the federal government, the state of Texas, and the Virgin Islands.

Before the Storm Season Begins

1. *Examine the structural condition of your house. Follow the principles of construction outlined in Chapters 3 and 4. Chapter 4 is particularly appropriate, since it concerns evaluation of a structure already built.*
2. *Check hurricane shutters.*
3. *Have on hand the following temporary flood-proofing materials; different items may be more appropriate for various types and locations of structures:*
   - *sandbags, already filled*
   - *plywood to cover windows*
   - *towels and caulking to stop seepage*
   - *woodbeams to brace fences, doors*
   - *blocks to raise furniture*
   - *plastic trashbags for waterproof storage*
4. *Trim dead tree limbs.*
5. *Review your insurance status.*
6. *Make an itemized list of personal property.*

7. Place policies and important records in a safe place.
8. Ask a friend or relative if their ''safer'' house can be used as a shelter by your family.
9. Ask an inland friend or relative if you can find shelter with them.
10. Arrange for transportation if you have none.

When a Hurricane Threatens

1. Listen for official weather reports.
2. Read your newspaper and listen to radio and television for official announcements.
3. Note the address of the nearest emergency shelter.
4. Evacuate pregnant women and the ill and infirm to safety where a physician is readily available.
5. Have plenty of clean clothes.
6. Be prepared to turn off gas, water, and electricity where it enters your home. Locate the switches ahead of time.
7. Fill tubs and containers with water (one quart per person per day).
8. Make sure your car's gas tank is full. Check battery water.
9. Secure your boat. Use long lines to allow for rising water.
10. Check fire extinguishers.
11. Lower water level in your swimming pool.
12. Remove canvas awnings.
13. Move valuables and personal papers to a high location.
14. Take down or lower your television antenna.
15. Secure movable objects on your property:
    - doors
    - shutters
    - outdoor furniture
    - garden tools
    - hoses
    - gates
    - garbage cans
16. Board up or tape windows and glassed areas (with large X on inside).
17. Remove furniture in the vicinity of windows.
18. Close the drapes.
19. Turn the controls of refrigerators and freezers to the coldest setting and keep the doors closed.
20. Cover freezer with blankets.
21. Wrap food in newspaper to increase insulation.
22. Make lots of ice.
23. Stock adequate supplies; remember, there will be a rush on local stores and many items will quickly run out:
    - transistor radio
    - flashlights
    - fresh batteries
    - candles
    - canned heat
    - matches

- *hammer*
- *nails*
- *boards*
- *screwdriver*
- *pliers*
- *ax**
- *hunting knife*
- *rope**
- *tape*
- *plastic dropcloths, waterproof bags, ties*
- *first-aid kit*
- *prescribed medicines*
- *containers for water*
- *water purification tablets*
- *disinfectant*
- *insect repellant*
- *gum, candy*
- *life jackets*
- *hard-top head gear*
- *charcoal bucket and charcoal*
- *fire extinguisher*
- *buckets of sand*
- *can opener and utensils*

Suggested Food Stock (For Family of Four)

- 2 cans, 13-oz. evaporated milk
- 1 carton, 14-oz. cream of wheat or oatmeal
- 4 cans, 7-oz. fruit juice
- 1 jar, 8 oz. peanut butter or cheese spread
- 2 cans tuna, sardines, chicken, or Spam
- 2 cans, 16-oz. pork and beans
- 3 cans, 10-oz. vegetable soup
- 1 jar, 2-oz. instant coffee or teabags
- 1 small can cocoa or Ovaltine
- 2 packages crackers
- 1 box, 16-oz. raisins or prunes
- 2 lbs. sugar

---

* An ax should be taken with you if you go to the upper floors or attic of your home. This can be used to cut an emergency escape opening in case of rising water entering the attic. The rope can be used for escaping to the ground when the water subsides.

- 1 waterproof container of salt
- pet food

If Evacuation Is Advised

1. *Leave as soon as you can. Follow official instructions only.*
2. *Take these supplies:*
   - *change of clothes*
   - *disposable diapers*
   - *baby formula*
   - *special medicine*
   - *identification tags, with name, address, and next of kin (wear them)*
   - *blankets and pillows in waterproof casing*
   - *radio*
   - *flashlight*
   - *fresh batteries*
   - *food, water, gum, candy*
   - *purse, wallet, valuables*
   - *rope, hunting knife*
   - *waterproof bags and ties*
   - *games and amusements for children*
   - *can opener and utensils*
   - *first-aid kit*
3. *Bring important documents and papers.*
4. *Disconnect all electric appliances except refrigerator and freezer. Turn controls of freezers and refrigerators to the coldest setting.*
5. *Disconnect gas supply.*
6. *Leave guns, alcohol, and narcotics at home; they will not be allowed in a shelter.*
7. *Leave food and water for pets. Seeing-eye dogs are the only animals allowed in shelters.*
8. *Shut off water and the main valve (where it enters your home).*

If You Stay

1. *Stay indoors and away from windows and glassed areas.*
2. *If you are advised to evacuate, DO SO AT ONCE.*
3. *Listen for continuing weather bulletins and official reports. Ignore rumors.*
4. *Use your telephone only in an emergency.*
5. *Follow official instructions only.*
6. *Keep a window or door slightly open on the side of house opposite the storm winds.*
7. *Remain in a downwind room. Use a strengthened interior room, if available.*
8. *Keep children dressed. Provide them with things to do.*
9. *Beware the eye of the hurricane. Remain indoors unless repairs are necessary.*
10. *Be alert for rising water.*
11. *If you detect gas:*

- *Do not light matches or turn on electrical equipment.*
- *Extinguish all flames.*
- *Shut off gas supply at the meter.*
- *Report gas service interruptions to the gas company. Gas should be turned back on only by a gas serviceman or licensed plumber.*

12. *Be careful what water you drink. The only safe water is the water you stored before it had a chance to come in contact with the floodwaters. An official announcement will proclaim when tap water is safe. Treat all water except stored water until you hear the announcement.*
    - *Boil water for thirty minutes before use.*
    - *If you are unable to boil water, treat water you will need with water purification tablets. Use five halazone tablets or two drops of chlorinated bleach per quart. Wait thirty minutes before drinking.*

After the Storm

1. *Listen for official radio advisories.*
2. *Avoid dangling wires.*
3. *Drive only if necessary and then with great caution.*
4. *Do not sightsee.*
5. *Walk around house to check damage.*
6. *Enter house with caution.*
7. *Clean up potential health hazards (perishables).*
8. *Open windows for circulation.*

Regulating America's Coast

Management, Insurance, Building Codes

Shoreline Development: Political Paradox

In the late 1960s and early 1970s, landmark federal legislation was passed for the purpose of managing the coastal zone. Protecting the environment, curbing unsound coastal development, and protecting people and property from coastal hazards were the goals of this legislation. But while vast expenditures have gone into these programs, conflicts between well-intentioned agencies have unfortunately frequently arisen. The paradox is that while one agency may have tried to hold back dangerous development, the policies and actions of other government agencies and programs have encouraged and promoted growth in these same coastal areas, greatly increasing the risks from hurricanes or other coastal hazards. The Florida Keys provide a simple example.

For years the Keys were sleepy tropical islands, uninhabited for the most part. Even though an 1846 hurricane pushed 5 feet (1.5 m) of water over the main street of Key West, there was no spectacular casualty count. By the 1930s, however, engineers were tying the Keys to the mainland via the East Coast Railroad line, the route of today's highway. Easier access brought more people, and four hundred of those people died when the 1935 hurricane sent 18 feet (5.5 m) of water over the Keys, destroying the rail line as well. Today we view the miles of causeway and thirty-eight bridges over the sea that tie the Keys to the mainland as an engineering marvel, and rightly so. We cannot, however, overlook the equally awesome marvels of nature. In the face of a hurricane, the causeway is like a very long, weak thread, certain to break in more than one place. The causeway is the escape route for most of the 65,000 persons likely to be on the Keys during a typical hurricane-season day. About half of these people, 30,000 souls, will be on Key West.

We can play number games using figures such as 12 hours lead time to begin evacuation, evacuation of 700 cars per hour, x number of evacuees by plane or boat, but the end result is always the same. Thousands, perhaps well in excess of 10,000, will be stranded on the Keys, and many will not live to see the end of the storm. Common sense seems to suggest that a wider upgraded causeway is needed to handle more people, and Congress authorized a $200-million grant to be administered through the Federal Highway Administration to widen and improve the causeway and bridges.

Such improvement is usually regarded as good, but is it? Better and bigger access brings more people. More people create a need for more efficient evacuation. More people create a demand for more services. And the carrying capacity of these islands was exceeded long ago. Natural water supply is inadequate for the population, and so dependence on an external water supply has become necessary. At the same time the causeway project was being approved, the Farmers Home Administration underwrote a new $63-million water line through the Keys. Tens of millions of dollars were lent at a bargain interest rate (5 percent) to the Florida Keys Aqueduct Authority for a pipeline system capable of delivering 13.5 million gallons (51 million liters) of water per day—*three times* the current consumption level! Were the bureaucrats of the Farmers Home Administration forward-looking promoters of progress and the free enterprise system, or were they, through ignorance, irresponsible promoters of a project that will ultimately result in the deaths of hundreds?

Utility lines must also stretch the long distance from mainland to key to key. Each of these man-made links increases the vulnerability of the island inhabitants' support system. The more things there are to go wrong, the more likely it is that something will go wrong. The survivors of a storm in the Keys would have to do without the essential goods and services that are dependent on a road transportation system, as well as water, utilities, and waste water treatment for an unpredictable amount of time after the storm. The number of people affected is a function of the size of the system, which in turn is determined by the size of the subsidies that supported the system's construction—$200 million to widen the causeway, $63 million for the enlarged water system, and tens of millions more for other services.

Unless there are policy reversals, the population on the Keys will continue to escalate, and within a few decades well over 100,000 people will live there, unless a large storm hits sooner. The problem grows in magnitude each year that passes without a storm, because the massive doses of federal dollars contribute to enlarging the support system, encouraging more development. The National Hurricane Center, which sometimes sounds like a broken record, has pointed out the likelihood of a high death toll in the next big hurricane to hit the Keys. When the big storm does come, the personal loss will be borne by the families and friends of the dead; the dollar loss will be borne by the American taxpayer.

Just as a paradox exists in the conflicting policies of the federal government, similar conflicts exist at the state and local levels. Perhaps with the exception of departments of natural resources and newly created offices of coastal zone management, most state officials have not given the coastal zone special attention in terms of the consequences of their actions. At the local level, the voters are often residents who derive their livelihood from development. They may represent only a small percentage of the total property owners, particularly in vacation-resort communities where property is held as second homes or for rental income. Beach communities with thousands of seasonal residents may have less than a hundred voters. Thus, the vested interests of the few will set local policy for many.

Infrastructure Growth: Shifting Federal Policies

Prior to the early part of this century, the federal government was not involved in land management, nor did it assume any of the risk for citizens who chose to live in natural hazard zones. The risk and ultimately the cost was borne by the victim. This policy of noninvolvement by the government changed gradually, first with the recognition of the national value of floodplain development, and then with assumption of responsibility for river floodplain control, navigation, and hydroelectric power development.

The Flood Control Act of 1936 set the trend for federal assumption of costs for water resources development, flood control, and disaster relief associated with floods. The emphasis then was on structural control, such as that provided by dams, levees, and reservoirs, just as later shoreline "protection" projects would rely on structural approaches involving seawalls, groins, and revetments. In both cases structural controls proved costly and often unsuccessful. For the last two decades, nonstructural management techniques have been employed more widely for river floodplains, just as the trend for shoreline management has also veered away from fixed structures.

Currently, the government is addressing the problems of improper land management and the increasing risk in the coastal zone through two major efforts, the National Flood Insurance Program (NFIP) and the Coastal Zone Management Act (CZMA). One of the goals of the National Flood Insurance Act of 1968 and the Flood Disaster Protection Act of 1973 has been to shift some of the costs and risks of flood losses, including storm-surge flooding, to those who create the risks—the occupants of the flood zone. At the same time, these programs attempt to put restraints on where and how structures are built, to avoid sensitive and dangerous coastal environments, and to encourage the design and the building of structures that are more resistant to coastal winds and waters than their inland counterparts. These programs are discussed in more detail in the following sections.

Unfortunately, many of the positive effects of these programs are offset by the fact that several other governmental agencies administer programs that not only encourage coastal and barrier island development, but stimulate it! Figure 9-1 summarizes the federal agencies that make up the infrastructure controlling such development. Many if not most of these agencies have no expertise in the coastal environment, and development of coastal areas is treated very much like development in the suburbs of an inland city.

The counterproductivity and waste of tax dollars by federal agencies with opposing goals is not unrecognized. The decade of the 1980s has already been marked by the signing of the Interagency Agreement on Hazard Mitigation. The goal of this agreement is to develop a common policy for flood disaster planning and postflood recovery in order that federal financial assistance minimizes future flood losses. The Federal Emergency Management Agency (FEMA) is responsible for promoting cooperation among such groups as the departments of Agriculture, Defense, Commerce, Housing and Urban Development, and the Interior; the Environmental Protection Agency; and the Small Business Administration.

The Interagency Agreement is a small first step, as it addresses primarily postflood planning and recovery. Eventually, such interagency unified policies should address all coastal hazards and require predisaster regulations designed to minimize losses. For many heavily developed coastal areas, such efforts are probably too late.

Basically, the federal government is beginning to move away from the financial backing of coastal development. The first major step in this direction occurred with the passage of the Coastal Barrier Resources Act by Congress in 1982. This bill

9-1. Federal Agencies: Infrastructure Subsidizers of Coastal Development

Agency	Coastal Development–Related Missions
Department of Agriculture	
Farmer's Home Administration (FmHA)	Water supply/sewer grants Business and industry loans
Soil Conservation Service (SCS)	Watershed protection and flood prevention loans and grants
Department of Commerce	
Economic Development Administration (EDA)	Public facilities, grants, and business loans
Office of Ocean and Coastal Resource Management (OCRM)	Coastal energy impact program grants and loans
Federal Emergency Management Agency (FEMA)	Disaster assistance, flood insurance
Department of Defense	
U.S. Army Corps of Engineers	Beach erosion control projects and navigation projects Grants, permits for shoreline structures, and dredging
Department of Energy (DOE)	Pipeline and transmission-line siting
Department of Housing and Urban Development (HUD)	Community development block grants Grants, loans, subsidies, and mortgage guarantees for housing
Department of Transportation (DOT)	
Federal Highway Administration (FHWA)	Highway research, planning, and construction subsidies
Coast Guard	Bridge permits, deepwater ports
Small Business Administration (SBA)	Recovery loans
Environmental Protection Agency (EPA)	Construction grants for sewage-treatment plants

(Modified from Natural Resources Defense Council, *Paving the Way for Coastal Development*.)

prevents the federal government from aiding barrier islands that have yet to be developed: no flood insurance can be sold for new structures, and no federal assistance can be provided for roads, sewers, bridges, or seawalls. Reasons for this bill's passage included the realization by a budget-conscious government that support of eroding, storm-vulnerable islands was economically foolhardy, as well as the

increasing awareness that federal support condoning island development was placing more and more citizens' lives in jeopardy. At the same time, an important part of
the ecosystem was being lost. Dauphin Island, Alabama, may have been the straw
that broke the camel's back. After Hurricane Frederick (1979), more than 90 million
dollars were spent in insurance claims, new bridge construction, sewer and water
system replacement, and other repairs to reopen an island that had only 300 homes
on it, an island that had been devastated by storms twice before in this century.

Future coastal dwellers, whether on a windswept barrier island or atop a beautiful
California seabluff, should recognize this rapidly evolving attitude of the federal government toward the shore. Practical ramifications of this could include decreasing
federal support of insurance, shoreline stabilization, and other amenities of coastal life.

Rules and Regulations: Know Before You Build or Buy

Peter Graber has written a series of excellent articles in *Shore and Beach* magazine
outlining the laws applicable to the coast, first in overview, then state by state. He
makes the point that new technologies and new environments require new laws and
sometimes a new legal framework in which to operate. This is certainly true for the
American coastal zone and continental shelf, as evidenced by the series of related
laws passed since the early 1950s. These laws have created a legal atmosphere
that can be and usually is more complicated for coastal citizens than for inland
counterparts.

The Coastal Zone Management Act of 1972 (CZMA; P.L. 92-583) set in motion an
effort to encourage all coastal states to manage their shorelines. The carrot dangled
was federal funds to be allotted to states that instituted suitable coastal zone management plans. Key requirements of the CZMA are coastal land-use planning based
on land classification, and the identification and protection of critical areas. The
designation of "areas of critical environmental concern" or "areas of particular
concern" is the heart of the planning classification. Other important land and water
use designations include the categories of "permissible uses," "areas of preservation," or vital areas, and "priority uses."

The CZMA program is administered by the Office of Coastal Zone Management
(OCZM) of the Department of Commerce, which provides funding for state planning
and implementation of such plans. In 1983 OCZM became OCRM: Office of Ocean
and Coastal Resource Management. Stress is placed on state leadership in the
planning process, and in fact the success of the program depends on the voluntary
participation of states and coastal communities. The OCRM has no federal regulatory powers or financial sanctions that it may impose. It can, however, provide federal grants and various kinds of technical assistance.

The basic responsibility for coastal zone management rests with the state. Most
coastal states are participating in the federal Coastal Zone Management program
and have enacted legislation to initiate regulation of land use in the coastal zone.
Some of these states have completed the mapping of critical areas and areas of
concern and require applications for permits to build in or to alter environments of
the coastal zone.

A few states, such as Georgia, Texas, and Virginia, opted not to participate in the
federal program. In general, the reason for their nonparticipation came from the wish
to have fewer restrictions on development. Although these states have coastal management programs in the sense that particular state laws govern coastal land use

and they have offices responsible for coastal management (figure 9-2), their programs are generally not as strong as those of states in the federal program. Virginia dropped out of the CZM program in 1979, Georgia in 1980, and Texas in 1981 after the state decided not to submit the Texas Coastal Program draft program for approval. In addition, some of the Great Lakes states are not participating in the Coastal Zone program either.

9-2. State Coastal Zone Management Offices

The following list of addresses by region is provided for persons who wish to contact their state office in charge of coastal zone management. In many cases this office is responsible for issuing clearance permits to build dwellings, protective structures, or similar alterations of the environment. (Asterisks indicate those states *not* participating in the federal CZM program.)

North Atlantic Region

Connecticut
Department of Environmental Protection
71 Capitol Avenue
Hartford, CT 06115
Phone: (203) 566-7404

Maine
State Planning Office
184 State Street
Augusta, ME 04330
Phone: (207) 289-3261

Massachusetts
Executive Office of Environmental Affairs
100 Cambridge Street
Boston, MA 02202
Phone: (617) 727-9530

New Hampshire
Office of State Planning
2½ Beacon Street
Concord, NH 03301
Phone: (603) 271-2155

New Jersey
Department of Environmental Protection
P.O. Box 1889
Trenton, NJ 08625
Phone: (609) 292-9762

New York
Coastal Management Unit
Department of State
162 Washington Street
Albany, NY 12231
Phone: (518) 474-4750

Rhode Island
Coastal Resources Management
   Program
Washington County Government
   Center
Tower Hill Road
South Kingston, RI 02897
Phone: (401) 789-3048

South Atlantic Region
Delaware
Department of Natural Resources and
   Environmental Control
P.O. Box 1401
Tatnall Building
Dover, DE 19901
Phone: (302) 736-3091

Florida
Department of Environmental Regu-
   lation
Twin Towers Office Building
2600 Blair Stone Road
Tallahassee, FL 32301
Phone: (904) 488-4807

* Georgia
Department of Natural Resources
2770 Washington Street
Atlanta, GA 30334
Phone: (404) 656-3508
   OR
Coastal Resources Division
Department of Natural Resources
1200 Glynn Avenue
Brunswick, GA 03520
Phone: (912) 264-4771

continued . . .

Maryland
Coastal Resources Division
Department of Natural Resources
Tawes State Office Building
Annapolis, MD 21401
Phone: (301) 269-2784

North Carolina
North Carolina Department of Natural
  Resources & Community Develop-
  ment
P.O. Box 27687
Raleigh, NC 27611
Phone: (919) 733-2293

South Carolina
South Carolina Coastal Council
Summerall Center
19 Hagood Street, Suite 802
Charleston, SC 29403
Phone: (803) 792-5808

* Virginia
Council on the Environment
Ninth Street Office Building
Richmond, VA 23219
Phone: (804) 786-4500

Gulf/Islands Region

Alabama
Office of State Planning and
  Federal Programs
State Capitol
Montgomery, AL 36131
Phone: (205) 832-6400

Florida
Department of Environmental Regu-
  lation
Twin Towers Office Building
2600 Blair Stone Road
Tallahassee, FL 32301
Phone: (904) 488-4807

Louisiana
Coastal Resource Program
P.O. Box 44396
Capital Station
Baton Rouge, LA 70804
Phone: (504) 342-4500

Mississippi
Bureau of Marine Resources
P.O. Box 959
Long Beach, MS 39560
Phone: (601) 864-4602

Puerto Rico
Department of Natural Resources
P.O. Box 5887
Puerto de Tierra, PR 00906
Phone: (809) 723-3090

* Texas
Natural Resources Advisory Council
200 East 18th Street
Austin, TX 78701
Phone: (512) 475-0414

Virgin Islands
Department of Conservation and
  Cultural Affairs
P.O. Box 4340
Charlotte Amalie
St. Thomas, VI 00801
Phone: (809) 774-3320

Great Lakes Region
* Illinois
Department of Transportation
Division of Water Resources
300 North State Street
Chicago, IL 60610
Phone: (312) 793-3123

* Indiana
Department of Natural Resources
Division of Outdoor Recreation
State Office Building
Indianapolis, IN 46204
Phone: (317) 232-4020

Michigan
Great Lakes Shorelands Section
Department of Natural Resources
Division of Land Resources
Stephens T. Mason Building
Lansing, MI 48926
Phone: (517) 373-1950

continued . . .

*Minnesota
Department of Natural Resources
Division of Waters
444 Lafayette Road
St. Paul, MN 55101
Phone: (612) 296-4800

New York
Coastal Management Unit
Department of State
162 Washington Street
Albany, NY 12231
Phone: (518) 474-4750

*Ohio
Ohio Department of Natural
    Resources
Fountain Square Court (Bldg. D)
Columbus, OH 43223
Phone: (614) 466-3770

Pennsylvania
Coastal Zone Management Office
Department of Environmental
    Resources
P.O. Box 1467
Harrisburg, PA 17120
Phone: (717) 783-9500

Wisconsin
Wisconsin Coastal Program
Department of Administration
Bureau of Coastal Management
101 South Webster
General Executive Facility 2
Madison, WI 53702
Phone: (608) 266-3687

Pacific Region
Alaska
Office of Coastal Management
Pouch AP
Juneau, AK 99801
Phone: (907) 465-3540

California
California Coastal Commission
631 Howard St., 4th Floor
San Francisco, CA 94105
Phone: (415) 543-8555

San Francisco Bay Conservation
    and Development Commission
30 VanNess Avenue
San Francisco, CA 94102
Phone: (415) 557-3686

Hawaii
Department of Planning and
    Economic Development
P.O. Box 2359
Honolulu, HI 96804
Phone: (808) 548-3042

Oregon
Coastal Program Manager
Land Conservation and Development
    Commission
1175 Court Street, NE
Salem, OR 97310
Phone: (503) 378-4097

Washington
Coastal Program Manager
Department of Ecology
State of Washington (PV-11)
Olympia, WA 98504
Phone: (206) 459-6273

If you own or are considering purchasing coastal property in a nonparticipating state you should take particular care to investigate the laws that regulate coastal land use. In addition, you may wish to learn why the state dropped out of the CZM program. As the political winds change, some of these states may rejoin the program, particularly if informed citizens call for better coastal management.

Every coastal state has a land-use management office (see figure 9-2). Before you build, alter topography (such as sand dunes) or vegetation, or install wells or

9-3. U.S. Army Corps of Engineers, District Offices

Atlantic Coast
Delaware
U.S. Army Engineer District, Phila-
  delphia
U.S. Custom House
2nd and Chestnut Streets
Philadelphia, PA 19106

Florida
U.S. Army Engineer District, Jack-
  sonville
P.O. Box 4970
Jacksonville, FL 32201

Georgia
U.S. Army Engineer District, Savannah
P.O. Box 889
Savannah, GA 31402

Maryland
U.S. Army Engineer District, Baltimore
P.O. Box 1715
Baltimore, MD 21203

New England
U.S. Army Corps of Engineers
New England Division
424 Trapelo Road
Waltham, MA 02154

New Jersey (Central and South)
U.S. Army Engineer District, Phila-
  delphia
U.S. Custom House
2nd and Chestnut Streets
Philadelphia, PA 19106

New York and New Jersey (North)
U.S. Army Engineer District, New York
26 Federal Plaza
New York, NY 10007

North Carolina
U.S. Army Engineer District, Wilm-
  ington
P.O. Box 1890
Wilmington, NC 28401

Puerto Rico
U.S. Army Engineer District, Jack-
  sonville
P.O. Box 4970
Jacksonville, FL 32201

South Carolina
U.S. Army Engineers District,
Charleston
P.O. Box 919
Charleston, SC 29402

Virginia
U.S. Army Engineer District, Norfolk
803 Front Street
Norfolk, VA 23510

Gulf Coast
Alabama
U.S. Army Engineer District, Mobile
P.O. Box 2288
Mobile, AL 36628

Florida
U.S. Army Engineer District, Jack-
  sonville
P.O. Box 4970
Jacksonville, FL 32201

Louisiana
U.S. Army Engineer District,
  New Orleans
P.O. Box 60267
New Orleans, LA 70160

Mississippi
U.S. Army Engineer District, Vicksburg
P.O. Box 60
Vicksburg, MS 39180

Texas
U.S. Army Engineer District, Galveston
P.O. Box 1229
Galveston, TX 77553

continued . . .

Pacific Coast

Alaska
U.S. Army Engineer District, An-
  chorage
P.O. Box 7002
Anchorage, AK 99510

California
U.S. Army Engineer District,
  Los Angeles
P.O. Box 2711
Los Angeles, CA 90053
  OR
U.S. Army Engineer District,
  San Francisco
100 McAllister Street
San Francisco, CA 94102

Hawaii
U.S. Army Corps of Engineers
Pacific Ocean Division
Building 230
Fort Shafter
Honolulu, HI 96813

Oregon
U.S. Army Engineer District, Portland
P.O. Box 2946
Portland, OR 97208

Washington
U.S. Army Engineer District, Seattle
4735 E. Marginal Way, South
Seattle, WA 98134

---

septic systems, contact your state agency. If you own waterfront property, its alteration (for example, shoreline "protection" devices) may require an additional permit
from the U.S. Army Corps of Engineers (figure 9-3). Some states are combining the
permit processes for state agencies and the army corps into a single permit application, thus cutting considerable red tape.

If you are considering the purchase of coastal property, it is worthwhile to check
on the classification of the property *before* you commit yourself to the purchase. The
state office of coastal zone management (see figure 9-2) is a good starting point.
You may also find a helpful guide in the booklet put out by H.U.D.'s Office of Interstate Land Sales, *Get the Facts Before Buying Land.*

The National Flood Insurance Act of 1968 (P.L. 90-448) as amended and altered
by the *Flood Disaster Protection Act of 1973* (P.L. 92-234) authorized the creation
of the National Flood Insurance Program (NFIP). The fundamental goal of the program was to reduce financial losses caused by flooding through an insurance program underwritten by the federal government.

Ever since the early part of this century, when the government first began to be
involved in land management, storm and flood victims have looked to the federal
government for disaster relief and reconstruction. Threatened coastal communities
have also looked to the U.S. Army Corps of Engineers to build and to maintain
structures to check shoreline erosion and to protect such development from storm
wave attack. The general public has shared the heavy financial burden for these
residents of high-risk coastal areas. The NFIP intended to reduce this tax burden by
requiring that communities adopt certain land-use and control measures in order to
qualify for federal flood insurance. The insurance program focuses on the identification of flood zones and the specification of a minimum elevation for construction
above an established flood level, plus certain flood-proofing requirements for structures.

Persons owning property in a flood zone who do not purchase flood insurance
may not, in the event of a flood, receive certain forms of federal financial assistance.

Such assistance as FHA (Federal Housing Administration) and VA (Veterans Administration) home mortgages, direct loans, and aid from the Small Business Administration or U.S. Department of Agriculture is available only if a community is participating in the National Flood Insurance Program and the property owner has purchased flood insurance. Communities not participating in the flood insurance program might also have difficulty in obtaining approval from EPA or the army corps for federal funds to support shoreline engineering, waste disposal, or water treatment systems within the flood zone. In spite of the fact that federal flood insurance is a very good deal from the home owners' standpoint, many individual home owners in qualified communities remain uninsured.

Community Entry into the National Flood Insurance Program

Establishing preliminary flood hazard areas that approximate the area inundated by a flood with a recurrence frequency of one in one hundred years, or one-percent chance of occurrence in any given year, is the first step. The Federal Emergency Management Agency (figure 9-4) will provide the community with one of their Flood Hazard Boundary Maps. Those communities with development or developable areas in the flood zone can participate by applying to enter a special "emergency program." Entry into this program allows owners of *existing* structures to purchase limited flood insurance coverage at an affordable rate. The community (incorporated town or village, county, or other governing unit) is required to adopt minimal floodplain management and construction regulations that will assure future building location and construction to be such as to minimize potential damage from flooding. Note that all structures are eligible for limited insurance under this initial "emergency program" stage, no matter how precarious their location or how poor their construction.

Once the community joins the "emergency program," the next step is a detailed engineering study of the community's flood hazards. The base flood or 100-year floodplain is mapped and divided into zones for insurance rate determination. This Flood Insurance Rate Map (FIRM) is published by the Federal Emergency Management Agency for insurance underwriters, banks and lending institutions, community officials, and the individual citizen. The community now converts from the "emergency program" to the "regular flood insurance program."

With entry into the regular program, all new structures and existing structures that undergo major modification must comply with local ordinances that meet or exceed the minimum requirements set by the National Flood Insurance Program. Do not forget that there will be additional requirements set by the state coastal zone management program, the health department, the building code, or other programs independent of flood insurance (see figure 9-2). In flood-prone areas of coastal high-hazard areas (V-zones), the key building requirement is that the lowest portion of the lowest floor beam be elevated above the base flood elevation (BFE, as shown on the Flood Insurance Rate Map).

The Flood Insurance Rate Map is detailed enough so that you can locate a specific property site, determine the base flood elevation at that site, and identify the flood hazard zone classification. These hazard zones are tinted on the map, darker tints representing higher flood hazard and classes from A (100-year flood zone) to C (lowest flood hazard). Subcategories within zones are indicated numerically (e.g., A1–A30). For more details on such maps, request *How to Read a Flood Insurance*

9-4. National Flood Insurance Program (NFIP) Addresses

National Office
National Flood Insurance Program
Federal Insurance Administration
Federal Emergency Management Agency
Washington, DC 20472

Federal Emergency Management Agency regional offices
(for each, address the Director, Office of Natural and Technological Hazards, FEMA)

Region I (CT, ME, MA, NH, RI)
J.W. McCormack Post Office & Courthouse Building
Boston, MA 02109
Phone: (617) 223-2609

Region II (NJ, NY, PR, VI)
26 Federal Plaza, Rm. 19–100
New York, NY 10278
Phone: (212) 264-4756

Region III (DE, MD, PA, VA)
Curtis Building
Sixth and Walnut Streets
Philadelphia, PA 19106
Phone: (215) 597-9581

Region IV (AL, FL, GA, MS, NC, SC)
1375 Peachtree Street, NE
Atlanta, GA 30309
Phone: (404) 881-2391

Region V (IL, IN, MI, MN, OH, WI)
One North Dearborn Street
Chicago, IL 60602
Phone: (312) 353-0757

Region VI (LA, TX)
Federal Center
Denton, TX 76201
Phone: (817) 387-5811

Region IX (CA, HI)
211 Main Street
Room 220
San Francisco, CA 94105
Phone: (415) 556-9840

Region X (AK, OR, WA)
Federal Regional Center
130 228th Street, SW
Bothell, WA 98011
Phone: (206) 481-8800

V-Zone Coverage/Individual Structure Rating
National Flood Insurance Program
Attn: V-Zone Underwriting Specialist
P.O. Box 34653
Bethesda, MD 20817
Phone: (800) 638-6620 toll free

For Copies of Post-Construction Elevation Certification
National Flood Insurance Program
Forms Order Unit
P.O. Box 34604
Bethesda, MD 20817

Rate Map (figure 9-5) from the NFIP/FEMA office in your region (see figure 9-4). Other recommended publications that you can obtain from this office include:

Design and Construction Manual for Residential Buildings in Coastal High Hazard Areas

Coastal Flood Hazards and the National Flood Insurance Program

Elevated Residential Structures

How to Read Flood Hazard Boundary Maps

In the Event of a Flood

Questions and Answers: National Flood Insurance Program

Actuarial (nonsubsidized/true risk) insurance rates are established on the basis of these zones. As the program has developed, these rates have been altered along with changes in the coastline caused by both nature and man. The trend for insurance rates in the coastal zone has been upward, and these adjustments (to make the rate actuarial) are not likely over yet. The National Flood Insurance Program has developed into the second-largest obligation against the federal treasury, behind Social Security. It is easy to see that a series of closely spaced hurricanes with widespread coastal destruction and associated severe inland flooding could result in staggering losses for the program. The fact that such climatic events have occurred in each of the last three centuries makes it imperative that the flood insurance program be actuarial and not heavily subsidized as in the past. As of 1980 the cumulative value of federal flood insurance policies was approaching $90 billion. The price tag for the total damage caused by a single *moderate* 1979 hurricane was $2 billion. Flood insurance claims were only a small part of the total, but imagine the cost of three such storms in one year with additional heavy inland flooding. It is not unlikely.

Waves: An Oceanographic Oversight

Bureaucracy does not always recognize the variations of nature. In establishing the federal flood insurance program, coastal storm-surge flooding was originally equated with inland flooding. Storm-surge flooding is the above-normal vertical rise of water level caused by winds pushing the water landward, and lower atmospheric pressure causing the rise itself. The storm-surge flood is a stillwater level, that is, the flood level assuming no waves will occur, even though, by the Army Corps of Engineers definition, the storm surge is recognized as the elevation to which high waves penetrate inland. Wave height was not included in defining the 100-year flood level for establishing insurance rates until recently, because there was no acceptable method of calculating wave heights. This is no longer the case.

By the Federal Emergency Management Agency's own estimate, the base flood elevations in use were probably closer to a 25-year flood than a 100-year standard, because waves can add significantly to actual water level. As a result, claims payments for construction in floor zones greatly exceeded income from premiums. The insurance in effect was receiving a substantial federal subsidy and was not reflecting true risk.

With the aid of the National Science Foundation, a new technique was developed to modify existing storm-surge calculations in order to include the wave height effect. An increase in base flood elevation (and required construction elevation) of 2 to 6 feet (.6 to 1.8 m) is the result on most open ocean shores.

Storm Waves and V-Zones

The V-Zone refers to all areas where there is great risk from the combined storm surge, wind-driven waves, scouring or erosion, plus the battering action of debris. The V-Zone is usually located along the open ocean shore but may also be found along shores of large embayments and sounds.

Insurance rates on all structures built or substantially improved after October 1, 1982, in the V-Zone will depend on the elevation of the structure in relation to a flood elevation that includes wave height. Existing maps are being revised to include wave heights for all V-Zones, but such mapping will not be completed until 1986.

If the insurance rate map for your area does not yet have wave heights for the V-Zone, the base flood elevation plus the wave height (BFEWH) may be calculated by an insurance agent utilizing data provided on the Post-Construction Elevation Certificate (see figure 9-4) to be submitted at the time of application for insurance. Likewise, an architect or engineer can do these calculations for you. Based on coastal engineers' knowledge of breaking waves, the following equation can be used, but is applicable only to structures in the V-Zone, and applies where the site elevation is less than the elevation of the 100-year storm water (BFE):

$$BFEWH = BFE + 0.55 (BFE - Site\ Elevation)$$

The V-Zone's critically hazardous conditions require enforcement of more restrictive conditions than in ordinary flood zones. These requirements include the elevation of structures on adequately anchored pilings or columns with the lowest portion of the building above base flood elevation plus wave height (BFEWH). The space below this floor must be free of obstructions (fill may not be used for support), or enclosed by break-away walls. Structures must be landward of the mean high-tide line, and alteration of sand dunes or mangrove stands that will increase flood damage is prohibited. No new mobile-home parks or individual mobile homes (except in existing mobile-home parks) may be located in a V-Zone. Even with such regulations, it remains to be seen whether damage claims payments will be less than premium income.

Note that the federal flood zone construction requirements are intended as minimum standards. State and local regulations can, and sometimes do, contain additional restrictions. A Florida Marine Advisory Program publication recommends a wave height adjustment formula that gives a higher elevation than the federal standard. Consider taking steps to go beyond these insurance requirements, as well as those minimums set by building codes. In fact, the Federal Emergency Management Agency provides incentive to go higher with your structure. Insurance rates are lower for each foot a structure is elevated above the wave height level, up to 4 feet (1.2 m) maximum.

A-Zone residents (inland from the V-Zone) are not totally immune from wave action either, although the threat is less severe. If you are near a V-Zone boundary you may want to approach site selection and construction as if you were in the V-Zone. A-Zone property is still subject to flooding, so elevating/flood-proofing new structures is a requirement for flood insurance. Flood-proofing an older structure is certainly a prudent thing to do; although new A-Zone structures do not require pilings or columns, such anchorage is highly recommended.

A logical conclusion at this point is to ask, "Who would build or buy a structure in a V-Zone?" It is particularly difficult to understand why some people would have their only home in such areas, as do thousands of retirees in Florida. Estimates are that 3,000 new structures a year will be built in V-Zones, and tens of thousands exist there already. Even with flood insurance and more accurately defined V-Zones, coastal development continues its rapid growth, magnifying the likelihood of a major disaster, and multiplying other demands on limited federal resources (e.g., seawalls to protect property in the V-Zone already subsidized through the federal flood insurance program). In other words, some coastal residents are protected in a double fashion with federal tax dollars: when the federally funded seawall fails, the federally funded insurance will pay for the house.

The Next Limit

The *Coastal Barrier Resources Act of 1982* prohibits new federal flood insurance for new construction or substantial improvements of structures located on *undeveloped* coastal barriers after October 1, 1983. The undeveloped coastal barriers were designated by Congress, based on preliminary maps prepared by the Department of the Interior. This law will limit the total coastal area in which federal flood insurance may be issued. Note that this legislation does *not* affect federal flood insurance on structures built prior to October 1, 1983, and that it applies only to certain undeveloped Atlantic and Gulf Coast barrier islands. The 1982 act also eliminated most other federal subsidies from these same undeveloped islands. The islands affected by this legislative act will most certainly *not* be desirable areas for future development from a home owner's viewpoint; make sure your new home is not on one of them.

One objective of this legislation is to protect the public from coastal hazards, potential loss of life, and almost certain property loss. Moreover, the move may also save long-term billions in tax dollars. Once again, however, a move to protect has set off a flurry of new coastal development. Incredibly, a nationally syndicated financial reporter advised those of her readers who own or were buying into real estate on tracts being listed as undeveloped to build on such property before the October 1, 1983, deadline! This advice ignores the purpose of the new law, namely to protect investments and possibly lives. It holds out the promise of beating the system. Those who followed this advice will have federal flood insurance at the risk of the lives of those living in the insured structure.

As was pointed out in the same article, the designation of the undeveloped areas does not prohibit construction, although most lending institutions are not likely to provide mortgages for construction in these areas. Why? Because most lenders know how unstable ocean-front environments are and invest only where there is a guarantee of return.

Obtaining Federal Flood Insurance

The following flood insurance application process for new construction and substantial improvements in V-Zones is taken from the *Federal Register*'s "Floodplain Management and Protection of Wetlands" report. The process is the same for the A-Zone, but no base flood elevation wave height is required.

1. Lender (or possibly permit official or insurance agent) informs builder that the property is in a flood area and insurance should be purchased.
2. If desired, prior to construction, builder may contact insurance agent for calculation of estimated premium at various flood elevations and designs.
3. Insurance agency provides the necessary forms to builder or buyer. (Post-Construction Elevation Certificate may be supplied by community permit office.)
4. Community official requires floodplain management criteria as condition of issuing

building permit. *Such criteria may not include wave height levels.*

5.Once a structure is built:

    a. Engineer, architect, surveyor or community official determines the applicable Flood Insurance Rate Map flood risk zone, and certifies elevation and structural design (for both insurance agent and community official). This is done by completing the Post-Construction Elevation Certificate

    b. Insurance agent submits insurance application, necessary certificates and premium to the National Flood Insurance Program.

    c. The National Flood Insurance Program reviews documents and provides insurance coverage.

We recommend that you check with your insurance agent very early in the process. Examine the flood insurance map for the location of your property with respect to the expected flood hazard.

You may wish to contact the Federal Emergency Management Agency office for your region (see figure 9-4) in search of advice or to request additional background material. We recommend the National Flood Insurance Program's pamphlet *Questions and Answers*, as well as its brochures on how to read flood maps.

Other Hazards

Federal flood insurance is emphasized here, but there is no insurance against the sea level rise and associated shoreline erosion, dune migration, overwash, inlet formation and migration, and other coastal hazards, unless there is associated flooding. You can find information on these processes and hazards, and one of the best sources of such information is your state's coastal zone management office (see figure 9-2). Your state may have an active Sea Grant Program Office, often located at the state university. Many sea grant offices will have specific site information on erosion rates, overwash frequency, inlet history, and water quality. In addition, other national organizations and federal agencies provide pertinent information (figure 9-5).

9-5: Other Information Sources on Coastal Zone Management

Federal Agencies/Offices
Office of Ocean and
    Coastal Resources Management
National Oceanic and
    Atmospheric Administration
2001 Wisconsin Avenue, NW
Washington, DC 20235

Eastern National Cartographic
    Information Center (E-NCIC)
U.S. Geological Survey
536 National Center
Reston, VA 22092
Phone: (703) 860-6336
(*map information*)

Coastal Barriers Task Force
Department of the Interior
Washington, DC 20240

Environmental Protection Agency
401 M Street, SW
Washington, DC 20460

Council for Environmental Quality
    and Hazard Mitigation
500 C Street, SW
Washington, DC 20472

Environmental Organizations
Natural Resources Defense Council
1725 I Street, NW, Suite 600
Washington, DC 20006

National Wildlife Federation
1412 16th Street, NW
Washington, DC 20036

Conservation Foundation
1717 Massachusetts Avenue, NW
Washington, DC 20036

National Park Service
780 Pension Building
440 G Street, NW
Washington, DC 20243

U.S. Fish and Wildlife Service
Department of the Interior
18th and C Streets, NW
Washington, DC 20240

Flood Insurance Coverage

Your regular home owner's insurance is *not* a flood insurance policy. Although your home owner's insurance may cover structural damage from wind or wind-driven rain (check your policy over with your insurance agent), it does not cover losses caused by the general and temporary flooding of normally dry land. Federal flood insurance offers the potential flood victim low-cost coverage against flood loss.

Federal flood insurance covers losses resulting from the flooding of coastal areas from storm surge, overflow of streams or tidal water, or unusual and rapid accumulation of surface water from any source. This form of insurance also includes coverage of damage resulting from mudslides caused by the accumulation of water on or under the ground, but it does not cover landslides. The latter is important to property owners on the West Coast or other areas where the shore is bluffed or property is threatened by unstable slopes. Both mudslides and landslides are likely in such areas, but only mudslides fall into the realm of flood insurance.

Flood insurance offers a less expensive, surer, and broader form of protection than does reliance on possible postdisaster loans or other assistance. If you own a residential, business, or farm structure that is principally above ground in an area of potential flooding, inquire as to the availability of flood insurance for both the structure and the contents.

Checklist of Coverage and Claims

1. *Check the location of your property on the federal Flood Insurance Rate Map or the Flood Hazard Boundary Map for your area. If your property lies in a flood-prone area,* you must purchase flood insurance to be eligible for any form of federal or federally related financial building or acquisition assistance *(e.g., FHA mortgages or SBA loans). Unless you are independently wealthy and willing to assume the total risk for flood loss, see your insurance agent and purchase flood insurance.*
2. *You will need a separate policy for each structure.*
3. *You may insure contents as well as the structure. Renters need to insure only contents.*
4. *Owners of condominium units (traditional townhouses or rowhouses) may insure their individual units (structure and/or contents).*

5. Mobile homes also are eligible for coverage provided they are on foundations, whether or not permanent. The wheels need not be removed.
6. If you purchase insurance on contents, make an itemized list of your personal property, including furnishings, clothing, and valuables. Make a photographic record of both the inside (photos of rooms with contents list on back of photo) and outside of your home. Such records may assist adjusters settling claims, will help prove uninsured losses that are tax deductible, and will assist you in determining how much coverage you will need. These records are useful for all types of insurance (e.g., fire, wind, and flood). If you have closed in the space under your house, you may want a photographic record to prove that the enclosure walls were the break-away type.
7. The following are not eligible for federal flood insurance: travel trailers and campers, fences, retaining walls, seawalls, septic tanks, and outdoor swimming pools; gas and liquid storage tanks, wharves, piers, bulkheads and similar structures; crops, shrubbery, land, livestock, roads; motor vehicles.
8. Keep your insurance policies and records (lists) of personal property in a safe place, such as a safe deposit box. If they blow away with your house in a hurricane, you will be delayed in recovering compensation, and such compensation may be reduced because nothing remains from which to verify your claim.
9. Know the name and location of the agency that issued the policy, and your agent, and tell some member of your family.
10. Federal flood insurance rates are set by the federal government. One insurance company or broker cannot charge you more than another, although the personalized service from one agent to another may vary.
11. Coverage generally does not become effective until five days from the date of application (fixed waiting period), except when property already covered is purchased.
12. In the event that your home, apartment, business, and/or contents have been destroyed or damaged, immediately call the insurance agency who sold the flood insurance policy. After consulting with you, the agent will assign an adjuster to inspect your property. Remember that in a disaster, such as after a hurricane, the adjusters will handle the most serious loss claims first.
13. In the time between flooding and waiting for an adjuster's inspection of a claim, it may be necessary to take cleanup/temporary repair steps to prevent additional property loss.

The remaining items are possible postflood steps that may be necessary and will relate to insurance. See also the storm checklists in Chapter 8.

14. Check your building for structural damage. Make temporary repairs to prevent collapse or further loss from rain, wind, or looting. The expense of such repairs also is covered by the flood policy, but you will need a record of receipts to document the repair cost. Take photographs of the damage prior to the temporary repair for additional documentation.
15. Before entering a damaged building, let it air out to remove escaped gas and foul odors. Gas leaks and live wires may be present. Do not use an open flame. Make sure electricity and gas supplies are shut off. Do not switch on lights or appliances until a utilities serviceman has checked your system.

16. *Begin immediate cleanup, even if your insurance adjuster has not surveyed the damage. Before discarding any perishable items that pose a health problem, make both a written and photographic record of the items. Damaged appliances, furniture, and hard goods should be hosed off and retained for the insurance adjuster's inspection. The adjuster will make recommendations as to repair or disposal of damaged items as well as resolving cash claims.*
17. *Remove sand and mud as soon as possible, preferably while still wet, in order for walls and floors to dry. Open all doors and windows to aid drying. Rugs and carpets should be dried quickly and thoroughly. Cleanup is necessary to reveal all damage.*

The Umbrella of Federal Emergency Management Agency

In 1979 President Jimmy Carter established the Federal Emergency Management Agency (FEMA) by executive order. This action consolidated responsibility for all national emergency preparedness, hazard mitigation, and disaster preparedness under a single agency. The National Flood Insurance Program was moved from Housing and Urban Development jurisdiction to FEMA in 1979 to join related programs.

FEMA's major objectives are to provide single-agency responsibility and contact with state and local government, to enhance the dual use of resources at all levels of government in planning and response to both peacetime and attack emergencies, and to provide greater effectiveness in hazard mitigation, preparedness, planning, relief, and recovery operations. The latter includes weather emergencies and geologic hazards, not the least of which are coastal hazards.

FEMA's authority does not end with the administration of flood insurance policies. The agency administers a state assistance program to aid states in improving floodplain management capabilities. It may negotiate purchase of insured real property that has suffered repeated damages from flooding, and turn such property over to the community or state where it will remain as open space. Likewise, a flood-damaged structure that cannot be rebuilt because of a local ordinance could be declared a "constructive total loss." A claim payment could be made up to the total amount of the policy provided that the site was converted to open space use. This option has not been used in the coastal zone but should not be ruled out. In South Nags Head, North Carolina, FEMA paid to have cottages moved back from the edge of a rapidly eroding shoreline *before* they fell victim to a retreating sand bluff. This approach to hazard mitigation could see wider application but only where structures are on deep lots.

FEMA also: provides technical assistance to save lives, protect property, ensure public health and safety; participates in relief to areas declared disaster areas by the president; provides aid and assistance to restore public facilities after a disaster; and acts as lead agency in governmental interagency disaster planning and recovery operations. Responsibilities extend well beyond this brief outline, including training and education programs. One important thrust in this latter area is the Hurricane Awareness Program. Another area is the Hurricane Preparedness Program, which provides funds for developing emergency evacuation plans in selected coastal areas.

In spite of improved awareness and more restrictions to qualify for insurance, and in spite of some site restrictions under the Coastal Zone Management program and similar hurdles, dangerous coastal zone development still has not really slowed. An additional step in trying to assure minimal structural integrity is the requirement of following an appropriate building code.

Building Codes: Minimum Safety Requirements

For at least forty centuries, the safety of building construction has been a matter of public concern in civilized countries. From this concern have grown rules and regulations called building codes. The most ancient of these codes about which we have firm information is the Code of Hammurabi, a famous king and lawmaker of Babylon in about 2100 B.C. In Babylon the architect was liable to pay for his mistakes with his life (figure 9-6). Fortunately for today's architects, modern codes are not quite so drastic.

The earliest building laws were concerned with collapse. For instance, the Romans restricted the height of buildings after the failure of high-rise speculative apartments built during the reigns of Julius and Augustus Caesar. Laws were passed that limited the heights of such structures to 70 feet (21 m), and later, when 70 feet was found unsatisfactory, to 60 feet (18 m).

The Romans had an effective way of assuring good construction on their stone arch bridges. These bridges were constructed, at least in part, by private enterprise, and the contractor had to put up a deposit to assure that the bridge would not collapse. At the end of forty years, if the bridge was still in good shape, the deposit would be returned. The Pons Fabricius, now known as the Ponte Quattro Capi, was built over the Tiber in Rome during the consulship of Cicero, 62 B.C., at the height of the Roman republic. It is a stone arch bridge that still survives intact, and contains an inscription recording the understanding that the contractor would have his deposit returned over a period of forty years. One can only wonder if the contractor lived long enough to collect his deposit, but it must have been an effective way of obtaining solid construction.

Later, regulations were introduced to prevent fire and restrict its spread, notably in the city of London in the fourteenth century. Regulations on sanitation, light, and ventilation are a modern development. The general lack of ancient codes or regulations provided the opportunity for architects and builders to experiment with new designs and materials, and in some cases to learn from their mistakes.

Most modern communities require that new construction adhere to the provisions of a recognized building code. Compiled by knowledgeable engineers, politicians, and architects, these codes regulate the design and construction of buildings and the quality of building materials. If you plan to build in an area that does not follow such a code, you would be wise to insist that your builder do so, to meet your own requirements. Local building officials in storm hazard areas often adopt national codes that contain building requirements for protection against high wind and water. The director of the National Hurricane Center has noted, however, that most of the codes in use do *not* give protection against storm surge.

It is emphasized that the purpose of these codes is to provide *minimum* standards to safeguard lives, health, and property. These codes protect you from yourself as well as your neighbor.

The existence of a building code is not a guarantee of safety; a code is only as good as its enforcement. Very frequently, perhaps more often than not, beach community building codes are too lightly enforced or enforced by individuals not well

A. If a builder build a house for a man and do not make its construction firm and the house which he has built collapse and cause the death of the owner of the house — that builder shall be put to death.

B. If it cause the death of the son of the owner of the house — they shall put to death a son of that builder.

C. If it cause the death of a slave of the owner of the house — he shall give to the owner of the house a slave of equal value.

D. If it destroy property, he shall restore whatever it destroyed, and because he did not make the house which he built firm and it collapsed, he shall rebuild the house which collapsed at his own expense.

E. If a builder build a house for a man and do not make its construction meet the requirements and a wall fall in, that builder shall strengthen the wall at his own expense.

Translated by R.F. Harper.
"Code of Hammurabi" p. 83 - seq.

Jacob Feld 1922.

9-6. Code of Hammurabi, about 2100 B.C. (From Feld, *Construction Failure*)

qualified to be building inspectors. Development is often rapid, compressed into the off-season, or during posthurricane reconstruction, and even well-qualified building inspectors may have difficulty keeping up with code inspections.

Building codes are necessary for guiding those people who simply do not know any better from cutting corners and thus their chances for a safe and sturdy structure (figure 9-7). It is emphasized that a code should contain the basic principles and guidelines to be followed, so written as to achieve safety and yet to permit creative

9-7. The value of a building code in protecting uninformed persons from their own actions is illustrated by
this newspaper advertisement. If the 2" x 2" lumber for sale were to be used in place of the 2" x 4"
lumber required by code, the result would be a much weaker house, vulnerable to high winds and water.
This ad appeared in a newspaper located in a region devastated by Hurricane Camille.

thinking and innovation on the part of the designer. This last part is important, for if
every nut and bolt were spelled out, the designer's hands would be tied, forcing him
or her to follow a set of rules in the same way an unthinking computer would design a
structure.

On the other hand, large structures usually will be engineered, while houses, dwellings, small shops, and other small structures rarely have the benefit of the calculations of such a professional. The builder of smaller structures often does not have
the theoretical knowledge to convert a code that lists only basic principles into brick
and mortar. Hence, a code must spell out sufficient details to guide the nontechnical
builder to a safe structure, yet give leeway for the theoretician's creative thinking.

Examples of major building codes and standards in use in the United States
follow:

The Standard Building Code

(formerly, Southern Standard Building
Code, used mainly on the southeast and Gulf coasts)
Southern Bldg. Code Congress International, Inc.
900 Montclair Road
Birmingham, AL 35213

The Uniform Building Code

(used mainly on the West Coast)
International Conference of Building
Officials
5360 South Workman Mill Road
Whittier, CA 90601

The Basic Building Code

(or BOCA Basic Building Code)
Building Officials and Code Administrators International, Inc.
17926 South Halstead Street
Homewood, IL 60430

The ANSI-A58.1: "Building Code Requirements for Minimum Design Loads in Buildings and Other Structures"

(by the American National Standards
Institute; not a code per se, in that
it is not a legal document by action
of a political body, but recommended in formulating codes)
American National Standards Institute
1430 Broadway
New York, New York 10018

NAVFAC DM-2: "Design Manual, Structural Engineering"

Naval Facilities Engineering Command
Department of the Navy
Washington, DC 20390

The National Building Code of the American Insurance Association
85 John Street
New York, New York 10038

The South Florida Building Code
(recognized as one of the most stringent U.S. codes, often used as a guide by other coastal communities)
Building Department, Dade County Courthouse
Dade County, FL 33130

The H.U.D. Code
("The Complete Guide to the H.U.D. Mobile Home Program," which includes "The Federal Mobile Home Construction and Safety Standards" code, a highly specific set of regulations for all manufactured houses including mobile homes; became law on June 15, 1976)
Department of Housing and Urban Development
451 7th Street S.W.
Washington, DC 20410

Comparison of Some of the Codes

None of the major building codes specify the force generated by storm surge, flooding of rivers, waves, or waterborne debris that a structure should resist. The National Flood Insurance Program specifies that new buildings are to be elevated or flood-proofed above certain flood levels. These levels are derived from FEMA's detailed on-site engineering surveys in the community and are portrayed on flood maps.

The community must require that all new construction and substantial improvements to existing structures conform to the rules, that is, in most instances be elevated to above the 100-year flood elevation shown on the map. Nonresidential structures in A-Zones can be flood-proofed in lieu of elevation. These requirements are met through a local building code.

Naturally, the foundations must not only raise the structure above the flood level and withstand the hydrodynamic forces of flowing water, but must also resist the impact of waterborne debris and the scouring effects of wave and storm surge action. There is literature that offers guidance on this, but it does not exist in the major codes. The codes do, however, treat wind forces in detail. For waterborne debris and scouring, we need to turn to other treatises, such as the Texas Coastal and Marine Council's *Model Minimum Hurricane-Resistant Building Standards for the Texas Gulf Coast*, with its chapters on wave and scour action and battering by debris.

The major national and certain regional building codes in the United States each use different methods of obtaining the wind loads to be used in designing a structure. Following is an overview of some of these methods.

The Standard Building Code uses a map (figure 3-34) to obtain an "annual extreme fastest-mile speed 30 feet [9 m] above ground—100-year mean recurrent interval." This is the highest, fastest speed of one mile (1.6 km) of air passing a weather station in a given year. Given this speed and the height above ground, a table (figure 3-35) is entered to obtain a basic wind-load pressure in pounds per square foot.

This basic wind-load pressure is then modified by "shape factors" (figure 3-36) to determine the design load. The wind-caused pressure felt by an object varies with its shape. A cylindrical object, for example, feels much less pressure than a flat surface.

The formula provided for obtaining the basic wind-load pressure is as follows:

$$P = 0.00256 \times V^2 \times (H/30)^{2/7}$$

where

P is the pressure in pounds per square foot (psf) from the force of the wind;
V is the wind speed in mph;
H is the height above grade (in feet) of the area where the pressure is being computed.

This formula is applicable only to heights 30 feet (9 m) or greater. Note that for a height of 30 feet the last term becomes unity and drops out, leaving the simplified formula: pressure P varies directly with the square of the velocity, V^2.

Appendix D of the Standard Building Code covers certain hurricane requirements such as continuity, stability, and anchorage, all related to the force of the wind.

The Uniform Building Code uses a map that gives an "allowable resultant wind pressure" for all parts of the continental United States. This figure is the combined inward and outward pressures on the exterior surfaces of an ordinary square building at 30 feet (9 m) above ground.

Then a table provides "wind pressure for various heights above ground." These values are used for horizontal pressure and uplift pressure on the building surfaces.

There are multiplying factors for certain structures such as chimneys, tanks, and towers, but no "shape factor" to the degree found in the Standard Code or South Florida Code.

The Basic Building Code uses a map similar but not identical to that in the Standard Code, which provides "basic wind speeds in mile per hour" at 30 feet (9 m) above ground. Unlike the Standard Code, whose speeds are based on 100-year recurrences, these basic speeds are based on a 50-year recurrence interval and hence are usually less (smaller). Given the basic wind speed and the height, a table is entered to provide the pressure in pounds per square foot.

Modifying factors are given for various types of structures such as signs, tanks, towers, chimneys, and for distribution on windward, leeward, and inclined surfaces. There is no special section on hurricanes, but they are recognized in a general way thus: "In geographical regions where local records indicate higher wind loads than established (by the map and table) the higher wind load shall be used." And also: "These provisions do not apply to structures of unusual shape, exposure, or structural characteristics. . . . In such cases special engineering investigations are required."

The National Building Code has adopted ANSI-A58.1, "Building Code Requirements for Minimum Design Loads in Buildings and Other Structures," in its entirety for wind loads.

The South Florida Building Code is similar in many ways to the Standard Building Code except that, being applicable to a given area, the wind velocity is specified as 120 mph. The basic wind-load pressure is obtained from the same formula, $P = 0.00256 \times V^2 \times (H/30)^{2/7}$, and this is to be multiplied by "shape factors" that are not always the same as those specified in the Standard Code.

Also covered are such wind-related items as stability, tie beams in masonry walls, permissible glass areas, and similar structures.

It would seem that of the above codes, the Standard Building Code and the South Florida Building Code are best suited to those geographical areas subject to hurricanes. Individual states or communities may have modifications of these codes or unique codes specifically for the coastal zone; the engineering firm of Dames and Moore, for example, has developed a tsunami building code for Hawaii (see also Appendix F of FEMA's *Design and Construction Manual for Residential Buildings in Coastal High Hazard Areas*). Check with your architect, builder, or state coastal zone office (see figure 9-2) for details.

Government Aid After the Storm: Helping You Recover

After a major storm, the president of the United States is likely to declare the affected area a major disaster area. Individuals, businessmen, and farmers in this area may be eligible for a wide variety of federal and state assistance programs. Quite often people are not aware of this and do not take advantage of available assistance.

After Hurricane Frederick hit the Gulf Coast and points north in September, 1979, the Federal Emergency Management Agency published a list of federal, state, and local agencies that could provide services or assistance to those who suffered losses. Although it was local in its applicability, other areas will have similar services that you should know about.

Unfortunately, much of this aid is used to stimulate a repetition of the earlier mistakes of unsafe development.

Future Policy Changes Will Affect Your Property

For forty years, regulatory policies have grown rapidly, although not as fast as development itself. New crises arise daily as the result of new problems brought on by development or the discovery that some policies do not achieve the goals for which they were designed. Thus, it is reasonable to expect that more regulation is in the offing for the coastal dweller. Do not expect a sustaining of the status quo. Ask any long-time coastal property-owner about the winds of change, natural and political.

Regulation changes will be enacted to improve relative safety through hazard mitigation and controlled development. Structures rebuilt or repaired after destruction or damage from storms, floods, and shoreline erosion will have to meet the new rules for local floodplain management regulations, coastal zone management, setback, health requirements, and other regulations that may be far different than when the original structure was built. Another possibility is that the community may take backward steps and loosen regulations controlling certain types of developments.

You cannot expect any island or coastal community you may buy into or build on to remain as it is. Living near the beach at a time of rising sea level will grow more costly to the individual with time. But living near the beach can be one of life's most beautiful experiences. Just make sure you know what you are doing.

The International System (SI) of Metric Units

Prefixes

Prefix	Symbol	Multiplication Factor
kilo	k	$1000 = 10^3$
centi	c	$0.01 = 10^{-2}$

SI Units

Quantity	Name of Unit	SI Symbol
length	meter	m
area	square meter	m^2
mass	kilogram	kg
force	Newton	N
time	second, hour	s, h
velocity	kilometer per hour	km/h
stress, pressure	Pascal = Newtons per square meter	$Pa = N/m^2$

Conversion to SI from US Customary Units

Quantity	Units	
	US Customary	SI Metric
length	1 in 1 ft	2.54 cm 0.3048 m
area	$1\ in^2$ $1\ ft^2$	$6.45\ cm^2$ $0.09290\ m^2$
velocity	1 mph (miles per hour)	1.609 km/h
force or weight	1 lb	4.448 N
mass	1 lb (mass)	0.4536 kg
stress or pressure	1 psi (pounds per square inch) 1 psf (pounds per square foot)	$6.895\ kN/m^2 = $ 6.895 kPa $47.88\ N/m^2 = 47.88$ Pa

Bibliography

Chapter 1

Adams, J.W.R. "Florida's Beach Program at the Crossroads." *Shore and Beach* 49 (1981):10–14.

Bascom, W. *Waves and Beaches*. Garden City, NY: Doubleday, Anchor Press, 1980.
> Perhaps the best popular book available on wave and beach principles and interactions.

Bird, E.C.F. *Coasts*. Cambridge, MA: Massachusetts Institute of Technology Press, 1969.

Davis, R.A. *Coastal Sedimentary Environments*. New York: Springer-Verlag, 1978.

Ingle, J.C. *The Movement of Beach Sand*. New York: Elsevier, 1966.

Kaufman, W., and Pilkey, O.H., Jr. *The Beaches Are Moving*. Garden City, NY: Doubleday, Anchor Press, 1979.

King, C.A.M. *Beaches and Coasts*. New York: St. Martin's Press, 1972.
> This volume, along with the following book by Komar, are the standard technical textbooks for courses in coastal geology.

Komar, P.D. *Beach Processes and Sedimentation*. Englewood Cliffs, NJ: Prentice-Hall, 1976.

Leatherman, S.P. "Barrier Beach Development: A Perspective on the Problem." *Shore and Beach* 49 (1981):2–9.

McCormick, C.L.; Neal, W.J.; Pilkey, O.H., Jr.; and Pilkey, O.H., Sr. *Living with the New York Shore*. Durham, NC: Duke University Press, 1983.

Morton, R.A.; Pilkey, O.H., Jr.; Pilkey, O.H., Sr.; and Neal, W.J. *Living with the Texas Shore*. Durham, NC: Duke University Press, 1983.

Pilkey, O.H., Jr.; Neal, W.J.; Pilkey, O.H., Sr.; and Riggs, S.R. *From Currituck to Calabash: Living with North Carolina's Barrier Islands*. 2nd ed. Durham, NC: Duke University Press, 1982.

Pilkey, O.H., Jr.; Pilkey, O.H., Sr.; and Turner, R. *How to Live with an Island*. Raleigh,

NC: Science and Technology Section, North Carolina Department of Natural and
Economic Resources, 1975.

Schwartz, M.L. *The Encyclopedia of Beaches and Coastal Environments*. Strouds-
burg, PA: Hutchinson Ross Publishing Company, 1982.

Shepard, F.P. *Submarine Geology*. 3rd ed. New York: Harper and Row, 1973.

Shepard, F.P., and Wanless, H.R. *Our Changing Coastlines*. New York: McGraw-Hill,
1971.

A state-by-state summary of the changes occurring along all of the continental
U.S. shorelines. Illustrated with many aerial photos.

Chapter 2

Bolt, B.A.; Horn, W.L.; MacDonald, G.A.; and Scott, F.A. *Geological Hazards*. 2nd
ed. New York: Springer-Verlag, 1977.

Clark, J.R. *Coastal Ecosystem Management*. New York: John Wiley and Sons,
1977.

California, Department of Navigation and Ocean Development. *Assessment and
Atlas of Shoreline Erosion along the California Coast*. Sacramento, CA: 1977.

Dolan, R.; Hayden, B.; and Lins, B. "Barrier Islands." *American Scientist* 68
(1980):16–25.

Godfrey, P.J. "Barrier Beaches of the East Coast." *Oceanus* 19 (1976):27–40.

Leatherman, S.P., ed. *Barrier Islands from the Gulf of St. Lawrence to the Gulf of
Mexico*. New York: Academic Press, 1979.

MacLeish, W.H. "The Coast." *Oceanus* 23 (1980):1–67.

McHarg, I. *Design with Nature*. Garden City, NY: Doubleday and Company, 1969.

Pilkey, O.H., Jr., and Neal, W.J. "Barrier Island Hazard Mapping." *Oceanus* 23
(1980):38–46.

Segrest, R.L., et al. *Handbook: Building in the Coastal Environment*. Brunswick, GA:
Georgia Coastal Area and Planning Commission, 1975.

Swift, D.J.P. "Barrier Island Genesis: Evidence from the Central Atlantic Shelf, Eastern U.S.A." *Sedimentary Geology* 14 (1975):1–43.

United States, Department of the Interior, Heritage Conservation and Recreation
Service. *Report of the Barrier Islands Work Group*; 1979.

United States, Department of the Interior, National Park Service. *Barrier Island Development*. Prepared for the National Park Service by S.P. Leatherman (Eastham,
MA: Cape Cod National Seashore, 1979).

United States, Department of the Interior, United States Geological Survey. *Hurricane
Frederick Tidal Floods of September 12–13, 1979, along the Gulf Coast*. Pre-
pared for the U.S.G.S. Hydrologic Investigation Atlas (HA-621 through HA-641) by
L.R. Bohman and J.C. Scott, 1980.

United States, Department of the Interior, United States Geological Survey. *Hurricane
Camille Tidal Floods of August, 1969, along the Gulf Coast*. Prepared for the
U.S.G.S. Hydrologic Investigation Atlas (HA-395 through HA-408) by K.V. Wilson
and J.W. Hudson, 1969.

United States, Department of the Interior, United States Geological Survey; Department of Commerce, National Oceanic and Atmospheric Administration. *Coastal
Mapping Handbook*. Edited for the U.S.G.S. and NOAA by M.Y. Ellis, 1978.

Yanev, P. *Peace of Mind in Earthquake Country*. San Francisco: Chronicle Books,
1974.

Chapter 3

American Wood Preservers Institute. *FHA Pole Construction*. McLean, VA: American Wood Preservers Institute, 1975.

Dade County, Board of County Commissioners. *The South Florida Building Code*. Dade County, FL: 1979.

International Conference of Building Officials. *The Uniform Building Code*. Whittier, CA: International Conference of Building Officials, 1973.

Masonry Institute of America. *Standard Details for One-Story Concrete Block Residences* (Publication 701). Los Angeles: Masonry Institute of America, 1977.

Masonry Institute of America. *Masonry Design Manual* (Publication 601). Los Angeles: Masonry Institute of America, 1979.

The first of the two references above is written for the layman and the designer. The second is a comprehensive, well-presented manual covering all types of masonry, including brick, concrete block, glazed structural units, stone, and veneer, which will probably be of more interest to the designer than to the layman.

Research Council on Performance of Structures. *Structural Failures: Modes, Causes, Responsibilities*. New York: American Society of Civil Engineers, 1973. See especially the chapter "Failure of Structures Due to Extreme Winds," pp. 49–77.

Saffir, H.S. "Hurricane Exposes Structure Flaws." *Civil Engineering*, February, 1971, pp. 54–55.

Southern Building Code Congress International, Inc. *The Standard Building Code*. Birmingham, AL: Southern Building Code Congress International, 1979.

Texas, Coastal and Marine Council. *Building Construction Checklist for the Texas Coast and Shoreline*. Austin, TX: 1978.

Texas, Coastal and Marine Council. *Model Minimum Hurricane-Resistant Building Standards for the Texas Gulf Coast*. Austin, TX: 1976.

United States, Department of Agriculture, United States Forest Service. *Houses Can Resist Hurricanes*, Research Paper FPL 33. Prepared for the U.S. Forest Service by L.O. Anderson and W.R. Smith (Madison, WI: Forest Laboratory, 1965).

An excellent paper, with numerous details on construction in general, including fastenings. Pole-house construction is treated in particular detail.

United States, Department of Agriculture, United States Forest Service. *Wood Structures Survive Hurricane Camille's Winds*, Research Paper FPL 123. (Madison, WI: Forest Products Laboratory, 1969).

United States, Department of Agriculture, United States Forest Service. *Long-Time Performance of Trussed Rafters with Different Connection Systems*, Research Paper FPL 204. Prepared for the U.S. Forest Service by T.L. Wilkinson (Madison, WI: Forest Products Laboratory, 1978).

United States, Department of Commerce, National Technical Information Services. *Checklist for Building Construction on Shore-Area Property*, Report No. 20. Prepared for NTIS by the University of Florida, 1977.

United States, Department of Defense, Defense Civil Preparedness Agency. *Wind-Resistant Design Concepts for Residences*, Report TR-83. Prepared for DCPA by D.B. Ward, 1976.

Vivid sketches and illustrations display construction problems and methods of tying structures to the ground. Aimed chiefly at home owners and builders, a large part of the text and illustrations is devoted to methods of strengthening residences. Recommendations are offered for relatively inexpensive modifications that will increase the safety of structures subject to severe winds. Chapter 8, "How to Calculate Wind Forces and Design Wind-Resistant Structures," should be of particular interest to the designer.

United States, Department of Defense, Defense Civil Preparedness Agency. *Interior Guidelines for Building Occupant Protection from Tornadoes and Extreme Winds*, Report TR-83A; 1975.

This supplement to Report TR-83 contains guidelines for architects and engineers based on a concept of strengthened interior spaces in public buildings and other high-occupancy buildings, including schools.

United States, Department of Defense, Defense Civil Preparedness Agency. *Tornado Protection—Selecting and Designing Safe Areas in Buildings*, Report TR-83B; 1976.

Less technical and more pictorial than Report TR-83A, this is intended for architects, engineers, and building administrators. One of its goals is to help determine the places in buildings offering the greatest protection against high winds caused not only by tornadoes, but also by hurricanes and other severe storms. Although TR-83A and TR-83B concentrate on larger buildings, they are of interest to the general public insofar as they provide a means by which to check on a building administrator's thoroughness in ensuring adequate protection in the school, office, or high-rise building he/she is responsible for.

United States, Department of Housing and Urban Development, Federal Insurance Administration. *Elevated Residential Structures Reducing Flood Damage through Building Design: A Guide Manual*; 1976.

This manual is intended for those who wish to design, build, and/or legislate in areas with special flood hazards to meet the requirements of the National Flood Insurance Program of September, 1976, FIA-184. FEMA will revise this publication as requirements change.

United States, Federal Emergency Management Agency. *Design and Construction Manual for Residential Buildings in Coastal High Hazard Areas*, FIA-7; 1981.

Walker, G.R.; Minor, J.E.; and Marshall, R.D. "The Darwin Cyclone: Valuable Lesson in Structural Design." *Civil Engineering*, December, 1975, pp. 82–86.

Walton, T.L., Jr. *Hurricane-Resistant Construction for Homes*. Gainesville, FL: Florida Sea Grant Publication, University of Florida, 1976.

A good summary of hurricanes, storm surge, and damage assessment, with guidelines for hurricane-resistant construction.

Chapter 4 _____

American Society of Civil Engineers. *Planning and Design of Tall Buildings*, vol. 2. New York: American Society of Civil Engineers, 1972.

Southern Building Code Congress International, Inc. *The Standard Building Code*. Birmingham, AL: Southern Building Code Congress International, Inc., 1979.

Texas, Coastal and Marine Council. *Model Minimum Hurricane-Resistant Building Standards for the Texas Gulf Coast*. Austin, TX: 1976.

United States, Department of Defense, Defense Civil Preparedness Agency. *Wind-Resistant Design Concepts for Residences*, Report TR-83. Prepared for DCPA by D.B. Ward, 1976.

See annotation for this entry under Chapter 3.

United States, Department of Defense, Defense Civil Preparedness Agency. *Interior Guidelines for Building Occupant Protection from Tornadoes and Extreme Winds*, Report TR-83A; 1975.

See annotation for this entry under Chapter 3.

United States, Department of Defense, Defense Civil Preparedness Agency. *Tornado Protection—Selecting and Designing Safe Areas in Buildings*, Report TR-83B; 1976.

See annotation for this entry under Chapter 3.

Chapter 5

American National Standards Institute. *Standard for Mobile Homes*, A119.1. New York: American National Standards Institute, 1974.

California, Seismic Safety Commission. *Seismic Protection for Mobile Homes*, Document SSC-46. Sacramento, CA: 1980.

National Fire Protection Association. *Standard for Installation of Mobile Homes, Including Mobile Home Park Requirements*, Paper No. 501A. Boston: National Fire Protection Association, 1975.

North Carolina, Department of Insurance. *Regulations for Mobile Homes and Modular Housing*. Raleigh, NC: 1979.

Pennington, W., and McDonald, J.R. *An Engineering Analysis: Mobile Homes in Windstorms*. Lubbock, TX: Texas Tech University, 1978.

United States, Department of Defense, Defense Civil Preparedness Agency. *Protecting Mobile Homes from High Winds*, Report TR-75; 1974.

United States, Department of Defense, Defense Civil Preparedness Agency. *Suggested Technical Requirements for Mobile-Home Tiedown Ordinances*, Report TM-73-1; 1974.

United States, Department of Housing and Urban Development. "Mobile Homes Construction and Safety Standards." *Federal Register* 40 (1975):58752–92.

Chapter 6

American Society of Civil Engineers. *Planning and Design of Tall Buildings*, vol. 2. New York: American Society of Civil Engineers, 1972.

American Society of Civil Engineers. *Structural Failures: Modes, Causes, Responsibilities*. New York: American Society of Civil Engineers, 1973.

Dade County, Board of County Commissioners. *The South Florida Building Code*. Dade County, FL: 1979.

Feld, J. *Construction Failure*. New York: John Wiley and Sons, 1968.

MacLeish, W.H. "Our Barrier Islands Are the Key Issue in 1980." *Smithsonian* 11 (1980):46–59.

Research Council on Performance on Structures. *Structural Failures: Modes, Causes, Responsibilities*. New York: American Society of Civil Engineers, 1973. The chapter "Failure of Structures Due to Extreme Winds" is especially appropriate.

Saffir, H.S. *Design Construction Requirements for Hurricane-Resistant Construction*, Preprint 2830. New York: American Society of Civil Engineers, 1977.

United States, Federal Emergency Management Agency. *Design and Construction Manual for Residential Buildings in Coastal High Hazard Areas*, FIA-7; 1981.

Chapter 7 _____

Bruun, P. "Sea Level Rise as a Cause of Shore Erosion." *Journal of Waterways and Harbor Division, American Society of Civil Engineers Proceedings* 88 (1962):117–30.

Emery, K.O. "Relative Sea Levels from Tide Gauge Levels Records." *Proceedings National Academy of Science* 77 (1980):6968–72.

Etkins, R., and Epstein, E.S. "The Rise of Global Mean Sea Level as an Indication of Climate Change." *Science* 215 (1982):287–89.

Fujita, T.T. "Proposed Characterization of Tornadoes and Hurricanes by Area and Intensity." SMRP Research Paper, University of Chicago, 1971.

Gornitz, V.; Lebedeff, S.; and Hansen, J. "Global Sea Level Trend in the Past Century." *Science* 215 (1982):1611–14.

Marshall, E. "By Flood If Not by Fire, CEQ Says." *Science* 221 (1980):463.

Pilkey, O.H. "Geologists, Engineers, and the Rising Sea Level." *Northeastern Geology* 3 (1980):150–58.

Pilkey, O.H., Jr.; Neal, W.J.; Pilkey, O.H., Sr.; and Riggs, S.R. *From Currituck to Calabash: Living with North Carolina's Barrier Islands*. 2nd ed. Durham, NC: Duke University Press, 1982.

Revelle, R. "Carbon Dioxide and World Climate." *Scientific American*, 247 (1982):35–42.

Simpson, R.H., and Riehl, H. *The Hurricane and Its Impact*. Baton Rouge, LA: Louisiana State University Press, 1981.

Swift, D.J.P., and Stanley, D., eds. *Marine Sediment Transport and Environmental Management*. New York: John Wiley and Sons, 1976.

United States, Department of Commerce, National Oceanic and Atmospheric Administration, National Weather Service. *The Deadliest, Costliest, and Most Intense United States Hurricanes of This Century (and Other Frequently Requested Hurricane Facts)*, NOAA Technical Memorandum NWS NHC 7. Prepared for NOAA by P.J. Hebert and G. Taylor (Miami, FL: 1978).

United States, Department of Commerce, National Oceanic and Atmospheric Administration, National Weather Service. *Hurricane Experience Levels of Coastal County Populations—Texas to Maine*, NWS Southern Regional Technical Report 2. Prepared for NOAA by P.J. Hebert and G. Taylor (Silver Spring, MD: 1975).

United States, Department of Defense, United States Army, Corps of Engineers. *Low-Cost Shore Protection—A Guide for Engineers and Contractors*; 1981.
This volume and the following two volumes are well-illustrated compendiums of shoreline stabilization methods that are principally of use on lagoon or other "quiet" water shorelines. The negative effects of various structures on adjacent beaches are, unfortunately, not addressed.

United States, Department of Defense, United States Army, Corps of Engineers. *Low-Cost Shore Protection—A Guide for Local Government Officials*; 1981.

United States, Department of Defense, United States Army, Corps of Engineers. *Low-Cost Shore Protection—A Property Owner's Guide*; 1981.

United States, Department of Defense, United States Army, Corps of Engineers.
Shore Protection Manual, 3 vols; 1977.
This three-volume set is considered by most to be the world's "bible" of coastal engineering.

Chapter 8

Baker, E.J. *Hurricanes and Coastal Storms*, Florida Sea Grant Report No. 23. Gainesville, FL: Marine Advisory Program, 1980.

Baker, Simon. *Storms, People, and Property in Coastal North Carolina*, UNC Sea Grant Publication 78-15. Raleigh, NC: North Carolina State University, 1978.

Foster, H.D. *Disaster Planning*. New York: Springer-Verlag, 1980.

Simpson, R.H., and Riehl, H. *The Hurricane and Its Impact*. Baton Rouge, LA: Louisiana State University Press, 1981.

Texas, Coastal and Marine Council. *Model Minimum Hurricane-Resistant Building Standards for the Texas Gulf Coast*. Austin, TX: 1976.

United States, Department of Commerce, National Technical Information Service. *The Tornado—An Engineering-Oriented Perspective*, NOAA Technical Memorandum ERL-NSSL-82. Prepared for NTIS by J.E. Minor, J.R. McDonald, and K.C. Mehta, 1977.

United States, Department of Housing and Urban Development. *When You Return to a Storm-Damaged Home*, HUD 148-FDAA (4); 1975.

United States, Federal Emergency Management Agency. *Emergency and Residential Repair Handbook*, HUD-527-FIA; 1979.

Chapter 9

Clark, J.R. *Coastal Ecosystem Management*. New York: John Wiley and Sons, 1977.

Conservation Foundation. *Coastal Environmental Management*. Washington, DC: Government Printing Office, 1980.

Feld, J. *Construction Failure*. New York: John Wiley and Sons, 1968.

Graber, P.H.F. "The Law of the Coast in a Clamshell." *Shore and Beach* 48 (1980).

Hildreth, R.G. "Coastal Natural Hazards Management." *Oregon Law Review* 59 (1980):201–42.

Miller, H.C. "Federal Policies in Barrier Island Development." *Oceanus* 23 (1980):47–55.

Miller, H.C. "The Barrier Islands." *Environment* 23 (1981):6.

Natural Resources Defense Council. *Paving the Way for Coastal Development*. New York: Natural Resources Defense Council, 1980.

Rhode, C. "Dauphin Island: At the Crossroads of Decision." *Mobile Magazine* (1980):1–12.

Sorkin, A.L. *Economics of Natural Disasters*. Lexington, MA: Lexington Books, 1981.

Texas, Coastal and Marine Council. *Model Minimum Hurricane-Resistant Building Standards for the Texas Gulf Coast*. Austin, TX: 1976.

United States, Department of Commerce, National Oceanic and Atmospheric

Administration, Office of Coastal Zone Management. *The First Five Years of Coastal Zone Management*, 1979.

United States, Department of Commerce, National Oceanic and Atmospheric Administration, Office of Coastal Zone Management. *Natural Hazard Management of Coastal Areas*. Prepared for OCZM by G.F. White and others, 1976.

United States, Department of Housing and Urban Development, Office of Interstate Land Sales. *Get the Facts Before Buying Land*.

United States, Department of the Interior, United States Geological Survey. *Facing Geologic and Hydrologic Hazards—Earth Science Considerations*, USGS Professional Paper 1240-B; 1982.

United States, Federal Emergency Management Agency. *Design and Construction Manual for Residential Buildings in Coastal High Hazard Areas*, FIA-7; 1981.

United States. "Flood Plain Management and Protection of Wetlands." *Federal Register* 46 (1981):51749–55.

Glossary

A zone: That portion of the 100-year floodplain not subject to wave action. May, however, be subject to residual forward momentum of breaking waves.

Bank: A local term for a barrier island.

Barrier island: Elongated islands essentially parallel to and fronting the shoreline of coastal plains. Made up of unconsolidated sediment, mostly sand.

Beach: The zone of unconsolidated material, usually sand, between the line of maximum upwash of fair-weather waves and the approximately 20- to 40-foot (6- to 12-m) water depth contour; the zone of active sand movement during storms.

Beach replenishment: The process of replacing the beach by pumping or trucking in new sand.

Beach ridge: A long ridge of sand dunes formed as the nearest dune line to the beach.

Berm: The nearly horizontal terrace on the upper beach, particularly characteristic of summer beaches, formed by the deposition of material by wave action.

Breakwater: A structure protecting a shore area, harbor, anchorage, or basin from waves.

Bulkhead: A structure similar to a seawall but built at a higher elevation in front of the first dune. Bulkheads are designed to withstand wave impact during storms but not on a daily basis. The distinction between a seawall and a bulkhead is that a seawall is intended to hold back the waves, and the bulkhead to hold back the land and occasionally the waves.

Coastal plain: The broad, gentle seaward-sloping plain bordering the ocean from New Jersey through Texas.

Continental shelf: The very gently dipping ledge of land between the beach and about 250 to 350 feet (80 to 100 m) water depth, at which point the continental slope begins. The North American continental shelf ranges from 5 to well over 100 miles (8 to 160 km) in width.

Dune: A hill of sand formed by the sweeping action of wind. The sand with which to build coastal dunes usually comes from the beach.

Dynamic equilibrium: The balance between coastal characteristics of wave size, sediment supply, the beach profile, and sea level; that is, the condition that if there is a change in any one of these, changes will also occur in the others to maintain a natural balance.

Egress: In reference to the coastal flood zone, the act of leaving and/or the path of escape from impending coastal hazards, usually hurricanes and associated storm-surge flooding; the escape route.

Estuary: The lower portion of a river valley where the environment changes gradually from freshwater to salt water. Estuaries are formed when the river valley is "drowned" by a rising sea level.

Finger canal: Canals dredged for the purpose of creating additional waterfront property as well as boat anchorages.

Groin: A wall built perpendicular to the shoreline to trap sand and thereby reduce local beach erosion rates. A groin is usually much shorter than a jetty.

Headland: An irregularity of land jutting out from the coast.

Ice ages: The period of geologic time (essentially the last 2 million years) during which glaciers alternately advanced and retreated over the land masses. At present we are in an interglacial time when the glaciers are relatively small.

Inlet: The channel between islands connecting the sound or lagoon with the open ocean.

Jetty: A structure, usually a wall of large stones, built perpendicular to the shoreline to protect inlets leading to harbors. Its protective function is to prevent sand from filling the channel.

Knot: A unit of speed, about 1.15 miles per hour (1.85 km/h).

Lagoon: A shallow body of salt water between a coastal barrier and the mainland.

Longshore current: The current in the surf zone that is formed by waves breaking at an angle on the beach rather than "head on," which moves water and sand essentially parallel to the shore.

Longshore drift: See **Longshore current.**

Maritime forest: The forest found on relatively high elevations of coastal areas. The forest is capable of surviving frequent winds and some salt spray.

New Jerseyization: A general term for the end result of a developed coast where shoreline engineering has been used to provide short-term erosion protection to property, resulting in the loss of beaches and dunes, and a general decline of aesthetics and safety, all at a high economic cost.

Nonbarrier coast: A coast that has no adjacent barrier islands. The Pacific Coast is an example.

Northeaster: A common type of storm with winds from the northeast, causing damage to East Coast shorelines.

100-year flood (or base flood) level: The maximum elevation that will be flooded by a storm; statistically, this is likely to occur once a century, that is, there is a 1 percent chance of this elevation being flooded in any given year.

Overwash: Storm waves that actually wash across the beach and onto adjacent land areas.

Overwash fan: Mass of sand carried onto the land by overwashing storm waves.

Overwash pass: Gap between dunes through which overwashing storm waves pass.

Primary coast: A coastline configuration produced by land processes such as erosion or deposition by streams or glaciers.

Primary dune: The first row of dunes closest to the open ocean beach.

Revetment: A facing of stone or concrete built to protect a scarp, embankment, or building against erosion. Frequently revetments protect the face of the first dune.

Ridge and runnel: The sand bar, commonly a few yards offshore, and the intervening trough. Waves break on the ridge, particularly at low tide.

Saffir–Simpson scale: A numerical scale to rank hurricanes.

Salt marsh: Coastal swamps flooded on a daily basis by salt water. Atlantic, Gulf, and Pacific marshes each have different species of marsh plants.

Scarp or Escarpment: A more or less continuous line of small to large cliffs or steep slopes facing in one general direction, which have been created by erosion.

Scour: Removal of underwater material by waves and currents, especially at the base or toe of a shore structure.

Seawall: A wall built parallel to the beach, designed to halt shoreline erosion by absorbing the impact of waves.

Secondary coast: A coastline configuration produced by marine processes such as erosion or deposition by waves, or the growth of coral reefs or mangrove thickets.

Setback line: A line located a minimum distance inland from the beach in front of which no construction is allowed.

Shoaling: Shallowing.

Shoreline accretion: Growth of the beach seaward; the opposite of erosion.

Shoreline retreat or Shoreline erosion: Long-range landward movement of shoreline. Does not include shorter-range predictable seasonal changes in beach shape.

Shoreline stabilization: An engineer's term for all procedures or construction methods that will stabilize the dynamic shoreline, i.e., halt beach erosion.

Sound: An arm of the sea between an island and the mainland; generally synonymous with lagoon.

Storm surge: A sea level rise above normal water level on the open coast during hurricanes caused by the action of wind on the water surface as well as by atmospheric pressure reduction. Wave height is superimposed on top of the storm-surge level.

Surge level: See **Storm surge.**

Talus: Coarse rock fragments mixed with soil at the foot of a cliff.

Tidal delta: Mass of sand carried through an inlet by tidal currents and deposited in the lagoon (flood-tidal delta) or on the inner continental shelf (ebb-tidal delta).

Tidal wave: A misleading synonym for both storm surge and tsunami.

Tornado: A localized, violently destructive windstorm occurring over land, characterized by a long, funnel-shaped cloud extending toward the ground, made visible by condensation and debris.

Tsunami: A sea wave produced by any large-scale, short-duration disturbance of the sea floor (earthquake, mass movement, volcanic eruption), and characterized by very long wave length (miles) duration and low amplitude on the open sea, but which may pile up water to heights of greater than 100 feet (30 m), coming onshore with great destructive force.

Typhoon: A tropical cyclone or hurricane of the western Pacific area and the China seas. Sometimes called ''cyclones'' or ''willie-willies,'' especially in Australia.

V zone (velocity zone): that portion of the land that would be inundated by wave surges (superimposed on a flood) and thus subject to additional hazards resulting from velocity wave action.

Water table: The top of the zone of water-saturated sand. Water wells must be sunk below the water table.

Wave energy: Increases with the wave height.

Index

Adams, James W.R., 3
Albemarle Sound, 4
American Red Cross, 105
Anchoring. *See* Connections
ANSI-A58.1, "Building Code Requirements for Minimum Design Loads in Buildings and Other Structures," 200
Arrowhead-plate cable system, 121
Ash Wednesday storm (1962), 22, 24, 125, 127, 137, 144-45, 161, 165, 167
Assessment and Atlas of Shoreline Erosion Along the California Coast, 28
Atlantic City, New Jersey, 13, 17, 145
Atlantic coast. *See* Barrier island shoreline; New England shoreline; specific communities
A zone, 57, 192

Barometric pressure, 34, 99, 162-63
Barrier island shoreline
    beach sand on, 8
    formation of, 13
    government protection of, 181, 193
    location of, 3
    migration of, 16-17, 22-23
    and seawalls, 17
    as secondary coasts, 3
    selecting a homesite on, 23-27
    and storms, 161, 165
Basic Building Code, The, 200, 202
Bay Ocean, Oregon, 18, 146
Beaches
    definition of, 4
    development on, 17-18
    replenishing, 150-55
    sand supply for, 5-9, 150-53
    and sea-level rise, 9-10

and wave energy, 4-5
Biloxi, Mississippi, 161
Bluffed shorelines
    composition of, 28-29
    failure of, 12-13, 28
    selecting a homesite on, 36
Bogue Island, North Carolina, 126
Bracing
    diagonal, 39-42, 73
    for existing homes, 98
    knee, 73
    lateral, 38, 47
    of pole houses, 73
    shear-wall, 42, 73
    for shelter modules, 101-2
    of wood structures, 38-42, 47
Breakwaters, 149-50, 153
    in Carthage, 2
    in southern California, 8, 149-50
Brick structures, 37, 54
    existing homes, 92, 96-97
    tying together, 59-61, 97
    unreinforced, 57-58, 92, 96
    in V zones, 57
Brigantine, New Jersey, 31
Budd, Thomas, 13
Building codes, 198-203. *See also* specific codes
    ancient, 198
    and high-rise buildings, 134
    and masonry construction, 59
    and pole houses, 76
    Roman, 198
Bulkheads, 155

Cape Cod, Massachusetts, 3, 13, 21

ABOUT THE AUTHORS

Orrin H. Pilkey, Sr., is a retired civil engineer with an extensive background in structural engineering, theory of ultimate strength design, and design of multistory frames. He received his B.S. in civil engineering from Texas A&M College and his M.S. in structural engineering from the University of Illinois. For several years prior to retirement, he was senior consulting engineer to the General Electric Company at NASA's Mississippi Test Support Facility in Bay St. Louis, Mississippi.

When Hurricane Camille struck the Gulf Coast in 1969, the Pilkeys' home in Waveland, Mississippi, was heavily damaged. Mr. & Mrs. Pilkey sought shelter at the NASA facility nearby, where his advice was sought on structural damage to the main administration building. As a result, Mr. Pilkey became deeply concerned over current building codes and practices in hurricane-prone coastal areas. He has since made a thorough and exhaustive study of safer construction methods in these regions.

Dr. Walter D. Pilkey, a native of Richland, Washington, recieved his B.A. in humanities from Washington State University (1957), M.S. in engineering sciences from Purdue University (1960), and Ph.D. from Pennsylvania State University (1962). From 1962 to 1969, he served as a research scientist at the ITT Research Institute, Chicago, Illinois. During 1963-1964, he was a visiting professor at Kabul University, Afghanistan.

Since 1969, Dr. Pilkey has been associated with the School of Engineering and Applied Science at the University of Virginia, where he is now Professor and Chairman of the Applied Mechanics Division. His research interests include the mechanics of solids, structural dynamics, crashworthiness, and turbidity currents. He has been an author or coauthor/editor of fourteen books and has authored or coauthored more than eighty technical papers.

During his sabbatical year (1975-76), he studied the shoreline protection systems, conservations efforts, and public laws of England and Europe. Considerable time was spent touring endangered shorelines and consulting with local authorities.

Dr. Orrin H. Pilkey, Jr., born in New York City, was raised in Richland, Washington, and received his B.S. in geology from Washington State University in 1957. His M.S. in geology was earned at Montana State University (1959) and his Ph.D. (geology), from Florida State University (1962). From 1962 to 1965, he served as research associate and assistant professor at the University of Georgia Marine Laboratory. Since 1965, he has been associated with the geology department at Duke University, where he has served as director of graduate studies and acting director of the Duke University Oceanographic Program (1978) as well as full professor of geology. During 1973-74, he was visiting professor at the University of Puerto Rico, Department of Marine Sciences; 1975-76, senior research geologist, U.S. Geological Survey, Woods Hole, Massachusetts.

Dr. Pilkey is editor of the *Journal of Sedimentary Petrology* and associate editor of *Marine Geology*. He is a member of a number of scientific societies, including the Geological Society of America, International Association of Sedimentologists, N.C. Academy of Science, the American Association of Petroleum Geologists, and the Society of Economic Paleontologists. He has been co-organizer of three continental shelf or continental slope symposia; a member of the Duke University scholarly exchange delegation to the People's Republic of China (1975), a member of two state government committees on shoreline development problems, and has done extensive research work in Tunisia, Egypt, and other areas around the Mediterranean Sea.

He is author or coauthor of more than eighty-five scientific papers and of several books.

Dr. William J. Neal, a native of Indiana, received his B.S. from the University of Notre Dame (1961), M.A. (1964) and Ph.D. from the University of Missouri (1968), all in geology. He is presently professor and chairman of the geology department at Grand Valley State Colleges in Michigan.

Dr. Neal has completed a senior postdoctoral fellowship at Duke University under a National Science Foundation grant, studying coastal land use and environmental geology. In 1967-68, he studied at McMaster University, Hamilton, Ontario, under a Canadian postdoctoral fellowship, and in 1969-71, he served as a research associate at Skidaway Institute of Oceanography in Savannah, Georgia. He is author or coauthor of numerous papers on sedimentology and the receipient of more than thirteen fellowships and/or research grants.